DOING PSYCHOLOGICAL RESEARCH

DOING PSYCHOLOGICAL RESEARCH

Joseph Horvat
Weber State University

Stephen Davis
Emporia State University

PRENTICE HALL, UPPER SADDLE RIVER, NJ 07458

Library of Congress Cataloging-in-Publication Data

Horvat, Joseph
    Doing psychological research / Joseph Horvat, Stephen Davis.
      p.   cm.
    Includes bibliographical references and index.
    ISBN 0-13-243692-2 (pbk.)
      1. Psychology—Research.   2. Psychology, Experimental.   I. Davis,
Stephen. II. Title.
    BF76.5.H67   1997
    150'.72—dc21   97–29377
                                                    CIP

Editor in chief: Nancy Roberts
Acquisition editor: Bill Webber
Editorial/production supervision, interior design,
   and electronic page makeup: Mary Araneo
Buyer: Tricia Kenny
Cover designer: Wendy Alling Judy

This book was set in 10/12 New Baskerville by A & A
Publishing Services, Inc., and was printed and bound by
Courier Companies, Inc. The cover was printed by
Phoenix Color Corp.

 © 1998 by Prentice-Hall, Inc.
Simon & Schuster/A Viacom Company
Upper Saddle River, New Jersey 07458

Printed in the United States of America
10 9 8 7 6 5 4 3 2 1

ISBN 0-13-243692-2

Prentice-Hall International (UK) Limited, *London*
Prentice-Hall of Australia Pty. Limited, *Sydney*
Prentice-Hall canada Inc., *Toronto*
Prentice-Hall Hispanoamericana, S.A., *Mexico*
Prentice-Hall of India Private Limited, *New Delhi*
Prentice-Hall of Japan, Inc., *Tokyo*
Simon & Schuster Asia Pet. Ltd., *Singapore*
Editora Prentice-Hall do Brasil, Ltda., *Rio de Janeiro*

To all of our students—
past, present, and future
and
To "Mom" from her wayward sons

Contents

Preface

Probably the most pressing of all problems for students in experimental psychology or research methods courses is the difficulty they often have developing ideas for an experiment. Even though psychology students may be confident that they understand the methods used in experimentation, that same confidence is nearly nonexistent when it comes to the development of a tangible, viable research idea. Questions students ask faculty members regarding research include "How do I get started on a research project?", "Do you know of something I could research?", and "How do people ever develop ideas for their theses or dissertations?" Students ask these types of questions far too frequently.

Experimental psychology and research methods texts within the field of psychology are typically excellent guides to the mechanics of experimentation. However, they are frequently less than ideal as practical aids in developing ideas for research. The purpose of this book is to help fill this void by providing students with paths to follow within the general framework of idea development. An important feature of this text is the presentation of various disciplines within psychology (i.e., cognitive, physiological, social) combined with the exercise of actually developing experimental research ideas within these various areas. For example, Chapters 4 through 11 contain tangible research ideas culled from the consideration of the sample research study that is a highlight of each chapter. Students are guided by a series of questions in order to aid them in developing their own ideas concerning the study presented, yet different from those suggested in our analysis of the study. In short, we want to help psychology students understand that the development of research ideas can become second nature and to help them to see these ideas to completion.

This text will actually help to teach idea development. The text, by its very nature, can be used as an important ancillary with any current experimental psychological or research methods text, or it can stand alone as a text for courses concerned with idea generation and the actual implementation of a research project.

Together we have over 50 years of teaching and research experience, and we rely on our experiences to help shape the creative process of research idea generation within this text. We use historically significant research, as well as research on the forefront of psychological science, to illustrate the point that one can use "old" or "new" research to develop ideas.

ACKNOWLEDGMENTS

The authors would like to thank a number of people who, without their help, this project would never have reached completion. First, we would like to thank all of our students throughout our careers whose questions, ideas, and problems were the basis for undertaking this endeavor. We would also like to extend our thanks to the reviewers, Dr. Paul Foos of the University of North Carolina-Charlotte, Dr. Paul Wellman of Texas A & M University, and Dr. Susan Lima of the University of Wisconsin, for their suggestions and praise of the project. We would like to thank Pete Janzow for his initial interest in the book and to Tamsen Adams for her persistence in seeing the project to fruition. Finally, we would like to thank our respective psychology faculties for their help in a variety of ways in making this book a reality.

Joseph Horvat
Stephen Davis

DOING PSYCHOLOGICAL RESEARCH

CHAPTER 1

Doing Psychological Research

Common bonds of most, if not all, students in an experimental or methods course in psychology revolve around apprehensions concerning their ability to conduct an original piece of psychological research. As with anything else, to become proficient at a task, one must become intimately familiar with that task. And, research has perhaps become the most important aspect in a student's career in the field of psychology.

Just how important is research in the field of psychology? As far as being accepted into a graduate program in psychology, research is considered to be the activity that is rated highest by prospective graduate schools (Keith-Spiegel, 1991) in determining acceptance of potential students. To gain employment or to advance in academic psychology, one must often publish research in appropriate journals. In the "real world," one is often asked to find an answer to a particular psychological problem, and research ideas are at the core of such successful pursuits. For the psychologist, research is considered to be the most important of all skills one can develop in one's professional life. Thus, the development of the skills needed to carry out an independent research program is a necessary requirement to a successful psychology career.

LEARNING A SKILL

Once they have overcome the initial fears of research, most students truly enjoy conducting their own projects. To develop an idea, carry that idea through all of its experimental stages, interpret the results, write a formal paper, and then present or publish the paper is a prideful accomplishment. However, problems often arise when one tries to develop an appropriate idea for research. Idea generation, like many skills one learns, is something that takes time and practice; it does not occur through osmosis. Can you imagine a person going out

1

right now and trying to run a marathon? What do you think their chances of success would be if this was the first time they had run in 10 years? Consider the person trying to use a computer for the very first time; it is a clumsy and frustrating act, to be sure. With appropriate practice, these tasks can become second nature. The same thing holds true for the development of an idea for psychological research. Initially, it can be difficult and frustrating. As with other skills, research idea generation requires special abilities that are developed through systematic practice. As one becomes more experienced in developing ideas for experiments, it becomes almost second nature to do so. Just like running a marathon, working with a computer, or even riding a bicycle for the very first time, once one has the skills necessary to carry out those tasks, those tasks become much easier.

Take the example of learning how to ride a bicycle. How difficult do you suppose it is to teach someone to ride a bicycle by just using verbal instructions? Without the aid of an actual bicycle, trying to teach another how to ride one is next to impossible. It is nearly as impossible to try and teach your young neighbors to ride a bike by having them watch you ride but not allowing them on the bike. Yet if we put the bicycle in the hands of the person we are trying to teach, the task becomes much easier. The same holds true with research. We can talk about it and teach about the multitude of studies that have been done in the past, but that is of no aid in developing the skills necessary to go "solo" with research.

This book is the bicycle and we are going to put that bike in your hands. After finishing this text, you will develop research idea generation skills that will last you a lifetime.

All research, whether it be in the field of chemistry, physics, anthropology, or psychology, shares many beliefs and ideas. So, in many respects, if individuals learn how to research something in chemistry, they will have the basic idea of how to approach research in other fields, such as psychology. One big difference between these associated fields and psychology is the fact that psychology is concerned with the study of the behavior of organisms. What can we study in psychology? Literally anything. It is a sure bet we will never exhaust all of the research possibilities within psychology in several lifetimes. It just takes a bit of knowledge, imagination, and creativity to become successful in developing a research idea. We know you can become successful!

ETHICAL CONSIDERATIONS

Are we allowed to investigate anything we want to investigate? The answer is generally yes, with some obvious restrictions. Why must there be such restrictions? Why are we not allowed to investigate any psychological phenomena in any manner we want as long as it is in the name of science? To answer these questions, let us assume you would like to conduct a study on the psychological effects a person experiences when having an arm pulled from the socket. Although there would certainly be some interesting behaviors to be studied from such a situation, would this study be ethical? That is, would/should/could we conduct such a study? Assuming it is an ethical study, how could we get individuals to participate?

Let us go through a hypothetical situation and explore some of these thoughts. Assume it is the last week of the term in your introductory psychology course and you currently have an F in the course. You are desperate and you would do just about anything to pass. Your professor comes in and announces she has an experiment to conduct and would like some volunteers. Because it is the last week of class and because students are busy, she needs to offer some type of inducement to secure enough participants for her study. She states those participating in her experiment will receive an A in the course. Immediately all hands fly up. Students are eager and willing to do their part in advancing psychology as a science! She then discloses what will be expected of all participants. Shoulders will be dislocated in an attempt to assess any and all psychological consequences of such an action. She goes on to tell you the procedure will be quite painful and the pain will last for approximately two months; however, there will be no permanent damage.

Your mind begins to reel. Sure it will hurt, but it is worth it to have an A in the class. The pain will not be permanent but the A will be. After all, you have never received an A in anything in your entire life. However, you rationalize, you do have two arms so you will not be totally disabled. With little additional thought you agree to participate in your professor's study.

Although this example is inane to say the least, it poses some interesting concerns. Is the study ethical? The professor did disclose what was going to happen and the student did, in fact, agree to voluntarily participate. But at what price? Months of induced pain on the part of the participants is reason enough to raise the highest degree of suspicion concerning the ethical nature of this study. There is no way a psychologist, or any other scientist, could or would conduct such an experiment. The American Psychological Association (*Ethical Principles of Conduct*, 1992) has developed and published a set of ethical principles that must be followed by all investigators engaging in psychological research. Rest assured, these principles would not allow such a study to be conducted.

In the example above, we are precluded from causing harm to participants by the ethical code of conduct as set down by APA (not to mention local, state, and federal laws). If an unscrupulous researcher were actually to conduct such an experiment, the participants in such a study would have a number of legal and ethical issues they could and should raise in a court of law.

Although this example is clear concerning its ethical prohibitions, many experiments may seem to be reasonable on the surface yet raise legitimate ethical considerations. Consider the example of requiring introductory students to participate in, let us say, three studies carried out by faculty and advanced students per term. How else could experimenters secure the necessary participants for their studies? Is this requirement, however, a form of coercion to which the student should not be subjected? Many universities have had to make just such decisions. The decisions usually favor some type of participation requirement with an appropriate codicil for those students believing, for whatever reason, the participation requirement is unjustified (e.g., requiring a short paper in lieu of participation).

A less obvious example of how ethical concerns are of primary importance in any study is found in the use of deception. Why would a trusted psychologist or psychology student use deception in research? Let us assume you wanted to study the relative helpfulness of people when the person needing help appears to be a "bum" versus an "executive" type of person. You could inform those participating this is indeed what you are studying, but what do you think the outcome would be of such disclosure? More than likely your participants would give a socially desirable answer like "It does not matter what the person looks like. I would be more than happy to help them under any circumstances." Thirty years of social psychological research has indicated the fallacy of such a statement. People are generally more likely to help someone who appears more "respectable" than someone who looks "less than respectable." Thus, it is often imperative to use deception in a research project; we cannot, for obvious reasons, always be forthcoming with information. However, is such a study ethical? Depending on the exact nature of the independent manipulations, it could or it could not be. *Ethical Principles of Conduct* may even be less than clear in aiding with a particular decision. As a result, colleges and universities have set up subject review committees or institutional review boards (IRBs) to help make appropriate judgments in such cases. Not surprisingly, all research must be approved by such a body to insure physical and psychological safety of all participants.

Ethical considerations are not for human participants only. In many cases, experimenters will use nonhuman participants in experiments. And, be assured, animals are also protected under the ethical principles.

The ethical code has several areas of direct concern for conducting psychological research. An abbreviated form of the ethical code of conduct is presented below to give you a general idea concerning what is and what is not ethical. We do warn you that what is presented here is only a synopsis of the ethical principles; we strongly suggest you spend considerable time reading the entire publication for a more complete presentation.

SYNOPSIS OF ETHICAL PRINCIPLES

The rights of the participant in a psychological experiment must be protected at all times; experimenters are held responsible for determining whether their research is ethical. Ethics committees help ensure this proposition is adhered to. Similarly, investigators are responsible for the conduct of all people working with them on the project. Likewise, potential consequences that might induce discomfort (mental, emotional, or physical) on the part of the participants must be shared with the participants at the outset of the experiment.

The experimenter must possess the specific competencies (and make certain those under his or her supervision possess adequate competencies) for the specific research project being conducted. Experimenters are not permitted to "go outside" of their respective competencies. If experimenters do not possess a specific competency necessary for a particular research procedure, they will make certain they obtain such competency prior to engaging in the research or make certain there is a person with the necessary competency performing the procedure in question.

The participant in a study has the right to decline or discontinue the experiment at anytime without fear of any type of retribution. They also have the right to have their individual data remain confidential unless there is agreement before hand about releasing such information. The obligations of both parties (the investigator and the participant) must be clarified and agreed upon in advance.

In most instances, full disclosure of the study must be provided to participants prior to their participation. When deception is used, the investigator must make certain there are no reasonable alternatives available and must disclose the reason for the deception to the participants as soon as possible.

Concerning animals, similar principles of conduct apply. Animals must be treated humanely in their care, use, and disposal. This requirement not only pertains to the experimenter but to any individual having access to the research animals. The experimenter is ultimately responsible for all individuals having contact with the animal. When dealing with animals, experimenters and their supervisees must not practice procedures that lay outside of their competencies.

As you can see, what we can and cannot do in an experiment is not left up to chance. We must be responsible in our experiments not only to make certain the results will be valid and reliable, but, and perhaps most importantly, to make certain our participants are cared for and treated properly. It is not difficult to abide by the ethical principles. We just need to be intimately familiar with them and make certain they take precedence when we devise our experiments. We will then be assured our research will achieve the highest degree of ethical consideration.

Finally, we must also realize that the ethical principles, like many other aspects in psychology, change over time. It is dynamic. What is ethical today may or may not be ethical tomorrow. You, as a researcher, must always be apprised of the latest edition of the code so your experiment will hold up to the highest degree of scrutiny. You must hold this responsibility in the highest regard.

REFERENCES

American Psychological Association. (1992). Ethical Principles of Conduct. *American Psychologist, 47,* 1607-1611.
Keith-Spiegel, P. (1991). *The complete guide to graduate school admission: Psychology and related fields.* Lawrence Erlbaum Associates, Inc.

CHAPTER 2

Where Do Research Ideas Come From?

So, you are faced with the challenge of doing a piece of research. Where is the idea for your project going to come from? In several of the following chapters, we will explore many psychological research areas to get an idea of the process that might be involved in a specific setting. In this chapter, however, we examine the general process of idea formation.

THINK IT THROUGH

Let's begin our search for research ideas by asking you to describe what you feel are potential sources for research ideas. List the sources that come to mind, then continue reading to see how many of your answers correspond to the ones we have proposed. You may well list some possibilities that we had not considered.

SOURCES OF RESEARCH IDEAS

One of the main features of this book is that it allows you to read *about* experiments. This activity also is an excellent source of ideas for research projects. Because psychology is the scientific study of human and animal behavior, its textbooks are filled with research findings used to support differing points of view. To locate potential research ideas, try reading your textbook in a slightly different manner. You should not read *just* for the facts and figures; think more deeply and concentrate on the cited research. Ask questions like the following: How was the research conducted? When and where was the research conducted? Who served as participants? What were the major findings? What seems to be a logical next step to make in this research? Questions such as these point directly to a myriad of potential projects. As you will see, one of our goals is to pique your interest in conducting research in a variety of areas by having you read about it in a textbook.

You will also find this text illustrates another excellent source of research ideas: reading research articles in the psychological journals. In this regard, our strategy is to reprint a published journal article and then dissect it in order to highlight potential research ideas. Unfortunately, you will not find research ideas conveniently listed and described in most journal articles. (Some suggestions for further research *may* be mentioned at the end of an article. You should pay close attention to these comments.) However, by repeatedly illustrating the process by which a research report can be analyzed and research ideas brought to light, we hope to prepare you to use this process on your own once you have completed this book and your research methods or experimental psychology course.

One of your routine, daily activities as a student can also be turned into a rich source of research ideas. Any ideas what this common activity might be? If you said simply going to class and listening to lectures, you are absolutely correct. According to Smith and Davis (1997), "Many excellent research projects are the result of a classroom lecture. Your instructor describes research in an area that sparks your interest and ultimately this interest leads to the development and conduct of a research project" (pp. 28–29). Hence, in addition to taking good notes on each lecture (or when reading your text), we encourage you to reserve a portion of each page in your notebook for research ideas. Many students use the left margin for this purpose. Jot your ideas down as they come to you. When class (or a chapter) is completed, sit down and go over your ideas and clarify them a bit more. It is important to review and firm up your ideas as soon as you can after the lecture or chapter. These ideas tend to be like plans in your dreams; they seem *great* at the moment, but you cannot remember them when you wake up.

You are walking across campus. The elections for student government officers will be held at the end of the week; campaign posters are everywhere. You wonder which posters are most effective in attracting voters' attention. Later you take a test in one of your classes and observe several students cheating. You wonder about the type of student who cheats (see Butler, Ridley, & Allen, 1996). After classes are over, you watch several of the athletic teams practicing. You wonder about the anxiety and self-confidence of the athletes; do these traits differ between individual and team sports (see Thomas & Kring, 1996)? You are probably already a step ahead of us and have concluded that everyday occurrences can provide a rich source of potential research ideas. All you have to do is keep your eyes and ears open. Incidently, the Butler et al. (1996) and Thomas and Kring (1996) studies were prompted by real-life occurrences. These studies were designed and conducted by undergraduate students. Their subsequent publication in a national journal attests to the fact that high-quality research is often prompted by everyday happenings. In fact, much of our research stems from such occurrences.

Many psychological theories, such as sociobiological theory, propose there are differences between the sexes. Such proposed differences offer a gold mine of research ideas and projects. For example, Lyerly, Smith, and Brownlow (1996) examined predicted sex differences in mate selection by examining the newspaper personal ads. Even if a particular ad does not predict sex differences, male-female comparisons may result in an excellent research project. For many decades, psychology has developed theories and attempted to produce generalizable research by almost exclusively testing male participants (see Tavris, 1992). How accurate are these theories and generalizations? Only additional research comparing the sexes will answer this question. It is noteworthy that this same concern also applies to animal research. Most animal projects, especially those using rats, are conducted with male animals in order to avoid potential problems introduced by the estrus cycle of female animals. As with human participants, one wonders if the generalization of results from male animals to female animals presents an accurate picture of the true state of affairs. Clearly, there are numerous potential research ideas here!

Just as psychological research has been dominated by male participants, it is arguable that modern psychology has been equally dominated by American research conducted on American participants (Shultz & Shultz, 1996). The generalizability of such research to other cultures and other countries is debatable. Today psychologists are taking cultural and ethnic differences more seriously (Lonner & Malpass, 1994). With international travel becoming a routine occurrence and with the advent of the Internet, the conduct of cross-cultural research has been made easier. You should be alert to such opportunities when they present themselves. If you are thinking you'll never be able to conduct such international projects, we encourage you to look around you. Multiculturalism and diversity have become major topics of interest in our own country. The different ethnic groups in the United States offer you an almost endless panorama of potential research ideas.

A final source of research ideas involves whether to use humans or animals as research participants. Before you determine this is a cut-and-dried decision with little relevance to the development of research ideas, let us relate a situation that happened a number of years ago to one of the authors. The daily session of an ongoing animal research project was about to begin. One student researcher entered the laboratory and announced in a particularly grumpy voice that no one was to talk to him and that he would be back in a few minutes. When he returned, he was drinking a *huge* soft drink and his spirits were greatly improved. The other researchers asked what was going on. The student replied that he suffered from hypoglycemia (low blood-sugar level) and that he needed to increase his sugar level (hence the large soft drink). The group was still discussing this situation after the training session concluded. Someone asked if hypoglycemia produced hostility and aggression. A check of the psychological literature indicated several correlational studies supporting this prediction. However, there were no real *experiments* in which hypoglycemia was created and hostility and aggression subsequently measured. These considerations led to a series of research projects (Davis, Cronin, Meriwether, Neideffer, & Travis-Neideffer, 1978; Davis, Gussetto, Tramill, Neideffer, & Travis-Neideffer, 1978; Neideffer, Davis, & Travis-Neideffer, 1980; Neideffer, Travis, Davis, Voorhees, & Prytula, 1977) in which hypoglycemia was experimentally created in rats by injecting insulin and aggressive responding in a subsequent aggression test was measured. The results indicated that as blood sugar was lowered (i.e., hypoglycemia created) by the insulin injection, aggressive responding increased. These studies represent instances in which the decision to conduct animal research stemmed from an examination of research conducted on humans. The reverse situation can also lead to fruitful research: a consideration of animal research may suggest projects using humans as the participants. For example, in developing the famous learned-helplessness paradigm, Seligman and Maier (1967) found dogs that were unable to escape electric shocks were unable to learn to solve subsequent problems; the inescapable shocks had rendered them helpless. This original research with dogs has led Martin Seligman to conduct research on depression in humans (Seligman, 1992).

THINK IT THROUGH

We hope the sources for research ideas we had in mind matched some of the ones you thought of. Now that we have explored sources for research ideas, you have one more major task to perform before you begin to implement your research project. What is that task? Why is it a crucial link in the research process? Give those questions some thought and jot down some answers before you read further.

LITERATURE REVIEW

Good experimental hypotheses and good research projects rest on a firm foundation of knowledge on the part of the researcher. "In all instances good researchers are familiar with the published literature and previous research findings. We do not seem to generate meaningful research ideas in areas with which we are not familiar" (Smith & Davis, 1997, p. 26). Yes, your next major task will be to conduct a literature review to determine what previous research has been done in your area of interest. The nature of the research that has been conducted will influence the design and conduct of your project.

As you conduct your literature review, there are several steps to keep in mind. First, in order to be thorough, you need to be organized. For example, you should first consult the *Thesaurus of Psychological Index Terms* (Walker, 1994). The terms you select from the *Thesaurus* will guide your search of the literature. Once you have selected the relevant key terms, your next step will likely be to work with the PsycLIT database. This database offers you a listing of the author(s), title, journal, volume, page numbers, and an abstract of all psychological research published since 1974. If you are interested in just the most current research you should see if your library has PsycFIRST. This database maintains only the last three years of research reports.

At this point, we caution you not to become overly enchanted with the computer printouts you receive from PsycLIT or PsycFIRST. Although these sources are convenient and easy to use, they do not provide all the information you need. As we indicated, they provide information about research conducted from 1974 to the present. Does that mean that research conducted prior to 1974 is of no value? No. It simply means you will be missing a significant portion of the psychological literature unless you are careful. How do you conduct a search of the pre-1974 literature? To obtain abstracts of these research reports, you will need to consult *Psychological Abstracts* (a monthly journal that provides the same information as PsycLIT.) You use the same index terms from the *Thesaurus* to enter *Psychological Abstracts* that you use in your computerized searches. The only difference is that you are conducting a manual search when you are dealing with *Psychological Abstracts.*

When you have isolated the published research that is relevant to the project you have in mind, you will need an organized procedure for obtaining it. Your initial stop will be the periodicals department in your own college library. What if your library does not subscribe to the journals you need? When confronted with this situation, keep in mind that most libraries have an interlibrary loan service which allows you to order journal articles and books from other libraries. Take advantage of this service. What if that option is not successful? A trip to a nearby library might prove fruitful. What if you are not successful there? Now it is time to consider writing, calling, or sending an e-mail to the author(s) to ask for a reprint of the article you are after. Although making personal contact in this manner may be more time consuming, it offers an advantage: you can ask the author for copies of other, related reports. Perhaps you will receive a preprint (a copy of a paper that is scheduled for publication in the future). In any event, you need to be thorough and organized in your quest to acquire the background literature for your research project. The more you know about the area in which you are going to conduct research, the better your project will be.

Your reading of the published research will reveal numerous gaps in our knowledge and understanding; jot them down. These gaps are the raw materials from which you will develop your research ideas.

REFERENCES

Butler, M., Ridley, T., & Allen, M. (1996). The demographics of cheating in college students. *Psi Chi Journal of Undergraduate Research, 1,* 11–14.

Davis, S. F., Cronin, E. L., Meriwether, J. A. Neideffer, J., & Travis-Neideffer, M. N. (1978). Shock-elicited attack and biting as a function of chronic versus acute insulin injection. *Bulletin of the Psychonomic Society, 12,* 149–151.

Davis, S. F., Gussetto, J. K., Tramill, J. L., Neideffer, J., & Travis-Neideffer, M. N. (1978). The effects of extended insulin dosage on target-directed attack and biting elicited by tail shock. *Bulletin of the Psychonomic Society, 12,* 80-82.

Lonner, W. J., & Malpass, R. (1994). When psychology and culture meet: An introduction to cross-cultural psychology. In W. J. Lonner & R. Malpass (Eds.), *Psychology and culture* (pp. 1-12). Boston: Allyn & Bacon.

Lyerly, C. C., Smith, S. M., & Brownlow, S. (1996). Looking for love in all the wrong places? Sex and race differences in mate selection through the personal ads. *Psi Chi Journal of Undergraduate Research, 1,* 15–25.

Neideffer, J., Davis, S. F., & Travis-Neideffer, M. N. (1980). Active avoidance responding as a function of insulin-induced hypoglycemia. *Bulletin of the Psychonomic Society, 15,* 324–326.

Neideffer, J., Travis, M. N., Davis, S. F., Voorhees, J. W., & Prytula, R. E. (1977). Sweet and sour rats: The effect of insulin dosage on shock-elicited aggression. *Bulletin of the Psychonomic Society, 10,* 311–312.

Seligman, M. E. P. (1992). *Helplessness: On depression, development, and death.* New York: Freeman.

Seligman, M. E. P., & Maier, S. F. (1967). Failure to escape traumatic shock. *Journal of Experimental psychology, 75,* 1–9.

Shultz, D. P., & Shultz, S. E. (1996). *A history of modern psychology* (6th ed.). Fort Worth, TX: Harcourt Brace.

Smith, R. A., & Davis, S. F. (1997). *The psychologist as detective: An introduction to conducting research in psychology.* Upper Saddle River, NJ: Prentice Hall.

Tavris, C. (1992). *The mismeasure of woman.* New York: Touchstone.

Thomas, E., & Kring, J. P. (1996). Anxiety and self-confidence in relation to individual and team sports: A reevaluation. *Psi Chi Journal of Undergraduate Research, 1,* 33–35.

Walker, A., Jr. (Ed.). (1994). *Thesaurus of psychological index terms.* Washington, DC: American Psychological Association.

CHAPTER 3

What Is Needed to Do Research?

Let's assume you have decided on your general research topic. Your specific research hypothesis may not be completely formulated, but that will come in due time; we will explore idea and hypothesis generation in specific areas of psychology in subsequent chapters. Right now, other considerations occupy our attention. In this chapter, we consider those "other" needs you may have as you set up your research project.

THINK IT THROUGH

What are some of these other needs? How important are they? How can they be met? What is the single most important need of a good research project? Write down some answers before reading further.

Certainly, money and equipment are important. After all, you may have to pay participants, purchase test animals, and pay laboratory technicians. Likewise, printing and postal charges have risen dramatically in recent years. In addition, your research may call for the use of a specialized piece of equipment. Hopefully, your faculty sponsor or department chair can assist you in acquiring necessary funding and equipment.

Although such considerations are essential, the generation of a good research idea is still the most important ingredient in a successful research project. Put another way, the *lack* of a good research idea cannot be counteracted by money and equipment. In this context, we would like to convince you that many excellent research projects can be undertaken with very meager budgets and limited or no equipment.

The best way to illustrate this point is to present a research project that started with a good idea but did not require extensive funds and elaborate equipment. Our featured article for this chapter is just such a project. The idea for this project (Kraus, Davis, & Burns, 1997) was born in the social psychology class taken by Malissa Kraus and Susan Burns, students at Emporia State University. After reading and hearing lectures about stereotypes and prejudice, Malissa and Susan wanted to conduct research on these topics. As you read about their ingenious research project, be particularly sensitive to the "other" needs they encountered.

Latency to Serve in Stores:
Effects of Sex, Race, and Clothing

Malissa S. Kraus, Stephen F. Davis, and Susan Burns
Emporia State University

The present study was designed to evaluate the effects of ethnicity and appearance on customer service in randomly selected stores in large shopping malls. African American, Hispanic American, and Caucasian confederates dressed in either business or casual attire recorded the latency to serve in a variety of single-entrance stores. The results indicated that race, sex, and type of attire were significant factors in determining how long the potential customer had to wait for service. Suggestions for more effective customer service are presented.

Physical attractiveness can be important in the formation of first impressions by salesclerks. For example, clothing or attire worn by a person influences one's perceptions about the wearer's socioeconomic status (Heitmeyer & Goldsmith, 1990). Additionally, there is evidence that sales personnel initially categorize customers on the basis of easily observable characteristics, such as clothing, ethnicity, and/or sex (Taylor, Fiske, Etcoff, & Reuderman, 1978).

Because potential customers are categorized on the basis of such characteristics, the process of stereotyping (Kaplan, Wanshula, & Zanna, 1992) clearly is at work in such instances. Unfortunately, stereotyping frequently leads to prejudice when individuals are judged on the basis of their group membership(s). Prejudice, in turn, frequently manifests itself in behaviors that adversely affect members of the targeted group; such behaviors are known as *discrimination*. Discrimination may occur in a variety of forms that range from subtle to blatant. For example, tokenism (hiring individuals only to satisfy guidelines; Summers, 1991) reflects subtle discrimination, whereas the finding that many physicians and nurses spend less time with AIDS patients than individuals suffering from other diseases (Hunter & Ross, 1991) is more blatant discrimination.

Once salesclerks classify shoppers on the basis of sex, ethnicity, and attire, it seems likely discrimination, in terms of quality of service, will follow. For example, negative attitudes toward and stereotypes of ethnic minorities may result in lack of attention and inferior service. Likewise, the quality of one's attire also may be positively related to quality of service. The present study sought to investigate these predictions.

METHOD

Participants

The accessible population consisted of the salesclerks in 84 one-entrance, service-oriented retail stores located in two large shopping malls in the Midwest. The stores were assigned to one of three categories: "male"—stores selling primarily male-oriented goods, such as electronics or sporting goods; "female"—stores selling primarily female-oriented goods, such as clothing or beauty aids; and "gender-neutral"—stores selling primarily gender-neutral goods, such as jewelry or home furnishings. The stores sampled in the present study were randomly selected from a larger number of stores from which permission and informed consent previously had been obtained from the manager. The number of each type of store evaluated in the two malls in shown in Table 3A–1.

Procedure

Three men (one African American, one Caucasian, one Hispanic) and three women (one African American, one Caucasian, one Hispanic) in their 20s served as confederates in the conduct of the experiment. The two styles of attire, business and casual, were adopted by each confederate. A description of each style of attire for the two sexes appears in Table 3A–2. None of the confederates had shopped in the malls used in the experiment. The assignment of confederates and attire to type of store and shopping mall was random with the restrictions that: (a) each confederate was to participate at each mall in only one style of clothing (i.e., if the African American man wore casual clothing in Mall 1, he wore business attire in Mall 2), and (b) casual and business clothing be worn an equal number of times in each mall.

Each confederate carried a silent, digital stopwatch in the palm of his or her hand. As the confederate crossed the threshold of each store and made

Table 3A–1 Number of each type of one-entrance store evaluated in each shopping mall

	Type of Store		
	Female	Male	Gender-Neutral
Mall 1	15	11	18
Mall 2	13	11	16

Table 3A–2 Style of attire, business versus casual, worn by the male and female confederates

Male—casual attire:	Non-namebrand, faded blue jeans, a worn sweatshirt, carried a used bluejean jacket, soiled tennis shoes with holes in toes, no socks.
Male—business attire:	Two-piece suit with a white button down collar shirt and conservative tie, dress socks and leather shoes.
Female—casual attire:	Same as male casual attire.
Female—business attire:	Skirted business suit and white blouse, hose, and matching leather pumps, gold jewelry.

eye contact with an available salesclerk, the stopwatch was activated. If an unoccupied salesclerk was not available upon entering the store, timing did not begin until a clerk was available and eye contact had been made. When a salesclerk approached the confederate and offered help, timing was stopped. An offer of assistance was defined as consisting of comments such as "May I help you?," "Is there something in particular you are looking for?," or "If I can be of assistance, or show you something, please let me know." If the salesclerk responded, "I will be right with you," the confederate did not stop timing. The latency-to-serve data was reported to a data recorder positioned in the mall walkways outside the stores.

RESULTS

A preliminary analysis compared the latency-to-serve data (seconds) between the two shopping malls. As the results of this analysis failed to yield a significant difference, $t(344) = 1.31$, $p > .05$, the malls were considered equivalent and this factor was not evaluated in subsequent analyses.

A four-factor analysis of variance (ANOVA) incorporating sex (male–female), race (African American–Hispanic–Caucasian), type of attire (business–casual), and type of store (masculine–feminine–gender neutral) was used to analyze the latency to serve data. This analysis yielded significance for the race, $F(2, 468) = 85.44$, $p < .001$, type of attire, $F(1, 468) = 33.18$, $p < .001$, sex x attire, $F(1, 468) = 24.05$, $p < .001$, and sex x race x attire, $F(2, 468) = 5.95$, $p = .003$, effects. The mean latencies to serve for the conditions represented in the significant triple interaction are shown in Figure 3A–1.

The Newman-Keuls procedure was used to probe the significant sex x race x attire interaction. The results of these contrasts indicated regardless of type of attire the Caucasian man and Caucasian woman were waited on significantly faster ($p < .01$) than all other groups, except the Hispanic man wearing business attire. The latency to serve the Caucasian man, the Caucasian woman, and the Hispanic man wearing business clothing did not differ reliably. Additional significant comparisons indicated the African American woman wearing either business or casual clothing, the African American man wearing casual clothing, and the Hispanic man wearing casual clothing received significantly ($p < .01$) *slower* service than the Hispanic woman wearing casual clothing. The Hispanic woman wearing business attire was waited on significantly *faster* ($p < .01$) than the Hispanic man wearing casual clothing and the African American man and the African American woman wearing casual clothing. Finally, the African American man dressed in casual attire received significantly slower ($p < .01$) service than did the African American man dressed in business clothing, the African American woman dressed in either business or casual clothing, and the Hispanic man dressed in casual attire. All other contrasts were not statistically reliable.

DISCUSSION

The results of this study indicate salesclerks continue to form unjust impressions of their customers based on easily observable characteristics including sex, attire, and race. These initial impressions, in turn, affect how promptly customers are served in retail stores. More specifically, the data appear to support an essentially negative evaluation of minority individuals in our country: These individuals experienced discrimination in the form of significantly longer response times from salespersons than did their Caucasian counterparts.

On the other hand, the logic of salesmanship suggests it is important for all customers to be accepted and appreciated as individuals of worth. If retail sales personnel appeal to this need initially, they can proceed to share their expertise regarding a particular product or service more effectively.

Two limitations of the present study are worthy of mention. The fact that the majority of the salesclerks were Caucasian suggests the need for replication in a setting where non-Caucasian salesclerks predominate. Perhaps discrimination against Caucasians would be evidenced. Likewise, because the two shopping malls sampled in this study were located in close proximity to predominately Caucasian housing suggests the need for replication in different geographic locations. These two limitations notwithstanding, the finding that certain customers were discriminated against remains unchanged.

Although generalizations beyond the confines of this particular sample are not encouraged, the results lend additional support to previous works showing a positive interaction within the buyer-seller dyad is necessary to facilitate quality customer service (Schurr & Ozanne, 1985). It is clear those retailers who become aggressive agents of change, making certain *all* customers are being offered quality service, will be the major beneficiaries in the ever-changing retail environment of the future.

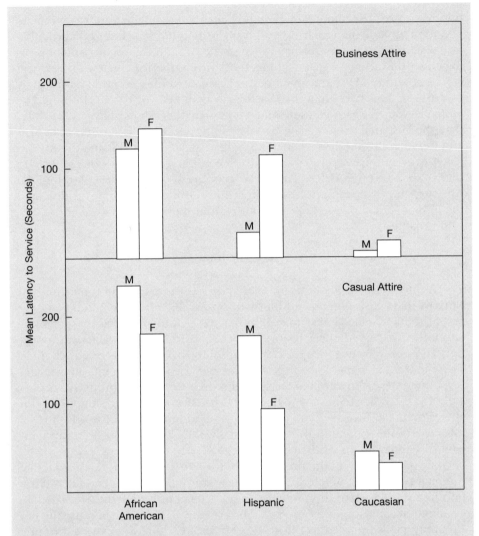

Figure 3A–1 Mean latency to service (seconds) as a function of sex (M = male confederate, F = female confederate) and ethnicity, by business attire (top panel) and casual attire (bottom panel).

REFERENCES

Heitmeyer, J. R., & Goldsmith, E. B. (1990). Attire, an influence on perceptions of counselors characteristics. *Perceptual and Motor Skills,* 923–929.

Hunter, C. E., & Ross, M. W. (1991). Determinants of health-care workers' attitudes toward people with AIDS. *Journal of Applied Social Psychology, 21,* 947–956.

Kaplan, M. F., Wanshula, L. T., & Zanna, M. P. (1992). Time pressure and information integration in social judgment: The effect of the need for structure. In O. Svenson

& J. Maule (Eds.), *Time pressure and stress in human judgment and decision making*. Cambridge: Cambridge University Press.

Schurr, P. H., & Ozanne, J. L. (1985). Influences on exchange process: Buyers preconceptions of a seller's trustworthiness and bargaining toughness. *Journal of Consumer Research, 11*, 937–953.

Summers, R. J. (1991). The influence of affirmative action on perception of a beneficiary's qualifications. *Journal of Applied Social Psychology, 21*, 1265–1276.

Taylor, S. E., Fiske, S. T., Etcoff, N. L., & Ruderman, A. J. (1978). Categorical and contextual bases of person memory and stereotyping. *Journal of Personality and Social Psychology, 36*, 778–793.

THINK IT THROUGH

Here are some questions to help place this research project in perspective and check your understanding.

1. What was the independent variable(s)? What was the dependent variable?
2. What control procedures were employed?
3. What were the main findings? What real-world implications do these findings have?
4. Was this an expensive project to conduct? Was elaborate equipment required?

The sex, race, type of store, and type of clothing worn by the confederates served as the independent variables. (Actually, sex, race, and type of store are not true independent variables because the experimenters did not directly manipulate them; however, they assumed this role in the present experiment.) The latency, as timed by the stopwatch, for a salesclerk to make appropriate contact was the dependent variable. Numerous control procedures were implemented in this research project; for example, (1) the confederates were the same age, (2) the confederates had never shopped in either of the malls, (3) each confederate wore only one style of clothing in each mall, (4) casual and business clothing were worn an equal number of times in each mall, and (5) timing did not begin until eye contact had been made with a salesclerk.

The results clearly indicate that sex, race, and clothing are factors that influence discrimination against shoppers by salesclerks. The implications are clear: store owners need to train their salesclerks more appropriately in order to avoid losing sales.

As you probably guessed, we purposely selected an inexpensive study that did not require elaborate equipment. Because the confederates were friends of the experimenters and volunteered to help with the research project, there was no expense, other than providing pizza after the project was completed, in order to pay them. The only piece of equipment employed in this study was an inexpensive stopwatch. This expenditure would hardly fall in the "major expense" category; in fact, you will likely find that such items may be borrowed from your own psychology department; Malissa and Susan did. Therefore, the major ingredient in this research project was an ingenious idea and the desire to put this idea to the experimental test.

THINK IT THROUGH

Now it's your turn. Let's take Malissa's and Susan's research one or two steps further. What are some good, inexpensive projects that you might want to conduct as a follow-up to the report you just read? Write down your thoughts and then we'll give you some possibilities.

As the two shopping malls were located near predominately Caucasian housing areas, it seems appropriate to replicate this research in other locales with different ethnic groups. Likewise, the study should be replicated using non-Caucasian salesclerks. It also would be interesting to determine the response of salesclerks to pairs of shoppers. In this regard, the many possibilities for forming pairs of shoppers offer intriguing research hypotheses.

As the shopping mall study clearly indicates, the key to a good project is the research idea, not how much money you spend on the project or the elaborate equipment you use. This logic is not limited to research in social psychology; it appears to be a generally applicable principle. To illustrate this point, we conclude this chapter with a brief examination of two additional projects of this nature from other areas of psychology.

TEACHING

Teaching offers more opportunities for excellent research projects than most people can imagine. For example, have you ever wondered how many people read the boxed sections in textbooks? Holly Miller conducted research to answer that question (Miller & Davis, 1993). She had two groups of college student participants read the same section from an economics text; then both groups took a test over this material. The test included questions on both regular text and boxed material. The only difference between the groups was the instructions; one group (Specified) was instructed to pay attention to the boxed material, whereas the other group (General) was not given these instructions. The results are shown in Figure 3–1.

As you can see from the figure, both groups did quite well on the questions from the regular text. However, performance on questions over the boxed material remained high only for the participants who were specifically instructed to pay attention to that material. This project represents another meaningful

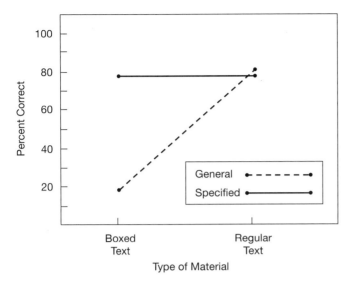

Figure 3–1 Mean percent correct responses to the regular-text and boxed-text questions for the general and specified groups.

research idea that did not require any equipment or, because the economics books were donated by a book publisher, any funds.

PHYSIOLOGICAL PSYCHOLOGY

Sometimes an easy to conduct, inexpensive, yet highly meaningful research project seems to drop out of the sky. Such was the case with a project proposed by Susan Nash. Susan had assisted with a project studying fetal alcohol syndrome in rats. That project entailed evaluating and comparing rat pups that had been exposed to alcohol before birth with pups that had not been exposed to alcohol before birth. When the project was completed, the pups remained in their cages until they matured. At that point, Susan proposed they be tested for alcohol preference. Because alcohol exposure occurred only during gestation, this research was designed to address whether prenatal exposure influenced adult preference (Nash, Weaver, Cowen, Davis, & Tramill, 1984). All Susan needed to do was place two drinking tubes (one containing plain water, one containing an alcohol-water mixture) on each animal's cage for 20 minutes each day for six days and record how much fluid was consumed. The results are shown in Figure 3–2 (higher data points = greater preference for the alcohol-water mixture). Clearly, the alcohol-exposed animals showed a greater preference for alcohol as adults. This was another meaningful experiment that required only a good research idea.

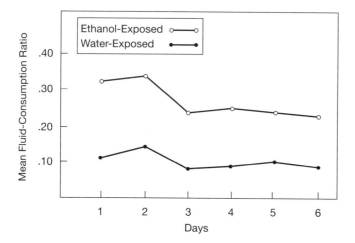

Figure 3–2 Daily group mean fluid-consumption Ratio (10% Ethanol mixture consumption divided by total fluid consumption). A ratio of .50 reflects consumption of equal amounts of the ethanol mixture and water, whereas ratios less than .50 reflect greater consumption of water.

Good research ideas are crucial to the success of your project; funding and equipment needs can be dealt with more easily. Your faculty advisor can be of great assistance in satisfying these "practical" needs; only *you* can develop the meaningful research idea. Please keep these thoughts in mind as you propose research ideas in response to our questions in the following chapters.

REFERENCES

Kraus, M. S., Davis, S. F., & Burns, S. (1997). Latency to serve in stores: Effects of sex, race, and clothing. *Emporia State Research Studies, 40,* 28–35.

Miller, H. R., & Davis, S. F. (1993). Recall of boxed material in textbooks. *Bulletin of the Psychonmic Society, 31,* 31–32.

Nash, S. M., Weaver, M. S., Cowen, C. L., Davis, S. F., & Tramill, J. L. (1984). Taste preference of the adult rat as a function of prenatal exposure to alcohol. *The Journal of General Psychology, 110,* 129–135.

CHAPTER 4

Comparative Research Idea Development

Since Professor Edmund Sanford constructed the first rat maze and student Willard S. Small published the initial report on rat behavior (Small, 1901), animal research has played an integral role in the development of psychological knowledge. For example, Domjan and Purdy (1995) indicate animal research has made pervasive contributions to such subareas of psychology as biological bases of behavior, sensation and perception, motivation, emotion, learning and memory, developmental psychology, psychopharmacology, psychopathology, treatment, and health and stress. Comparative psychologists do not study only laboratory rats; the animals they study range from worms to primates.

As Purdy (1996) points out, there are numerous reasons for becoming involved in comparative psychology research. Among these reasons are:

1. You learn something about anatomy, physiology, and behavior.
2. You acquire techniques of good animal care and maintenance.
3. You practice ethical and responsible treatment of animals.
4. You design experiments which comply with federal and local guidelines.
5. You are more competitive in the tight competition for admission to graduate school.

How does one become involved in animal research? Here are some suggestions (see Purdy, 1996) that may open some doors for you. (Keep in mind these tips are applicable to other research areas as well.)

1. Take an inventory of the faculty at your school to see who is conducting animal research. Once you have found a faculty member you would like to work with, camp out on his or her office doorstep and volunteer your services.

2. Be willing to start small and work your way up. You may have to begin your research career by performing somewhat menial tasks, such as cleaning cages and feeding the animals. Be flexible and patient; your turn to assume more involved roles and possibly work with different species will come.

3. Be thinking of your own original research ideas. Do not hesitate to discuss your proposed projects with your faculty supervisor. Although some of your ideas will not turn into research projects, some will. Keep generating new ideas!

What if your school does not have animal research facilities? Are you out of luck with regard to conducting this type of research? Absolutely not! Here are some creative solutions that will allow you to conduct animal research when you have very limited facilities and limited funds.

1. Select an organism to study that does not require extensive (and expensive) equipment and facilities for housing, maintenance, and testing. Here are some possibilities.

   a. *Goldfish.* A review of the published research reveals an extensive body of work on goldfish; this species has been studied in a variety of tasks. Establishing and maintaining a fish laboratory is significantly easier than establishing and maintaining a rat laboratory. Fish are less expensive to purchase, feed, and maintain.

   b. *Invertebrates.* It may surprise you to find an extensive literature describing the use of such animals as ants, earthworms, roaches, fruit flies, and houseflies in psychological research has been developed. (Because the feature article for this chapter deals with honeybees, we discuss them next in a separate section.) Such animals can be used for research on a myriad of topics in conditioning, as well as sensation and perception. Invertebrates offer the following advantages as research animals: (1) they are easy to acquire, (2) they are inexpensive, (3) housing and maintenance requirements are minimal, and (4) most test equipment can be built by the researcher. Charles Abramson, a psychologist at Oklahoma State University, is a leader in the use of invertebrates for psychological research. References to his work appear at the end of the chapter; they will provide many good tips and suggestions on conducting invertebrate research.

   c. *Honeybees.* Extensive research on honeybees indicates this species is capable of very complex learning. As you will see in the research article we have selected for inclusion in this chapter, the cost of doing honeybee research can be quite minimal.

2. If the facilities at your school simply preclude the conduct of animal research, then you should consider the possibility of conducting field research. Regardless of where you live, the world around you is filled with endless possibilities for great research projects. For example, you can

study foraging behavior, predator vigilance, communication, and mating behavior, in a wide range of animals and settings. Research of this nature is limited only by your own creativity.

3. Another option for becoming involved in animal research is to work in an animal laboratory at another institution. Many laboratory directors are thrilled to have a volunteer join their lab group. If you can locate such a laboratory close to your own school, you can work out the arrangements for this type of experience during the regular school year. Otherwise, you may have to consider a summer placement. Because you are a volunteer, you should not expect to be paid for your efforts; if you do receive some sort of funding, you should be thankful. (The research involvement and professional growth you receive are more valuable than money.) Also, you should check to see if you can receive academic credit, possibly as an "independent research" course, for such a placement.

We encourage you to explore the possibilities of comparative psychology research; the possibilities are endless. The feature article for this chapter (Huber, Couvillon, & Bitterman, 1994) describes the recent use of honeybees to study a long-standing topic of interest to learning psychologists: place learning (where the experimental target is located in the environment) and position learning (where the experimental target is located in relation to the test animal). This report presents the results of four experiments dealing with place learning (Experiments 1 and 2) and position learning (Experiments 3 and 4).

Place and Position Learning in Honeybees *(Apis mellifera)*

Brigitte Huber, P. A. Couvillon, and M. E. Bitterman
Békésy Laboratory of Neurobiology, University of Hawaii

Foraging honeybees *(Apis mellifera)* were trained individually to choose between 2 identical targets set close together on a large table in a heterogeneous surround. Discrimination was facilitated by the introduction of a small object that was nearer to 1 target than the other. It was also facilitated by the introduction of a longer object or a curved shield that was not differentially placed with respect to the tar-

This research was supported by Grant IBN-9308132 from the National Science Foundation. We thank Peter D. Balsam for helpful comments.

Correspondence concerning this article should be addressed to M. E. Bitterman, Békésy Laboratory of Neurobiology, 1993 East–West Road, Honolulu, Hawaii 96822. Electronic mail may be sent to jeffb@ahi.pbrc.hawaii.edu.

gets but designed to encourage a fixed orientation to them. The results support a distinction between place learning and position learning in honeybees.

When a honeybee is trained to choose between two targets that differ in some integral property, such as color, the locations of the targets must be interchanged to demonstrate discrimination of color apart from location. Discrimination of location, which may be evident in a preference displayed at the outset of training or established by differential reinforcement (Couvillon, Klosterhalfen, & Bitterman, 1983; Klosterhalfen, Fischer, & Bitterman, 1978), is interesting because location is not an integral property of a target but may be given in relation either to its surround *(place learning)* or to the orientation of the animal *(position learning)*.

Place and position learning were first clearly distinguished in some early experiments with rats (Blodgett & McCutchan, 1947; Tolman, Ritchie, & Kalish, 1946). Trained on an elevated T maze whose situation in a visually heterogeneous environment is changed from trial to trial, rats can learn readily to go always to a fixed place, whether a left or a right turn at the choice point is required to take them there on any given trial. They also can learn—more readily in a homogeneous environment than in a heterogeneous one (Restle, 1957)—to turn always to the left or always to the right at the choice point, although the same turn takes them to different places on different trials. Learning always to turn left or right at a choice point has traditionally been characterized as *response* learning rather than position learning on the assumption that the motor system is uniquely involved. That assumption is clearly expressed by Leonard and McNaughton (1990) in a recent essay on the neurobiology of spatial representation in rats: "The response strategy," they wrote, "employs a specific sequence of motor acts, largely independently of the distribution of sensory cues, to attain a goal of navigation" (p. 375). Our own preference is for the more neutral term, position learning, because persuasive evidence for the motor interpretation is lacking. It seems at least equally plausible that choice may be based on "position in visual space," as Wehner (1981, p. 536) suggested in his analysis of pattern discrimination in honeybees.

Place learning in honeybees has been studied in landmark experiments of several different kinds. One useful technique is to feed foragers on a target near a distinctive object or array of objects, and then to record their searching behavior in the absence of the target after some objects have been altered, repositioned, or removed (e.g., Cartwright & Collett, 1982; Cheng, Collett, Pickhard, & Wehner, 1987; Collett & Kelber, 1988; Wehner, 1981). Another technique is to train foragers to choose between two identical targets, with nearby objects to indicate which of the targets contains food on any trial (e.g., Couvillon & Bitterman, 1992). Evidence of position learning in honeybees comes from experiments with confined foragers limited to walking in a maze (Weiss, 1954) or in a Y-shaped discrimination chamber (Sigurdson, 1981). In the present experiments with free-flying subjects, place and position learning are contrasted in the same foraging situation.

EXPERIMENT 1

The subjects of this experiment were trained to discriminate between two identical targets at different locations on a homogeneous surface in a differentiated surround.

Method

Subjects. The subjects were 36 foraging honeybees *(Apis mellifera)*, all experimentally naive, from our own hives in the vicinity of the laboratory. They were recruited and trained individually.

Procedure. The experimental situation is sketched in Figure 4A–1. The targets were displayed on the 90×180 cm wooden top of a table set outdoors at one end of the south wall of our laboratory building. The table was about 120 cm from the wall under the eaves of the building in a two-sided enclosure that was differentiated by shaded windows, metal shelving, a rack of timing and recording equipment, air conditioning units, and shrubbery. Animals approached from the south by flying around the east wall of the enclosure. The targets were petri dishes (5.5 cm in diameter), with their covers sprayed with gray paint.

The pretraining procedure in this and all subsequent experiments was as follows: An animal was selected at random from a group of foragers at a feeding station equipped with a jar of 10%–12% sucrose solution that was out of sight of the training situation. The animal was captured in a match box, carried to the table, and placed at a large drop of 50% sucrose solution on a single target situated at the center of the table. There the animal was permitted to feed to repletion (during which time it was marked with an identifying spot of colored lacquer) and then to fly back to the hive. Typically, the animal returned to the table in a few minutes and continued to shuttle back and forth between the hive and the table as long as sucrose was available there. If it did not return to the table after its first placement, it was picked up at the feeding station (where it usually could be found) and placed again on the target. Choice training began on the visit after the animal's first return to the table of its own accord and continued for a total of 16 training visits.

One group of animals (Group 40: $n = 12$) was trained with a pair of targets placed 40 cm apart (edge-to-edge) at the center of the table in an east–west arrangement, as shown in Figure 4A–1. One of the targets (S+) contained a 100-µl drop of 50% sucrose solution from which feeding to repletion was permitted, and the other target (S–) contained a 100-µl drop of water, unacceptable to the animals and distinguishable from the sucrose only by taste. If S– was chosen on any trial, an error was recorded, and correction was permitted; the sub-

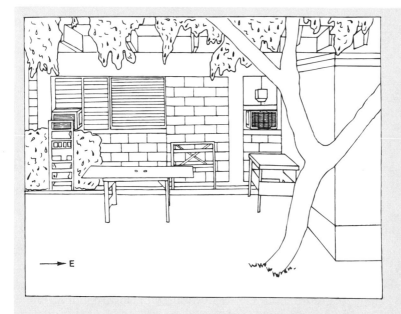

Figure 4A–1 A sketch of the experimental situation, which shows the two targets, 10 cm apart, centered on the 90 × 180 cm top of the training table.

ject fed to repletion on each trial, which ended with the subject's return to the hive. A second group of animals (Group 10; $n = 12$) was trained as was Group 40, except that the targets were only 10 cm apart. For a third group of animals (Group 10V; $n = 12$), the targets also were 10 cm apart, but the placement of the pair during training was varied (without rotation—the east–west orientation was maintained) over the four quadrants of the table in balanced quasi-random fashion, four trials in each quadrant. Six of the 12 animals in each group were trained with the east target as S+ and the rest, with the west target as S+ and the rest, with the west target as S+. The targets used on each visit were washed and exchanged for others in a set of identical targets after the visit in order to randomize extraneous stimuli.

On the visit after the 16th training visit, there was a 10-min extinction test in which each target now contained a 100-μl drop of water. For Groups 40 and 10, the targets were situated as they were in training; for Group 10V, the targets were at the center of the table, exactly as for Group 10. When an animal encountered water on one of the targets, it left the target, then returned to the same target or went to the other, left again, and returned again to one of the targets (sometimes only briefly, with no attempt to drink), and so forth; the interval between successive responses increased as the test continued. All actual contacts with each target, however brief, during a 10-min period were recorded by the experimenter, who pressed one of two hand-held switches that activated counters programmed to print stored frequencies at 30-s intervals. Work with each animal was terminated at the conclusion of the extinction test.

Results

In Figure 4A–2 (which includes selected acquisition data from this and from subsequent experiments), the performance of Groups 10 and 40 is plotted in terms of the mean number of erroneous choices in successive blocks of four acquisition trials. Group 40 made significantly fewer errors than was expected by chance ($p < .05$, binomial expansion), but Group 10 did not ($p > .05$). In Figure 4A–3, the performance of the two groups in the extinction test is plotted in terms of the mean cumulative number of responses to each target in successive 30-s intervals. Group 40 significantly preferred S+, $F(1, 11) = 11.18$, $p < .01$, but Group 10 did not ($F < 1$). These results can be understood on the assumption that the 40-cm separation was sufficient to permit place learning (differentiation of the targets in terms of features of the larger surround adjacent to them), although the 10-cm separation was not.

The mean number of errors made by Group 10V did not decline signifi-

Figure 4A–2 The course of acquisition under five conditions in which the position of the pair of targets remained the same. 40 = Group 40; 10 = Group 10; L = Groups LP and LN (both trained with the landmark); B = Groups BN, BS, BD, and B0 (all trained with the bar); S = Group S (trained with the shield).

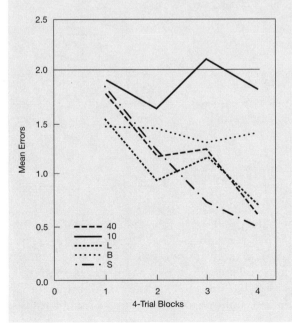

Figure 4A–3 Performance in the extinction test of the three groups trained with the targets alone in Experiment 1.

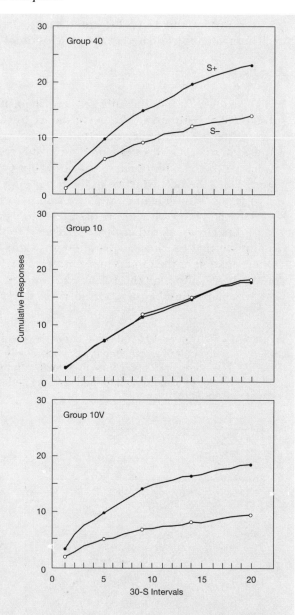

cantly over blocks of acquisition trials ($p > .05$), but in extinction (Figure 4A–3), the animals showed a significant preference for S+, $F(1, 11) + 9.48$, $p = .01$. The extinction measure, which is based on many more responses than the acquisition measure, is, of course, the more reliable of the two, and it may be expected also to be the more sensitive, given that it is made at the end of acquisition. The preference of Group 10V for S+ is unlikely to reflect place learning because the location of the pair of targets was varied widely in training and was never, as in the test, at the center of the table. A better explanation may be that the Group 10V animals adopted a common orientation to the targets that served as the basis for position learning. The common orientation was perhaps more likely to develop in Group 10V than in Group 10 because continued inspection of the situation on departure was promoted by the variation in training locations; Lehrer (1991) found that variation in training conditions increases the frequency with which departing foragers turn back and look at the feeding situation. It is possible also, of course, that the variation facilitated the development of a common orientation by promoting inspection on approach. A detailed videographic analysis of behavior both on arrival and departure will be instructive.

EXPERIMENT 2

In Experiment 1, 10-cm separation of two targets presented always at the center of the table was assumed to permit neither place nor position learning. In Experiment 2, the separation was the same, but a small object was introduced that was nearer one of the targets than the other and might serve, therefore, as a local landmark. The arrangement was expected to permit place learning.

Method

Subjects. The subjects were 32 foraging honeybees, all experimentally naive, from our own hives. They were recruited and trained individually.

Procedure. Two groups of animals were trained with two targets 10 cm apart (edge-to-edge) at the center of the table in the east–west arrangement and, as shown in the top portion of Figure 4A–4, with a landmark 5 cm away from one of the targets—east for half the animals in each group and west for the rest. The landmark was a blue wooden block, 4 cm wide × 4 cm high × 9 cm long, with its long dimension in the north–south orientation. For Group LP ($n = 8$), the target nearer the landmark was S+. For Group LN ($n = 8$), the target nearer the landmark was S−. In extinction the configuration was the same as in training.

Two other groups of 8 animals each—Groups LPR and LNR—were trained as were the first two, except that the location of the target and landmark configuration on the table was changed from trial to trial, and it was rotated in 90° steps as well, all in balanced quasi-random sequence. On one trial in each quadrant, the configuration was as shown in Figure 4A–4, with the targets in the east–west orientation and the landmark to the west; on a second trial in each quadrant, the targets were in a north–south orientation with the landmark to the north; on a third trial in each quadrant, the targets were in an east–west orientation with the landmark to the east; and on a fourth trial in each quadrant, the targets were in a north–south orientation with the landmark to the south.

Figure 4A–4 The target and landmark configuration
of Experiment 2, the
target and bar con-
figuration of Experi-
ment 3, and the tar-
get and shield
configuration of
Experiment 4.

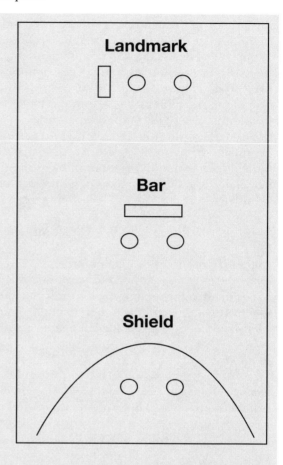

The extinction test was given with centered targets in the east–west arrangement, with the landmark to the east for half the animals in each group and to
the west for the rest.

Results

In acquisition, Groups LP and LN developed a significant preference for S+
($p = .01$); their pooled performance, which was much the same (and much like
that of Group 40), is plotted in Figure 4A–2. Their performance in extinction,
which also was much the same, is pooled in Figure 4A–5. Analysis of variance
yields a significant preference for S+, $F(1, 14) = 22.27$, $p < 1$) nor a significant
Group × Stimulus interaction ($F < 1$). It is clear that the introduction of a distinguishing landmark compensated for reduced separation of the targets that
impaired the performance of Group 10 in relation to that of Group 40. It is
clear also that the landmark could serve equally well as a positive or a negative
signal. Equal performance in landmark-positive and landmark-negative training
has previously been reported by Couvillon and Bitterman (1992).

Figure 4A–5 Performance in the extinction test of the groups trained with the landmark in Experiment 2.

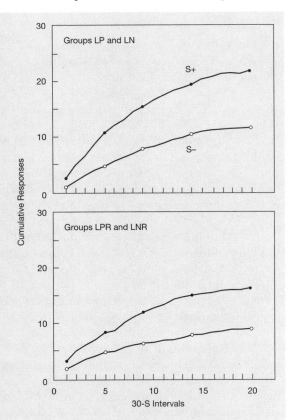

The performance of Groups LPR and LNR, for which the landmark and target configurations were displaced and rotated from trial to trial, did not improve significantly in acquisition ($p > .05$). Their performance in extinction (pooled in Figure 4A–5) did, however, show a significant preference for S+, $F(1, 14) = 45.33$, $p < .0001$, with neither a significant group effect ($F < 1$) nor a significant Group × Stimulus interaction ($F < 1$). It is clear from the extinction results that displacement and rotation did not prevent the development of a preference; the critical determinant of performance, apparently, was proximity to the landmark, which defined the place at which sucrose was to be found.

EXPERIMENT 3

In Experiment 3, we looked again for differential response to targets separated by 10 cm but with a local object—a bar—that was placed symmetrically with respect to the targets. The bar was not a landmark in the special sense that the block used in Experiment 2 could be called a landmark, because the bar did not in itself distinguish between the targets, although it probably did help to define their location as a pair. The bar was introduced on the intuition that it might encourage a fixed orientation to the targets and thus facilitate position learning.

Method

Subjects. The subjects were 40 foraging honeybees, all experimentally naive, from our own hives. They were recruited and trained individually.

Procedure. The target and bar configuration is diagrammed in Figure 4A–4. The bar was a blue block, $18 \times 4 \times 4$ cm. For animals in Group BN ($n = 8$), the bar was situated 5 cm north of the two targets, which were at the center of the table (10 cm apart in the east–west arrangement), both in training and in testing. For animals in Group BS ($n = 8$), the bar was 5 cm south of the targets both in training and testing. For half the animals in each group, the east target was S+; for the rest, the west target was S+.

Two other groups were trained as were Groups BN and BS, except that the bar position was balanced within rather than between groups—north for half the animals in each group and south for the rest. Again the east target was S+ for half the animals in each group, and the west target for the rest. For the animals of Group BD ($n = 8$), the position of the bar was different in extinction than in training—south for animals trained with the bar to the north, and north for animals trained with the bar to the south. For the animals of Group B0 ($n = 8$), the bar was absent in extinction.

A fifth group of animals (Group BR; $n = 8$) was trained with the location of the target and bar configuration changed from trial to trial—four trials in each of the four quadrants of the table—and rotated in $90°$ steps as well (all in balanced, quasi-random sequence). On one trial in each quadrant, the configuration was as shown in Figure 4A–4, with the bar to the north; on a second trial, the bar was to the south; and on a third and a fourth trial, the orientation of the targets was north–south with the bar either to the east or to the west. As the target and bar configuration is diagrammed in Figure 4A–4, the left target was S+ for half the animals and the right target, for the rest. In extinction the targets were at the center of the table in the east–west arrangement with the bar to the north.

Results

The pooled acquisition results for Groups BN, BS, BD, and B0, each of which was trained with a centered and unrotated configuration, are plotted in Figure 2. The number of errors was significantly less than chance ($p < .0001$), but there was not the same systematic improvement in performance in this case as in the landmark case. In extinction, Groups BN and BS, whose pooled performance is plotted in Figure 6, both showed a significance preference for S+, $F(1, 14) = 37.62$, $p < .0001$, with neither a significant group effect ($F < 1$) nor a significant Group $\times$ Stimulus interaction ($F < 1$). Whereas the two targets were equidistant from the bar, the bar could not have functioned as a simple landmark. Our hypothesis is that the bar in some way facilitated orientation to the

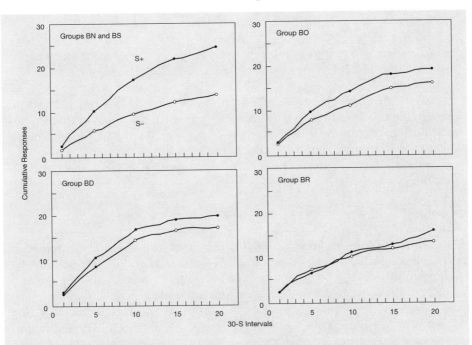

Figure 4A–6 Performance in the extinction test of the groups trained with the bar in Experiment 3.

targets, making position learning possible. The extinction results for the other three bar groups also are plotted in Figure 4A–6. The fact that none of them showed a significant preference for S+ ($F < 1$ in each case) suggests that the orientation assumed to permit position learning in Groups BN and BS was jointly controlled by the bar and by some more remote feature of the context. The results for Groups BD and B0 show the continuing importance of the bar; displacing it, or removing it entirely, impaired discrimination. The results for Group BR, whose preference for S+ was not different from chance either in training or in the extinction test, show that a fixed relation between the target and bar configuration and the larger context was essential.

EXPERIMENT 4

In Experiment 4, a salient local surround—a tall, white, curved shield—was substituted for the bar. The shield was intended to exert more powerful control of the direction of approach to the targets and at the same time to minimize the influence of the larger environment at the point of choice. Our hope was that it might provide a standard set of conditions for studying the relation between position learning and learning about other target properties.

Method

Subjects.   The subjects were 8 foraging honeybees, all experimentally naive, from our own hives. They were recruited and trained individually.

Procedure.   For a single group of 8 animals, designated as Group S, a white curved shield, 50 cm high and 71 cm wide, was set to the north of the two targets. Both in training and in testing, the targets were centered on the table in the east–west arrangement, 10 cm apart and 10 cm from the shield. The geometry is shown in Figure 4A–4. The east target was S+ for half the animals, and the west target was S+ for the rest.

Results

The course of learning in Group S is shown in Figure 4A–2. The number of errors was significantly less than chance ($p < .0001$), and the plot shows the same pronounced improvement as was found in Group 40 and in the landmark groups (Groups LP and LN) for which the placement of the target was unchanged during training. In the extinction test the animals showed a strong and significant preference for S+, $F(1, 7) = 92.56$, $p < .0001$. The extinction curves are plotted in Figure 4A–7.

DISCUSSION

In Experiment 1, the locations of the two identical targets alone at the center of the table were clearly discriminated when they were separated by 40 cm (Group 40) but not when they were separated by only 10 cm (Group 10). The simplest explanation is that the animals of Group 40 were responding on the basis of contextual stimuli, which were not sufficiently different for targets that were closer together; that is, there was place learning in Group 40 but not in

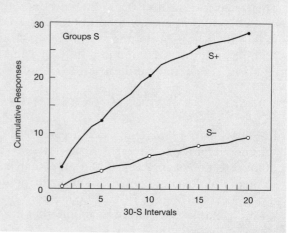

Figure 4A–7 Performance in the extinction test of the group trained with the shield in Experiment 4.

Group 10. Direct evidence of place learning was found in Experiment 2, in which the addition of a local landmark that was closer to one of the targets than to the other made discrimination possible even with a separation of only 10 cm. Rotation of the target and landmark configuration during training to some extent impaired acquisition as measured in terms of errors but did not prevent the development of a clear preference for the rewarded location as evidenced by the subsequent extinction test; that is, control by the local landmark transcended control by features of the surroundings, as Cheng et al. (1987) also reported, although remote features sometimes may play a dominant role (Cartwright & Collett, 1982), as a function, one must suppose, of their relative salience. How landmarks work remains to be determined, of course.

Our first indication of location learning that is not place learning was provided in Experiment 1 by Group 10V, for which the placement of the pair of targets, separated by 10 cm, was systematically varied (without rotation) in the course of training. Preference for S+ in the extinction test suggested the development of a common orientation to the targets, which then could be differentiated in terms of position. Experiment 3 showed that discrimination could be facilitated also by the use of a local object—the bar—that did not in itself distinguish the two targets but seemed in conjunction with the surroundings to promote the development of a fixed orientation to the targets. The popular snapshot metaphor (Cartwright & Collett, 1982) does not help us to understand why the bar and landmark configurations ought to be differentially susceptible to rotation. In Experiment 4, with the bar replaced by a high curved shield, a substantial preference for S+ appeared both in training and extinction; like the bar, the shield did not in itself distinguish the two targets but can be supposed to have exerted more powerful control of the direction of approach to them. As has already been noted, the idea that honeybees discriminate position in the visual field was suggested some years ago by Wehner (1981), who stressed the importance for honeybees and other flying insects of "fixating objects of interest" (p. 393) and speculated on the way in which direction of approach is determined.

Our own interest in the problem has been stimulated by the results of experiments on the discrimination of what are best now referred to as *color–location* compounds (Couvillon et al., 1983; Klosterhalfen et al., 1978). Although the term *position* rather than *location* was used in the reports of those experiments, the discrimination may as well have been of place, because the targets were presented in locally differentiated surroundings. (The distinction between position and place learning was not considered at the time.) The color–location results are intriguing because they differ from those of color–odor experiments; for example, dimensional transfer is found with color–location compounds but not with color–odor compounds (Klosterhalfen et al., 1978). The differences can perhaps be understood on the assumption that color and odor are integral target properties and that position functions like one, but place (if that is what actually was studied) does not. It will be interesting to do experiments of the same kind both under the place-learning conditions of Experiment 2 and the position-learning conditions of Experiment 4.

REFERENCES

Blodgett, H. C., & McCutchan, K. (1947). Place versus response learning in the simple T-maze. *Journal of Experimental Psychology, 37,* 412–422.

Cartwright, B. A., & Collett, T. S. (1982). How honey bees use landmarks to guide their return to a food source. *Nature, 295,* 560–564.

Cheng, K., Collett, T. S., Pickhard, A., & Wehner, R. (1987). The use of visual landmarks by honeybees: Bees weight landmarks according to their distance from the goal. *Journal of Comparative Physiology A, 161,* 469–475.

Collett, T. S., & Kelber, A. (1988). The retrieval of visuo-spatial memories by honeybees. *Journal of Comparative Physiology A, 163,* 145–150.

Couvillon, P. A., & Bitterman, M. E. (1992). Landmark learning by honeybees. *Journal of Insect Behavior, 5,* 123–129.

Couvillon, P. A., Klosterhalfen, S., & Bitterman, M. E. (1983). Analysis of overshadowing in honeybees. *Journal of Comparative Psychology, 97,* 154–166.

Klosterhalfen, S., Fischer, W., & Bitterman, M. E. (1978). Modification of attention in honeybees. *Science, 201,* 1241–1243.

Lehrer, M. (1991). Bees which turn back and look. *Naturwissenschaften, 78,* 274–276.

Leonard, B., & McNaughton, B. L. (1990). Spatial representation in the rat: Conceptual, behavioral, and neurophysiological perspectives. In R. P. Kestner & D. S. Olton (Eds.), *Neurobiology of comparative cognition* (pp. 363–442). Hillsdale, NJ: Erlbaum.

Restle, F. (1957), F. (1957). Discrimination of cues in mazes: A resolution of the "place vs. response" question. *Psychological Review, 64,* 217–228.

Sigurdson, J. E. (1981). Automated discrete-trials techniques of appetitive conditioning in honeybees. *Behavior Research Methods & Instrumentation, 13,* 1–10.

Tolman, E. C., Ritchie, B. F., & Kalish, D. (1946). Studies in spatial learning: II. Place learning versus response learning. *Journal of Experimental Psychology, 36,* 221–229.

Wehner, R. (1981). Spatial vision in arthropods. In H. Autrum (Ed.), *Comparative physiology and evolution of vision in invertebrates: C. Invertebrate visual centers and behavior II* (pp. 287–616). Berlin: Springer.

Weiss, K. (1954). Der Lernvorgang bei einfachen Labyrinthdressuren von Bienen und Wespen [The learning of simple mazes by bees and wasps]. *Zeitschrift für Vergleichende Physilogie, 36,* 9–20.

THINK IT THROUGH

Answering the following questions will help you check your understanding of this article. We suggest you jot down your answers as you read each question, then continue reading the chapter.

1.   What is the distinction between place and position learning?

2. What was the purpose of Experiment 1? What did the researchers find and how are these results related to Experiment 2?
3. What did the results of Experiment 2 show? How are these results related to the design of Experiment 3?
4. What did the results of Experiment 3 show and how did these results contribute to the design of Experiment 4?
5. What did the results of Experiment 4 demonstrate?
6. In what way have these experiments contributed to our general understanding of the behavior of honeybees?
7. Why were all four experiments necessary to help answer the research questions?
8. What might the next steps in this research program be?

This article presents a good illustration of the hypothetico-deductive model in operation. Based on previous research and current theory, a researchable hypothesis is devised and put to the experimental test. The results of that experiment are used to modify the theory (if modification is needed) and aid in the deduction of new hypotheses. These new hypotheses are tested and the cycle continues. In these experiments Huber et al. studied the discrimination learning of free-flying honeybees. In Experiment 1, they found honeybees could discriminate a petri dish containing sucrose from an identical dish containing water if the dishes were separated by 40 cm, but not if the dishes were separated by only 10 cm. When plain water was placed in both dishes (i.e., extinction), the honeybees trained with the dishes 40 cm apart continued to show a preference for the dish that formerly contained sucrose. The honeybees trained with the dishes 10 cm apart did not show a preference during extinction. For a third group of honeybees, the dishes were 10 cm apart but were not always located in the center of the table top where testing took place. Although these honeybees did not show a decline in errors (i.e., going to the water dish) during training, they showed a preference for the former sucrose dish during extinction. The authors attribute this preference to more frequent inspection by these animals. The results of Experiment 1 prompted Experiment 2 in which a landmark (the blue bar) was used in conjunction with two, 10-cm-apart dishes. When the landmark was consistently placed by the sucrose dish *or* by the water dish, the honeybees made fewer errors in choosing between the two dishes. The landmark assisted them in learning the place they were going. In Experiment 3, the blue bar was placed symmetrically in relation to the two dishes. In this instance, it was not used to distinguish between the dishes, but rather to help define the location of the dishes and assist in position learning. Although the presence of the bar did not influence the number of errors made during training, it did result in a significant preference for the former S+ (sucrose) dish during extinction. In Experiment 4, a tall, white, curved shield was substituted for the blue bar. It was thought the larger shield would exert more powerful control over the direction of approach to the dishes and, therefore, facilitate the discrimination between them. The results supported this prediction: the number of errors decreased during extinction and the honeybees displayed a significant preference for the former S+ dish during extinction.

In addition to being a good example of the hypothetico-deductive method of research, this report also serves as an excellent example of programmatic research. When programmatic research is conducted, the researcher identifies a specific area of interest and confines his or her activities to that area. As in the article you just read, when programmatic research is conducted, experiments tend to build on each other until a more complete picture is developed. The present researchers, especially Couvillon and Bitterman, have studied the behavior of honeybees for years. Through their programmatic research they have developed a wealth of information that is very valuable in suggesting new studies to be conducted and the appropriate methodology to be used in them. Because psychology is becoming so diversified and specialized, most researchers find themselves devoting their research attention to programmatic research in one specified area.

Now, let's stand back and examine this article from several different perspectives. First, do you feel you could you conduct a study using honeybees as the test animals? There are several reasons to say yes. For example, the expense involved in such projects can be quite minimal.

THINK IT THROUGH

How carefully did you read this article? List the equipment Huber et al. used in these experiments. Which pieces of equipment are easy to acquire? Which ones are more difficult or expensive?

Equipment List for Honeybee Studies

1. _____

2. _____

3. _____

4. _____

5. _____

The basic equipment used in these studies included a match box to capture the test animal, two petri dishes for sucrose and water, colored lacquer to mark the test animal, a table, and the two counters used to record the frequencies of going to the S+ (sucrose) and S– (water) dishes during the 30-second intervals. The first four items can be obtained easily and at very little expense. However, programmable counters may be expensive or more difficult to acquire. Assuming you do not have funds to purchase such equipment, you might want to check with faculty in your department (or other departments, if necessary) to see if such equipment is available and can be borrowed. If this search is unsuccessful, consider another option: adapt an old computer for this task. As more powerful computers become available, most psychology departments are beginning to accumulate a huge surplus of older (e.g., IBM 286 computers) but still functional, computers. A skillful programmer should be able to set up such a computer to serve the same functions as the programmable counters. If these searches fail to yield positive results, you might want to consider the use of mechanical, hand-held tally counters. Although these counters are not as sophisticated (or reliable) as a programmable counter or a computer, they will provide you with meaningful data.

THINK IT THROUGH

So far so good, except your campus does not have an abundance of bee hives for you to use. That problem seems insurmountable. Should you abandon your dreams of becoming a renowned honeybee researcher? Is there still some way you can conduct the honeybee project you have in mind?

Remember our earlier discussion of conducting field studies? This problem offers you a perfect opportunity to conduct a field study. All you need to do is find a local honey producer who is willing to let you use a few of his or her bees. As no harm will come to any of the bees, that should not be an especially difficult task.

What are the next steps with this line of honeybee research? Here are some suggested follow-up studies that could be conducted.

1. Huber, Couvillon, and Bitterman demonstrated that honeybees can learn to go to the correct target when the targets are spaced 30 cm apart, but not when they are only 10 cm apart. Where in the 20-cm range between 10 and 30 cm is the break point where discrimination fails? Only additional research can answer this question.
2. Was the use of petri dishes as targets a crucial variable? Can honeybees learn place and position discriminations as easily (or even better) when different targets are used? What types of stimuli might be used as targets?
3. How important are weather conditions to this type of learning in honeybees? Notice the present article does not describe the existing weather

conditions. Conditions such as the degree of cloudiness may influence the results of these experiments.

4. Could this series of experiments be replicated in the more controlled conditions of the laboratory?

5. Replication of these studies in the more controlled laboratory environment would allow one to evaluate the relevance of other cues in the environment.

6. Of what other forms of discrimination learning are honeybees capable? For example, can they learn to discriminate between sucrose and water targets on the basis of color or shape?

7. Could other organisms be used to study similar behaviors?

THINK IT THROUGH

List five ideas below that can be researched that are related to the ideas mentioned above and list three novel ideas (not related to any of the above ideas) that could also be researched. What types of materials and time would each of these eight ideas require?

Related ideas:

1. _____

2. _____

3. _____

4. _____

5. _____

Novel ideas:

1. _____

2. _____

3. _____

After listing your various research ideas, have one of your professors read them and give you additional and alternate suggestions. Take the suggestions and modify or change them to fit your study.

REFERENCES

Domjan, M., & Purdy, J. E. (1995). Animal research in psychology: More than meets the eye of the general psychology student. *American Psychologist, 50,* 496–503.

Huber, B., Couvillon, P. A., & Bitterman, M. E. (1994). Place and position learning in honeybees (*Apis mellifera*). *Journal of Comparative Psychology, 108,* 213–219.

Purdy, J. E. (1996, June). *Getting undergraduates involved in basic and applied research with animals.* Paper presented at the annual meeting of the American Psychological Society, San Francisco, CA.

Small, W. S. (1901). Experimental study of the mental processes of the rat. II. *American Journal of Psychology, 12,* 206–239.

ADDITIONAL READINGS

Abramson, C. I. (1986). Invertebrates in the classroom. *Teaching of Psychology, 13,* 24–29.

Abramson, C. I. (1990). *Invertebrate learning: A laboratory manual and source book.* Washington, DC: American Psychological Association.

Abramson, C. I. (1994). *A primer of invertebrate learning: The behavioral perspective.* Washington, DC: American Psychological Association.

Abramson, C. I., Onstott, T., Edwards, S., & Bowe, K. (1996). Classical-conditioning demonstrations for elementary and advanced courses. *Teaching of Psychology, 23,* 26–30.

CHAPTER 5

Social Research Idea Development

Perhaps no other area represents such a wealth of psychological research, and hence such a potential wealth of ideas for projects, as does the diverse area of social psychology. Social psychologists study such topics as attitudes, attraction, emotionality, helping behavior, suggestibility, conformity, obedience, aggression, and prejudice, just to name a few. If there is a study to be done on people, you can bet a social psychologist will be involved.

How, then, can we come up with a single study to aid you in developing research ideas within social psychology? If we take a 1984 quote from R. Lance Shotland (Myers, 1996), which tends to represent most social psychologists' views, our task becomes much easier: "Probably no single incident has caused social psychologists to pay as much attention to an aspect of social behavior as Kitty Genovese's murder," (p. 517).

With all of the murders occurring nationwide in a single year, what was it about this particular incident that catapulted it to notoriety status in social psychology? In 1964, a young woman by the name of Kitty Genovese was viciously raped and stabbed outside her New York apartment building. What made this murder uniquely interesting for social psychologists was the fact that her attacker originally fled after Ms. Genovese began screaming and yelling for help. When no one came to her aid the attacker returned, raping her for a second time, and stabbing her eight more times. It was not until the attacker finally left did any of the people living in the apartment building call police.

You might say "No one helped the woman because no one heard her pleas for help." That certainly would help to explain the lack of any type of response. However, it was later found that no less than 38 of her neighbors heard her screams but decided, for then unknown reasons, to ignore her obvious need of help!

THINK IT THROUGH

Would you personally have helped this woman had you heard her screams? Perhaps you would, but research tends to suggest most people would not. Before reading the featured article in this chapter, think of some of the reasons why a person would not go to the aid of this woman in trouble, let alone call the police. List five different reasons that would explain such a lack of interest in the plight of the dying woman. Next, list five situations in which a person would almost certainly help another who is in mortal danger.

As you read the article and the rest of this chapter, determine how accurate your reasons and situations were. As you read the chapter, determine why those hypotheses that were determined to be correct were correct and why those that were determined to be incorrect were incorrect. You will probably find some interesting answers.

Bystander Intervention in Emergencies: Diffusion of Responsibility[1]

John M. Darley and Bibb Latanté
New York University, Columbia University

Ss overheard an epileptic seizure. They believed either that they alone heard the emergency, or that 1 or 4 unseen others were also present. As predicted the presence of other bystanders reduced the individual's feelings of personal responsibility and lowered his speed of reporting ($p < .01$). In groups of size 3, males reported no faster than females, and females reported no slower when the 1 other bystander was a male rather than a female. In general, personality and background measures were not predictive of helping. Bystander inaction in real-life emergencies is often explained by "apathy," "alienation," and "anomie." This experiment suggests that the explanation may lie more in the bystander's response to other observers than in his indifference to the victim.

[1]This research was supported in part by National Science Foundation Grants GS1238 and GS1239. Susan Darley contributed materially to the design of the experiment and ran the subjects, and she and Thomas Moriarty analyzed the data. Richard Nisbett, Susan Millman, Andrew Gordon, and Norma Neiman helped in preparing the tape recordings.

Several years ago, a young woman was stabbed to death in the middle of a street in a residential section of New York City. Although such murders are not entirely routine, the incident received little public attention until several weeks later when the New York Times disclosed another side to the case: at least 38 witnesses had observed the attack—and none had even attempted to intervene. Although the attacker took more than half an hour to kill Kitty Genovese, not one of the 38 people who watched from the safety of their own apartments came out to assist her. Not one even lifted the telephone to call the police (Rosenthal, 1964).

Preachers, professors, and news commentators sought the reasons for such apparently conscienceless and inhumane lack of intervention. Their conclusions ranged from "moral decay," to "dehumanization produced by the urban environment," to "alienation," "anomie," and "existential despair." An analysis of the situation, however, suggests that factors other than apathy and indifference were involved.

A person witnessing an emergency situation, particularly such a frightening and dangerous one as a stabbing, is in conflict. There are obvious humanitarian norms about helping the victim, but there are also rational and irrational fears about what might happen to a person who does intervene (Milgram & Hollander, 1964). "I didn't want to get involved," is a familiar comment, and behind it lies fears of physical harm, public embarrassment, involvement with police procedures, lost work days and jobs, and other unknown dangers.

In certain circumstances, the norms favoring intervention may be weakened, leading bystanders to resolve the conflict in the direction of nonintervention. One of these circumstances may be the presence of other onlookers. For example, in the case above, each observer, by seeing lights and figures in others apartment house windows, knew that others were also watching. However, there was no way to tell how the other observers were reacting. These two facts provide several reasons why any individual may have delayed or failed to help. The responsibility for helping was diffused among the observers; there was also diffusion of any potential blame for not taking action; and finally, it was possible that somebody, unperceived, had already initiated helping action.

When only one bystander is present in an emergency, if help is to come, it must come from him. Although he may choose to ignore it (out of concern for his personal safety, or desires "not to get involved"), any pressure to intervene focuses uniquely on him. When there are several observers present, however, the pressures to intervene do not focus on any one of the observers; instead the responsibility for intervention is shared among all the onlookers and is not unique to any one. As a result, no one helps.

A second possibility is that potential blame may be diffused. However much we may wish to think that an individual's moral behavior is divorced from considerations of personal punishment or reward, there is both theory and evidence to the contrary (Aronfreed, 1964; Miller & Dollard, 1941, Whiting & Child, 1953). It is perfectly reasonable to assume that under circumstances of group responsibility for a punishable act, the punishment or blame that accrues to any one individual is often slight or nonexistent.

Finally, if others are known to be present, but their behavior cannot be closely observed, any one bystander can assume that one of the other observers is already taking action to end the emergency. Therefore, his own intervention would be only redundant—perhaps harmfully or confusingly so. Thus, given the presence of other onlookers whose behavior cannot be observed, any given bystander can rationalize his own inaction by convincing himself that "somebody else must be doing something."

These considerations lead to the hypothesis that the more bystanders to an emergency, the less likely, or the more slowly, any one bystander will intervene to provide aid. To test this proposition it would be necessary to create a situation in which a realistic "emergency" could plausibly occur. Each subject should also be blocked from communicating with others to prevent his getting information about their behavior during the emergency. Finally, the experimental situation should allow for the assessment of the speed and frequency of the subjects' reaction to the emergency. The experiment reported below attempted to fulfill these conditions.

PROCEDURE

Overview. A college student arrived in the laboratory and was ushered into an individual room from which a communication system would enable him to talk to the other participants. It was explained to him that he was to take part in a discussion about personal problems associated with college life and that the discussion would be held over the intercom system, rather than face-to-face, in order to avoid embarrassment by preserving the anonymity of the subjects. During the course of the discussion, one of the other subjects underwent what appeared to be a very serious nervous seizure similar to epilepsy. During the fit it was impossible for the subject to talk to the other discussants or to find out what, if anything, they were doing about the emergency. The dependent variable was the speed with which the subjects reported the emergency to the experimenter. The major independent variable was the number of people the subject thought to be in the discussion group.

Subjects. Fifty-nine female and thirteen male students in introductory psychology courses at New York University were contacted to take part in an unspecified experiment as part of a class requirement.

Method. Upon arriving for the experiment, the subject found himself in a long corridor with doors opening off it to several small rooms. An experimental assistant met him, took him to one of the rooms, and seated him at a table. After filling out a background information form, the subject was given a pair of headphones with an attached microphone and was told to listen for instructions.

Over the intercom, the experimenter explained that he was interested in learning about the kinds of personal problems faces by normal college students in a high pressure, urban environment. He said that to avoid possible embarrassment about discussing personal problems with strangers several precautions had been taken. First, subjects would remain anonymous, which was why they had been placed in individual rooms rather than face-to-face. (The actual reason for this was to allow tape recorder simulation of the other subjects and the emergency.) Second, since the discussion might be inhibited by the presence of outside listeners, the experimenter would not listen to the initial discussion, but would get the subject's reactions later, by questionnaire. (The real purpose of this was to remove the obviously responsible experimenter from the scene of the emergency.)

The subjects were told that since the experimenter was not present, it was necessary to impose some organization. Each person would talk in turn, presenting his problems to the group. Next, each person in turn would comment on what the others had said, and finally, there would be a free discussion. A mechanical switching device would regulate this discussion sequence and each subject's microphone would be on for about 2 minutes. While any microphone was on, all other microphones would be off. Only one subject, therefore, could be heard over the network at any given time. The subjects were thus led to realize when they later heard the seizure that only the victim's microphone was on and that there was no way of determining what any of the other witnesses were doing, nor of discussing the event and its possible solution with the others. When these instructions had been given, the discussion began.

In the discussion, the future victim spoke first, saying that he found it difficult to get adjusted to New York City and to his studies. Very hesitantly, and with obvious embarrassment, he mentioned that he was prone to seizures, particularly when studying hard or taking exams. The other people, including the real subject, took their turns and discussed similar problems (minus, of course, the proneness to seizures). The naive subject talked last in the series, after the last prerecorded voice was played.[2]

When it was again the victim's turn to talk, he made a few relatively calm comments, and then, growing increasingly louder and incoherent, he continued:

> I-er-um-I think I-I need-er-if-if could-er-er-somebody er-er-er-er-er-er-er give me a little-er-give me a little help here because-er-I-er-I'm-er-er-h-h-having a-a-a real problem-er-right now and I-er-if somebody could help me out it would-it-would-er-er s-s-sure be-sure be good . . . because-er-there-er-er-a cause I-er-I-uh-I've got a-a one of the-er-sei———er-er things coming on and-and-and I could really-er-use some help so if somebody would-er give me a little h-help-uh-er-er-er-er-er c-could some-

---

[2]To test whether the order in which the subjects spoke in the first discussion round significantly affected the subjects' speed of report, the order in which the subjects spoke was varied (in the six-person group). This had no significant or noticeable effect on the speed of the subjects' reports.

body-er-er-help-er-uh-uh-uh (choking sounds). . . . I'm gonna die-er-er-I'm . . . gonna die-er-help-er-er-seizure-er-[chokes, then quiet].

The experimenter began timing the speed of the real subject's response at the beginning of the victim's speech. Informed judges listening to the tape have estimated that the victim's increasingly louder and more disconnected ramblings clearly represented a breakdown about 70 seconds after the signal for the victim's second speech. The victim's speech was abruptly cut off 125 seconds after this signal, which could be interpreted by the subject as indicating that the time allotted for that speaker had elapsed and the switching circuits had switched away from him. Times reported in the results are measured from the start of the fit.

Group size variable.   The major independent variable of the study was the number of other people that the subject believed also heard the fit. By the assistant's comments before the experiment, and also by the number of voices heard to speak in the first round of the group discussion, the subject was led to believe that the discussion group was one of three sizes: either a two-person group (consisting of a person who would later have a fit and the real subject), a three-person group (consisting of the victim, the real subject, and one confederate voice), or a six-person group (consisting of the victim, the real subject, and four confederate voices). All the confederates' voices were tape-recorded.

Variations in group composition.   Varying the kind as well as the number of bystanders present at an emergency should also vary the amount of responsibility felt by any single bystander. To test this, several variations of the three-person group were run. In one three-person condition, the taped bystander voice was that of a female, in another a male, and in the third a male who said that he was a premedical student who occasionally worked in the emergency wards at Bellevue hospital.

In the above conditions, the subjects were female college students. In a final condition males drawn from the same introductory psychology subject pool were tested in a three-person female-bystander condition.

Time to help.   The major dependent variable was the time elapsed from the start of the victim's fit until the subject left her experimental cubicle. When the subject left her room, she saw the experimental assistant seated at the end of the hall, and invariably went to the assistant. If 6 minutes elapsed without the subject having emerged from her room, the experiment was terminated.

As soon as the subject reported the emergency, or after 6 minutes had elapsed, the experimental assistant disclosed the true nature of the experiment, and dealt with any emotions aroused in the subject. Finally the subject filled out a questionnaire concerning her thoughts and feelings during the emergency, and completed scales of Machiavellianism, anomie, and authoritarianism (Christie, 1964), a social desirability scale (Crowne & Marlowe, 1964), a social responsibility scale (Daniels & Berkowitz, 1964), and reported vital statistics and socioeconomic data.

RESULTS

Plausibility of Manipulation

Judging by the subjects' nervousness when they reported the fit to the experimenter, by their surprise when they discovered that the fit was simulated, and by comments they made during the fit (when they thought their microphones were off), one can conclude that almost all of the subjects perceived the fit as real. There were two exceptions in different experimental conditions, and the data for these subjects were dropped from the analysis.

Effect of Group Size on Helping

The number of bystanders that the subject perceived to be present had a major effect on the likelihood with which she would report the emergency (Table 5A–1). Eighty-five percent of the subjects who thought they alone knew of the victim's plight reported the seizure before the victim was cut off, only 31% of those who thought four other bystanders were present did so.

Every one of the subjects in the two-person groups, but only 62% of the subjects in the six-person groups, ever reported the emergency. The cumulative distributions of response times for groups of different perceived size (Figure 5A–1) indicates that, by any point in time, more subjects from the two-person groups had responded than from the three-person groups, and more from the three-person groups than from the six-person groups.

Ninety-five percent of all the subjects who ever responded did so within the first half of the time available to them. No subject who had not reported within 3 minutes after the fit ever did so. The shape of these distributions suggest that had the experiment been allowed to run for a considerably longer time, few additional subjects would have responded.

Table 5A–1 Effects of Groups' Size on Likelihood and Speed of Response

Group size	N	% responding by end of fit	Time in sec.	Speed score
2 (*S* & victim)	13	85	52	.87
3 (*S*, victim & 1 other)	26	62	93	.72
6 (*S*, victim, & 4 others)	13	31	166	.51

Note.—p value of differences: $\chi^2 = 7.91$, $p < .02$; $F = 8.09$, $p < .01$, for speed scores.

Figure 5A–1 Cumulative distributions of helping responses.

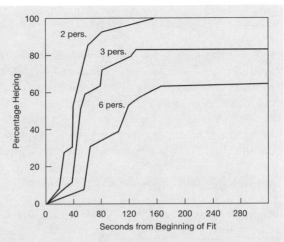

Speed of Response

To achieve a more detailed analysis of the results, each subject's time score was transformed into a "speed" score by taking the reciprocal of the response time in seconds and multiplying by 100. The effect of this transformation was to de-emphasize differences between longer time scores, thus reducing the contribution to the results of the arbitrary 6-minute limit on scores. A high speed score indicates a fast response.

An analysis of variance indicates that the effect of group size is highly significant ($p < .01$). Duncan multiple-range tests indicate that all but the two- and three-person groups differ significantly from one another ($p < .05$).

Victim's Likelihood of Being Helped

An individual subject is less likely to respond if he thinks that others are present. But what of the victim? Is the inhibition of the response of each individual strong enough to counteract the fact that with five onlookers there are five times as many people available to help? From the data of this experiment, it is possible mathematically to create hypothetical groups with one, two, or five observers.[3] The calculations indicate that the victim is about equally likely to get help from one bystander as from two. The victim is considerably more likely to have gotten help from one or two observers than from five during the first minute of the fit. For instance, by 45 seconds after the start of the fit, the victim's chances of having been helped by the single bystanders were about 50%, compared to none in the five observer condition. After the first minute, the likelihood of getting help from at least one person is high in all three conditions.

[3]The formula for the probability that at least one person will help by a given time is $1 - (1 - P)^n$ where n is the number of observers and P is the probability of a single individual (who thinks he is one of n observers) helping by that time.

Effect of Group Composition on Helping the Victim

Several variations of the three-person group were run. In one pair of variations, the female subject thought the other bystander was either male or female; in another, she thought the other bystander was a premedical student who worked in an emergency ward at Bellevue hospital. As Table 5A–2 shows, the variations in sex and medical competence of the other bystander had no important or detectable affect on speed of response. Subjects responded equally frequently and fast whether the other bystander was female, male or medically experienced.

Sex of the Subject and Speed of Response

Coping with emergencies is often thought to be the duty of males, especially when females are present, but there was no evidence that this was the case in this study. Male subjects responded to the emergency with almost exactly the same speed as did females (Table 5A–2).

Reasons for Intervention or Nonintervention

After the debriefing at the end of the experiment each subject was given a 15-item checklist and asked to check those thoughts which had "crossed your mind when you heard Subject 1 calling for help." Whatever the condition, each subject checked very few thoughts, and there were no significant differences in number or kind of thoughts in the different experimental groups. The only thoughts checked by more than a few subjects were "I didn't know what to do" (18 out of 65 subjects), "I thought it must be some sort of fake" (20 out of 65), and "I didn't know exactly what was happening" (26 out of 65).

It is possible that subjects were ashamed to report socially undesirable rationalizations, or, since the subjects checked the list *after* the true nature of the experiment had been explained to them, their memories might have been blurred. It is our impression, however, that most subjects checked few reasons because they had few coherent thoughts during the fit.

Table 5A–2 Effects of Group Composition of Likelihood and Speed of Response[a]

Group size	N	% responding by end of fit	Time in sec.	Speed score
Female *S*, male other	13	62	94	74
Female *S*, female other	13	62	92	71
Female *S*, male medic other	5	100	60	77
Male *S*, female other	13	69	110	68

[a]Three-person group, male victim.

We asked all subjects whether the presence or absence of other bystanders had entered their minds during the time that they were hearing the fit. Subjects in the three- and six-person groups reported that they were aware that other people were present, but they felt that this made no difference to their own behavior.

Individual Difference Correlates of Speed of Report

The correlations between speed of report and various individual differences on the personality and background measures were obtained by normalizing the distribution of report speeds within each experimental condition and pooling these scores across all conditions ($n = 62–65$). Personality measures showed no important or significant correlations with speed of reporting the emergency. In fact, only one of the 16 individual difference measures, the size of the community in which the subject grew up, correlated ($r = -.26$, $p < .05$) with the speed of helping.

DISCUSSION

Subjects, whether or not they intervened, believed the fit to be genuine and serious. "My God, he's having a fit," many subjects said to themselves (and were overheard via their microphones) at the onset of the fit. Others gasped or simply said "Oh." Several of the male subjects swore. One subject said to herself, "It's just my kind of luck, something has to happen to me!" Several subjects spoke aloud of their confusion about what course of action to take, "Oh God, what should I do?"

When those subjects who intervened stepped out of their rooms, they found the experimental assistant down the hall. With some uncertainty, but without panic, they reported the situation. "Hey, I think Number 1 is very sick. He's having a fit or something." After ostensibly checking on the situation, the experimenter returned to report that "everything is under control." The subjects accepted these assurances with obvious relief.

Subjects who failed to report the emergency showed few signs of the apathy and indifference thought to characterize "unresponsive bystanders." When the experimenter entered her room to terminate the situation, the subject often asked if the victim was "all right." "Is he being taken care of?" "He's all right isn't he?" Many of these subjects showed physical signs of nervousness; they often had trembling hands and sweating palms. If anything, they seemed more emotionally aroused than did the subjects who reported the emergency.

Why, then, didn't they respond? It is our impression that nonintervening subjects had not decided *not* to respond. Rather they were still in a state of indecision and conflict concerning whether to respond or not. The emotional behavior of these nonresponding subjects was a sign of their continuing conflict, a conflict that other subjects resolved by responding.

The fit created a conflict situation of the avoidance-avoidance type. On the one hand, subjects worried about the guilt and shame they would feel if they did not help the person in distress. On the other hand, they were concerned not to make fools of themselves by overreacting, not to ruin the ongoing experiment by leaving their intercom, and not to destroy the anonymous nature of the situation which the experimenter had earlier stressed as important. For subjects in the two-person condition, the obvious distress of the victim and his need for help were so important that their conflict was easily resolved. For the subjects who knew there were other bystanders present, the cost of not helping was reduced and the conflict they were in more acute. Caught between the two negative alternatives of letting the victim continue to suffer or the costs of rushing in to help, the nonresponding bystanders vacillated between them rather than choosing not to respond. This distinction may be academic for the victim, since he got no help in either case, but it is an extremely important one for arriving at an understanding of the causes of bystanders' failures to help.

Although the subjects experienced stress and conflict during the experiment, their general reactions to it were highly positive. On a questionnaire administered after the experimenter had discussed the nature and purpose of the experiment, every single subject found the experiment either "interesting" or "very interesting" and was willing to participate in similar experiments in the future. All subjects felt they understood what the experiment was about and indicated that they thought the deceptions were necessary and justified. All but one felt they were better informed about the nature of psychological research in general.

Male subjects reported the emergency no faster than did females. These results (or lack of them) seem to conflict with the Berkowitz, Klanderman, and Harris (1964) finding that males tend to assume more responsibility and take more initiative than females in giving help to dependent others. Also, females reacted equally fast when the other bystander was another female, a male, or even a person practiced in dealing with medical emergencies. The ineffectiveness of these manipulations of group composition cannot be explained by general insensitivity of the speed measure, since the group-size variable had a marked effect on report speed.

It might be helpful in understanding this lack of difference to distinguish two general classes of intervention in emergency situations: direct and reportorial. Direct intervention (breaking up a fight, extinguishing a fire, swimming out to save a drowner) often requires skill, knowledge, or physical power. It may involve danger. American cultural norms and Berkowtiz's results seem to suggest that males are more responsible than females for this kind of direct intervention.

A second way of dealing with an emergency is to report it to someone qualified to handle it, such as the police. For this kind of intervention, there seem to be no norms requiring male action. In the present study, subjects clearly intended to report the emergency rather than take direction action. For such indirect intervention, sex or medical competence does not appear to affect one's qualifications or responsibilities. Anybody, male or female, medically trained or not, can find the experimenter.

In this study, no subject was able to tell how the other subjects reacted to the fit. (Indeed, there were no other subjects actually present.) The effects of group size on speed of helping, therefore, are due simply to the perceived presence of others rather than to the influence of their actions. This means that the experimental situation is unlike emergencies, such as a fire, in which bystanders interact with each other. It is, however, similar to emergencies, such as the Genovese murder, in which spectators knew others were also watching but were prevented by walls between them from communication that might have counteracted the diffusion of responsibility.

The present results create serious difficulties for one class of commonly given explanations for the failure of bystanders to intervene in actual emergencies, those involving apathy or indifference. These explanations generally assert that people who fail to intervene are somehow different in kind from the rest of us, that they are "alienated by industrialization," "dehumanized by urbanization," "depersonalized by living in the cold society," or "psychopaths." These explanations serve a dual function for people who adopt them. First, they explain (if only in a nominal way) the puzzling and frightening problem of why people watch others die. Second, they give individuals reason to deny that they too might fail to help in a similar situation.

The results of this experiment seem to indicate that such personality variables may not be as important as these explanations suggest. Alienation, Machiavellianism, acceptance of social responsibility, need for approval, and authoritarianism are often cited in these explanations. Yet they did not predict the speed or likelihood of help. In sharp contrast, the perceived number of bystanders did. The explanation of bystander "apathy" may lie more in the bystander's response to other observers than in presumed personality deficiencies of "apathetic" individuals. Although this realization may force us to face the guilt-provoking possibility that we too might fail to intervene, it also suggests that individuals are not, of necessity, "non-interveners" because of their personalities. If people understand the situational forces that can make them hesitate to intervene, they may better overcome them.

REFERENCES

Aronfreed, J. The origin of self-criticism. *Psychological Review*, 1964, *71*, 193–219.
Berkowitz, L., Klanderman, S., & Harris, R. Effects of experimenter awareness and sex of subject on reactions to dependency relationships. *Sociometry*, 1964, *27*, 327–329.
Christie, R. The prevalence of machiavellian orientations. Paper presented at the meeting of the American Psychological Association, Los Angeles, 1964.
Crowne, D., & Marlowe, D. *The approval motive*. New York: Wiley, 1964.
Daniels L., & Berkowitz, L. Liking and response to dependency relationships. *Human Relations*, 1963, *16*, 141–148.

Milgram, S., & Hollander, P. Murder they heard. *Nation*, 1964, *198*, 602–604.
Miller, N., & Dollard, J. *Social learning and imitation.* New Haven: Yale University Press, 1941.
Rosenthal, A. M. *Thirty-eight witnesses.* New York: McGraw-Hill, 1964.
Whiting, J. W. M., & Child, I. *Child training and personality.* New Haven: Yale University Press, 1953.

What are your initial impressions about this pioneering piece of social psychological research? Was it rather ingenious the way Drs. Darley and Latané decided to research this response of apathy on the part of Genovese's neighbors? What were the initial thoughts of these two researchers that helped them decide to employ a confederate and contrived participants in order to study bystander apathy?

To help answer these questions let us go back and look at what your responses were to the question initially posed at the beginning of the chapter. What were your five reasons for people not helping? If you suggested that the more people there are in a situation requiring a significant amount of help the less likely any one person is to actually help in that situation, you are correct. Generally, the more people there are who could potentially help in any given situation, the more likely there will be a diffusion of responsibility on the part of bystanders in that situation. Put another way, the more people there are to help a person requiring aid in a given situation, the greater will be the bystander apathy in that situation. It appears that people reason that "Others are around to help so I am not going to get involved!" Have you ever personally witnessed this type of response? If you have, you can certainly understand the psychological significance of attempting to answer the bystander apathy question. After all, that is what psychological research is all about: trying to answer questions regarding behavior.

With the concept of diffusion of responsibility in mind, it is actually a fairly elementary step to bring the Genovese murder into the laboratory. Although both Darley and Latané are undoubtedly bright individuals, there is really nothing exceptional about the pragmatics of their work. They wanted to solve a complex problem, and, by applying sound research methods, they were able to devise a study to answer their question accurately. They were right; the notion of diffusion of responsibility was confirmed by their study!

THINK IT THROUGH

Instead of using an intercom to study this diffusion-of-responsibility phenomenon, what other methods could be employed? In particular, could we use VCRs, video monitors, and video cameras instead of intercoms? How could we use these more modern devices, and what do you think the results of such studies would be? List some different methods that could be used to conduct this study in the "real world."

Let us assume we wanted to replicate this study using VCRs, video monitors, and video cameras. One way we could accomplish this task would be to bring in four participants at a time (three would be confederates). We would then inform them, as part of our cover story, "we are interested in studying how accurate people are in judging body language through the use of video monitors." We would go on and explain to them "you will each be in a room with three video monitors and one video camera; the camera is being used to send your reactions to the other three participants and the monitors are being used so you will be able to view the behaviors of the other three. Thus, each of you will be able to view the behaviors of the other people taking part in this study on the monitors that are provided in your respective rooms." After viewing the behaviors on the monitors for 10 minutes, participants will be asked to rate the behaviors of one another on a bogus questionnaire purportedly needed in order to study a variety of "body language dimensions."

In reality, we would be studying bystander apathy. We would have a "command center" in which there would be three VCRs sending prerecorded tapes of the confederates to our actual participant. Obviously, the participant would not be told we are using tapes of the behavior of our confederates. She or he would believe what she or he is viewing on her or his monitors is live and not taped. Likewise, the participant would believe his or her behavior is being sent (via the video camera in their room) to the other three people taking part in the study. About two or three minutes into the experiment, one of the confederate's tapes would depict that confederate experiencing what appears to be some type of seizure. We would chronicle the behavior of the actual participant to determine if they would rush to the aid of our confederate (supporting the notion of prosocial behavior) or simply do nothing at all (supporting the notion of diffusion of responsibility). We could even vary the number of confederates we employ to determine the point at which diffusion of responsibility becomes critical (i.e., are people less likely to help if there are 2, 3, 5, or 15 potential helpers present).

If we employed these changes, what do you think the outcome of our study would be? Would our participants be more or less likely to help the person in need compared to the participants in the Darley and Latané study? Remember, in this proposed scenario, the message sent would both be visual and auditory which is a significant departure from the Darley and Latané study where participants only heard a person experiencing a seizure.

On the other hand, how could we do a similar study in a "real world" situation? Could we have a person feign a seizure on a city street (varying the number of bystanders) and observe what happens? As with any study, the possible parameters and changes are limitless. A little methodological ingenuity can go a long way in devising different studies on the same theme.

What are some of the ethical issues to be dealt with in the Darley and Latané experiment and the ones we have suggested? Could a person be potentially harmed, psychologically, after participating in such a study? Just think if you were a participant in the Darley and Latané study and you decided, for whatever reason, not to help. Upon being debriefed as to the true nature of the study, you feel somewhat foolish. (Obviously, the exact nature of the study could not be given to you in advance because if you knew what the study was really investigating your behavior would most certainly be different.) In fact, you may feel like you are a social failure. You always thought of yourself as a caring, concerned, compassionate person, but now you are confronted with the stark fact that you are not.

Today, such studies are often approved by institutional review boards (IRBs) as long as several requirements are met. First, the participants must be completely debriefed as to the exact nature of the experiment. Second, a statement from the experimenter informing the participant "their behavior is typical" would also be necessary. Third, they should be informed that the nature of the study they have just completed does not necessarily replicate the real world and their behavior could certainly be different when confronted with a real-life situation. Finally, remember the participant must be free to withdraw from a study at any time (although, in reality, this behavior is highly infrequent). With these protections in place, an IRB could approve this study.

Even though many IRBs would approve such a study, the ethics of such studies are somewhat suspect, and, should you consider doing such a study, it would be important for you to have your IRB approve your study. Many such boards are becoming less inclined to give approval to such studies because of the chance of psychological harm to the participants. In the future, studies like those conducted by Darley and Latané are not likely to be approved; they are simply too intrusive.

Ethical considerations are always a primary concern in conducting research. It is of particular concern when the people being studied do not know they are participating in a study. The reason for this is the person has not given their permission to participate in a study and, as a result, she or he cannot withdraw from the study (how can one withdraw from a study if she or he does not know she or he is actually participating in a study?). Similarly, they cannot be easily debriefed. How, then, can we study such a phenomena?

THINK IT THROUGH

One way to obviate the ethical considerations raised would be to make studies less intrusive. Instead of having a person feign a seizure, perhaps we could conduct a study in which, under the guise of some other study, we have confederates make simple requests of participants. We could have a confederate ask the participant to get the confederate a drink of water. We could even vary the number of confederates in our study to see if such simple requests are more or less as the number of "bystanders" are varied. Similarly, we could ask a confederate to request the participant place a phone call for a confederate. These two suggestions are highly diminished in the actual demands placed upon the participant when compared to what was needed from the participants in the Darley and Latané study, but they will certainly free us from the ethical concerns raised above.

At the beginning of this chapter, you were asked to suggest five situations you could devise a study around to try and increase helping behavior. Such prosocial aspects in experiments are often looked upon more favorably by IRBs (when compared to studying why people do not help). As a result, these suggested experiments might not only have a better chance of being approved, but they will also put a different perspective on this interesting area of psychological research.

You could also use some type of scenario/questionnaire format to study bystander apathy. This approach will be discussed in Chapter 10. If you are interested in this form of research, we suggest you read that chapter for additional suggestions. Such formats are not considered to be nearly as intrusive and, thus, are likely to win your IRB's approval.

Psychology is a dynamic science. As such, its ethics are expected to change (the American Psychological Association periodically updates the Ethical Principle when it is determined such updates are needed). As ethical considerations change, so must we. Should a particular method become ethically suspect, this does not necessarily mean that we must abandon that area of research. We simply must adapt our methods to conform to current ethical standards.

What about sex and ethnicity? Can these variables influence bystander apathy and/or prosocial behavior? Just think of the different manipulations that can (and have!) been used to study these variables (Eagly & Crowley, 1986). What if the person was an African American woman in need of help and the bystanders were Caucasian men or women? What if the person in need of help was a Native American man and the bystanders were African American men or women? Gender and ethnicity are always important variables to study; they are easily introduced as important variables in any project (see Chapters 2 and 3).

If you do not believe such variables would have any effect on the outcome of a study, you only need to refer to the riots that occurred in south central Los Angeles during the summer of 1992. A Caucasian trucker by the name of Reginald Denny was innocently driving through the area during the riots when he was pulled out of his truck and was savagely beaten by a group of African American rioters. A news helicopter happened upon the beating and began to broadcast live shots of the incident (the crew was Caucasian). At no time did the news crew provide any direct aid to Mr. Denny; they simply continued to film the brutal beating. Few people know that Denny was actually saved by an African American couple who intentionally drove into the riot (after watching the live broadcast of the beating) and placed him in their car and drove him to the hospital. These two people risked their lives to save the life of a person of a different race. It would be interesting to know more about this type of altruistic and prosocial behavior in similar situations. Social psychologists have studied such behavior (Batson, 1991; Eisenberg & Fabes, 1991) with quite interesting results.

THINK IT THROUGH

How could we use animals in investigating bystander apathy? List at least four different methods that employ animals to study this area of human behavior. It might, at first, appear to be an impossible task, but if you put some creative thought into this task, we are certain that you can develop at least four methods!

One way we could use animals would be to use the animal as the participant instead of a human as the participant. Could we use an animal, such as a dog or a cat, in some type of feigned distress and determine if people are more or less likely to help an animal or a human? Yes, we could, and we would likely obtain some rather surprising results! We could also study what types of animals are likely to receive more attention (e.g., a dog or a cat). What ethical considerations could result from such a study? Do we have ethical concerns when using animals? We only need to go back and reread Chapter 2 for the answer to this question. In conducting an experiment such as this, we would probably not be confronted with ethical issues as long as the animal is protected from harm. Therefore, animals *can* be used to investigate bystander apathy. Good research can often be seen as variations on a theme.

What were your four methods for using animals in a bystander apathy experiment? Did any of the four methods you developed mirror the suggested methods? Why or why not?

THINK IT THROUGH

List five ideas related to those mentioned above that can be researched, and list three novel ideas (not related to any of the above) that could also be researched. What types of materials and time would each of these eight areas require? Are there any ethical concerns in the studies you have proposed? If so, how can you go about eliminating these concerns?

Related ideas:

1. _____

2. _____

3. _____

4. _____

5. _____

Novel ideas:

1. _____

2. _____

3. _____

After listing your various research ideas, have one of your professors read them and give you additional and alternate suggestions. If you have an interest in this area of research, you will find it exciting to develop and pursue your ideas to fruition with the aid of your favorite professor and your ethics committee.

Review the literature to identify additional readings if you are interested in pursuing research in the area of social psychology. Some are related to bystander apathy and some are related to other areas (e.g., obedience and interpersonal attraction). We have listed several that should be of interest to you. And, do not hesitate to ask your professor for additional suggestions.

REFERENCES

Batson, C. D. (1991). *The altruism question: Toward a social psychological answer.* Hillsdale, NJ: Earlbaum.

Berscheid, E, & Walster (Hartfield), E. (1978). *Interpersonal attraction.* Reading, MA: Addison-Wesley.

Bond, C., DiCandia, C., & McKinnon, J. R. (1988). Response to violence in a psychiatric setting. *Personality and Social Psychology Bulletin, 14,* 448–458.

Darley, J. M., & Latané, B. (1968). Bystander Intervention in Emergencies: Diffusion of Responsibility. *Journal of Personality and Social Psychology, 8,* 377–383.

Eagly, A. H., & Crowley, M. (1986) Gender and helping behavior: A meta-analytic review of the social psychological literature. *Psychological Bulletin, 100,* 283–308.

Eisenberg, N., & Fabes, R. A. (1991). Prosocial behavior and empathy: A multimethod developmental perspective. In M. S. Clark (Ed.) *Review of personality and social psychology* (Vol. 12, pp. 34–61). Newbury Park, CA: Sage.

Myers, D. G. (1996). *Exploring Psychology.* New York: Worth.

ADDITIONAL READINGS

Milgram, S. (1976). *Obedience to authority: An experimental view.* New York: Harper & Row.

Salovey, P., Mayer, J. D., & Rosenhan, D. L. (1991). Mood and helping: Mood as a motivator of helping and helping as a regulator of mood. In M. S. Clark (Ed.) *Review of personality and social psychology* (Vol. 12, pp. 215–237). Newbury Park, CA: Sage.

CHAPTER 6

Developmental Research Idea Development

Developmental psychology is concerned with the systematic changes that occur throughout an individual's entire life. During the course of our lives we change physically, cognitively, emotionally, socially, and behaviorally. We only need to think back five or six years to understand the veracity of such a statement; we are quite different today than we were only a few years ago. We do not stop developing after adolescence; we continue to develop until we die. Likewise, even though we were not aware of it, we changed dramatically during our prenatal development. The changes that occur from conception until death constitute the milieu of the developmental psychologist.

The article you are about to read investigates ethnic identity in children on a cognitive level. *Do not* read the abstract, introduction, results, or discussion sections of the article at this time. Read *only* the method section; after reading this section, we will ask you a few questions prior to having you read the rest of the article.

The Measurement of Children's Racial Attitudes in the Early School Years

John E. Williams, Deborah L. Best, and Donna A. Boswell
Wake Forest University

Williams, John E.; Best, Deborah L.; and Boswell, Donna. The Measurement of Children's Racial Attitudes in the Early School Years. *Child Development,* 1975, 46, 494–500. The Preschool Racial Attitude Measure II (PRAM II) is a procedure for assessing the attitudes of preliterate children toward light-skinned (Euro-American) and dark-skinned (Afro-American) human figures. Although designed for research with preschool children, it is also appropriate to the test-taking ability of children in the early school grades. In the main, developmental, study 483 children in the first 4 grades of a single, integrated, public school were administered PRAM II by Euro- and Afro-American examiners. Among Euro-American children, it was found that pro-Euro/anti-Afro (E+/A–) bias reached a peak at the second-grade level and subsequently declined. Afro-American children also were found to display evidence of E+/A– bias, but to a lesser degree, and with no appreciable age trends being observed. Evidence regarding race-of-examiner effects was inconclusive. A second study established the representative nature of the data in the developmental study by a comparison of the PRAM II scores of the second-grade children in the developmental study with the mean scores of other groups of second graders ($N = 255$) in other geographical locations.

The Preschool Racial Attitude Measure II (PRAM II) is a procedure for assessing the evaluative responses of preliterate children to light-skinned (Euro-American) and dark-skinned (Afro-American) human figures (Williams, Best, Boswell, Mattson, & Graves 1975). PRAM II is a lengthened version of the racial-attitude assessment procedure described by Williams and Roberson (1967) and subsequently named PRAM I. Although originally designed for work with preschool children, the PRAM procedures have also been employed successfully with children in the lower school grades (Shanahan 1972; Traynham 1974), whose test-taking ability is more compatible with the PRAM picture-story format than with the paper-and-pencil procedures employed with older children and adults. In the PRAM procedures the child indicates his racial attitude by the selection of light- and dark-skinned figures in response to stories containing

---

Child Development, 1975, 46 494–500 © 1975 by the Society for Research in Child Development, Inc. All rights reserved. Used by permission of *Child Development.*

This study was supported by grants to the first author from the National Institute of Child Health and Human Development (HD-02821) and the Wake Forest Graduate Council. The authors are indebted to Mr. Grady E. Stone, Jr., principal, and the teachers of Wesley B. Speas Elementary School for their support and cooperation. Requests for reprints of this paper, for copies of the PRAM II manual, and for information concerning the loan or purchase of test materials should be sent to John E. Williams, Department of Psychology, Wake Forest University, Winston-Salem, North Carolina 27109.

positive and negative evaluative adjectives (e.g., good, nice, kind; bad, naughty, mean). The rationale of the procedure is supported by studies (Edwards & Williams 1970; Gordon & Williams 1973; McMurtry & Williams 1972) in which it has been demonstrated that the "semantic space" of the preschool child embraces an evaluative dimension similar to that previously found among older children and adults (DiVesta 1966; Osgood, Suci, & Tannenbaum 1957).

The PRAM II procedure provides the child with 24 opportunities to choose between Euro- and Afro-American figures in response to evaluative adjectives, and generates a score range of 0–24 within which low scores are indicative of pro-Afro/anti-Euro (A+/E–) bias, high scores are indicative of pro-Euro/anti-Afro (E+/A–) bias, and mid-range scores, around 12, are indicative of no consistent racial bias. The first 12 items (Series A) and the second 12 items (Series B) comprise equivalent short forms of the procedure. In the PRAM II standardization study (Williams et al. 1975), the PRAM II procedure was administered to Euro-American and Afro-American preschoolers, mean age 64 months, by Euro- and Afro-American examiners in Winston-Salem, North Carolina. The mean racial-attitude scores obtained in the preschool study are shown in Table 6A–1 where several effects can be observed. First, it is noted that all mean scores were on the high side of the neutral point of 12, and were thus indicative of tendency toward E+/A– bias in all groups. Second, it can be seen that the degree of E+/A– bias was lower among Afro-American children than among Euro-American children. Third, it is observed that there was evidence of a race-of-examiner effect, with both groups of children displaying somewhat more E+/A– bias in the presence of a Euro-American examiner. The first two effects noted had been predicted on the basis of research with PRAM I (H. McAdoo 1970; J. McAdoo 1970; Vocke 1971; Walker 1971; Williams & Edwards 1969; Williams & Roberson 1967; and others cited in Williams et al. 1975). The significant race-of-examiner effect was not expected and, in fact, has proved not to be replicable in a subsequent study designed specifically to study this effect (Best 1972).

The general purpose of the present study was to chart the development of racial attitudes in Euro- and Afro-American children beyond the preschool

Table 6A–1 Mean PRAM II Racial-Attitude Scores for 272 Preschool Subjects Classified by Race of Subject and Race of Examiner

Race of Subject	Race of Examiner		
	Euro-American	Afro-American	Total
Euro-American	18.66(68)	15.38(68)	17.02(136)
Afro-American	15.28(68)	14.18(68)	14.73(136)
Total	16.97(136)	14.78(136)	15.88(272)

NOTE.–*N*'s are given in parentheses.

level through the administration of the PRAM II procedure to children in the first four grades of a single elementary school. A secondary purpose was to compare the racial attitudes of second-grade children in several different geographical localities in order to verify the representative nature of the data obtained in the main developmental study.

METHOD

Developmental study.—The general design of this study was to test all first- and third-grade children, and samples of second- and fourth-grade children, in a single public elementary school in Winston-Salem, North Carolina. At the second- and fourth-grade levels, all Afro children were tested, but only approximately one-half of the Euro children. The other half of the Euro second and fourth graders were not available because of their participation in another research study. The school involved was chosen because of the receptivity of the school administration to the study, and because the school draws its pupils from many of the same areas of the city as those served by the kindergarten programs involved in the PRAM II preschool standardization study. At the time of the study in fall 1972, the local school system had been racially integrated for several years. The racial composition of the children in all classrooms in the school studied was approximately 70% Euro-American and 30% Afro-American, with the racial composition of the school faculty approximately the same.

The PRAM II procedure[1] (Williams et al. 1975) and the Peabody Picture Vocabulary Test (PPVT) (Dunn 1965) were individually administered, in that order, by female Euro-American and Afro-American college students. At each grade level, an effort was made to follow the design of the PRAM II preschool standardization study by having approximately half of the children in each race-of-subject group tested by Euro examiners, with the others being tested by Afro examiners. This joint variation in race of subject and race of examiner led again to four major research groups at each grade level: Euro children/Euro examiner; Euro children/Afro examiner; Afro children/Euro examiner; Afro children/Afro examiner. Each subject group was composed of approximately the same number of boys and girls.

A total of 483 children were tested. For purposes of statistical analysis, the data for 25 subjects were randomly excluded so that, at each grade level, the numbers of Euro children tested by Euro and Afro examiners were equal, and the numbers of Afro children tested by Euro and Afro examiners were equal. The data analysis was, thus, based on 458 children: 152 first graders, 80 second graders, 158 third graders, and 68 fourth graders. The number of children in each of the four race-of-subject/race-of-examiner groups at each grade level is shown in Table 6A–2.

---

[1]The PRAM II materials and procedures are described more fully by Williams et al. (1975) and in a manual which is available upon request.

Table 6A–2 Mean PRAM II Racial-Attitude Scores for Children in Grades 1–4 Classified by Race of Subject and Race of Examiner

Race of Subject	Race of Examiner		
	Euro	Afro	Total
Grade 1:			
Euro	19.0(49)	17.6(49)	18.3(98)
Afro	15.3(27)	13.3(27)	14.3(54)
Total	17.7(76)	16.1(76)	16.9(152)
Grade 2:			
Euro	19.4(19)	18.6(19)	19.0(38)
Afro	14.4(21)	11.9(21)	13.2(42)
Total	16.8(40)	15.1(40)	15.9(80)
Grade 3:			
Euro	18.3(56)	14.5(56)	16.4(112)
Afro	13.3(23)	11.9(23)	12.6(46)
Total	16.8(79)	13.7(79)	15.3(158)
Grade 4:			
Euro	16.2(18)	15.1(18)	15.6(36)
Afro	13.3(16)	13.6(16)	13.5(32)
Total	14.9(34)	14.4(34)	14.6(68)

NOTE.–*N*'s are given in parentheses.

Geographical area study.—The subjects in this study were Euro- and Afro-American second-grade students in several communities in North Carolina, South Carolina, and New York. These communities were not chosen systematically but were "targets of opportunity" where the investigators had access to second-grade children. All subjects were administered the PRAM II procedure and the PPVT following standard instructions by Euro-American college students. A total of 255 children from communities outside Winston-Salem were tested; the number of students tested in each community is shown in Table 6A–4.

RESULTS

Each child's PRAM II performance was scored in standard fashion by counting one point for the selection of a light-skinned (Euro) person in response to a positive evaluative adjective, and one point for the selection of a dark-skinned (Afro) figure in response to a negative evaluative adjective. With 24 response opportunities, these scores could range from 0 to 24, with high scores indicating E+/A– bias, low scores indicating A+/E– bias, and mid-range scores indicating no bias. The Peabody Picture Vocabulary Test was scored in standard fashion to yield a vocabulary IQ.

Developmental study.—The reliability of the racial-attitude scores among all children tested was estimated by correlating the children's scores on the first 12 items (Series A) of the PRAM II procedure with their scores on the last 12 items (Series B). These correlations ranged from .64 to .78 at the various grade levels, yielding Spearman-Brown estimates of .78–.88 for the reliability (internal consistency) of the total racial-attitude scores. The means and standard deviations for Series A and Series B were also found to be highly similar and not significantly different. When the PRAM II total scores were examined in relation to vocabulary IQ scores, negligible correlation coefficients were obtained.

The mean PRAM II racial attitude scores for each of the four race-of-subject/race-of-examiner groups at each grade level are shown in Table 6A–2. It will be observed that, at each grade level, the marginal mean for Euro children was higher than the comparable mean for Afro children, and that the marginal mean for Euro examiners was higher than the mean for Afro examiners.

The statistical analysis of these data was conducted by performing a 2×2 factorial analysis of variance at each grade level. The results of these analyses can be summarized as follows: the main effect of race of subject was significant ($p < .01$) at grade levels 1, 2, and 3, but not at 4; the main effect of race of examiner was significant ($p < .01$) only at the third-grade level; the interaction effect between race of subject and race of examiner was not significant at any grade level. Thus, while the evidence of a race-of-subject effect was quite clear in the first three grades, the evidence of a race-of-examiner effect remained unclear.

Since race of examiner was not a major influence on the scores obtained, the two race-of-examiner groups at each grade level were pooled in order to examine the developmental trends more carefully, with the mean scores obtained by Euro and Afro preschoolers in the PRAM II standardization study (Williams et al. 1975) used for reference purposes. For the Euro-American children, the respective mean scores for the five age groups (preschool through fourth grade) were: 17.0, 18.3, 19.0, 16.4, and 15.3. A simple analysis of variance of the scores in the five Euro groups revealed statistically significant variability ($p < .01$) among the mean scores. Further analysis by t tests revealed that the degree of E+/A– bias in the Euro group increased significantly ($p < .01$) from the preschool to the second-grade level, and decreased significantly ($p < .01$) from the second to the third. At the third- and fourth-grade levels, the Euro-American children were displaying significantly ($p < .01$) less bias than at the first-grade level. For the five age groups of Afro-American children, the respective means were: 14.7, 14.3, 13.2, 12.6, and 13.5. There was thus some evidence of a trend toward a gradual diminution in E+/A– bias from the preschool level through the early school years. However, a simple analysis of variance of the scores in the five Afro groups provided no statistical bias for concluding that such a trend existed.

The school-age data were also examined by computing the percentages of Euro and Afro children at each grade level who obtained racial-attitude scores failing in the following score ranges: 0–7, definite A+/E– bias; 8–9, probably A+/E– bias; 10–14, no bias; 15–16, probably E+/A– bias; and 17–24, definite E+/A– bias. These percentages are shown in Table 6A–3 together with the corresponding data from the preschool standardization study. These data were further summarized by combining the "definite" and "probable" bias categories to create three general categories; A+/E– bias (scores of 0–9), no bias (scores of 10–14), and E+/A– bias (scores of 15–24), and E+/A– bias (scores of 15–24). The percentages of children at the five grade levels scoring in each of these three categories are shown in Figure 6A–1. Here it can be seen that approximately three-quarters of the Euro preschool through second-grade children show E+/A– bias, with a sharp reduction in grades 3 and 4 to only slightly more than one-half. There also appears to be a related increase in the proportion of Euro children in the no-bias category, from approximately one-fifth of the preschool through second graders to approximately one-third of the third and fourth graders.

The data of the Afro children seen in Figure 6A–1 show little evidence of consistent age trends. While the proportion of Afro children showing E+/A– bias appears to decrease between the first- and third-grade levels, it appears to increase again at the fourth-grade level. Likewise, the proportion of children in the no-bias category appears to increase from the second-grade to third-grade

Table 6A–3 Percentages of PRAM II Scores of Euro- and Afro-American Children at Each of Five Grade Levels Falling into Each of Five Scoring Categories

Score Range	Scoring Category	Change Expectancy[a]	Race of Subjects	Grade Level				
				Preschool	1	2	3	4
0–7	Definite A+/E– bias	3.3	Euro	3.7	3.1	0.0	2.7	2.8
			Afro	10.3	16.7	21.4	10.9	9.4
8–9	Probable A+/E– bias	12.1	Euro	2.9	3.1	0.0	4.5	8.3
			Afro	2.2	5.6	7.1	8.7	9.4
10–14	No bias	69.2	Euro	21.3	16.3	21.1	35.7	36.1
			Afro	35.3	22.2	23.8	45.7	34.3
15–16	Probable E+/A– bias	12.1	Euro	14.0	12.2	10.5	10.7	11.1
			Afro	12.5	14.8	16.7	15.2	28.1
17–24	Definite E+/A– bias	3.3	Euro	58.1	65.3	68.4	46.4	41.7
			Afro	39.7	40.7	31.0	19.6	18.8

[a]These are the percentages which would be expected from a group of unbiased children, responding purely by chance, based on the binomial distribution.

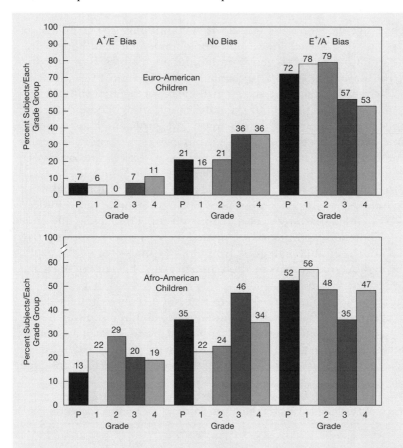

Figure 6A–1 Percentages of children in five school grades (preschool through fourth) displaying pro-Afro/anti-Euro (A+/E–) bias, no bias, or pro-Euro/anti-Afro (E+/A–) bias.

levels but to decrease again at the fourth-grade level. Of particular interest is the absence of any simple age trend in A+/E– bias, which appears to increase from preschool to second grade, and to decrease again at the third- and fourth-grade levels. It can also be observed that, at each grade level studied, the proportion of Afro children displaying E+/A– bias was considerably higher than the proportion displaying A+/E– bias.

Geographical area study.—The mean PRAM II racial attitude scores for the groups of second-grade children in the geographical area study are shown in Table 6A–4, together with the mean scores obtained from the second-grade children tested by Euro-American examiners in the Winston-Salem study. A simple analysis of variance of the scores of the four groups of Afro-American children yielded a nonsignificant result, while the analysis conducted for the six Euro groups

Table 6A–4 Mean Pram II Racial-Attitude Scores of Second-Grade Children Tested by Euro-American Examiners

	Race of Subjects	
Location and Characteristics of School	Euro-American	Afro-American
1. Winston-Salem, N.C.: public, integrated	19.2(34)[a]	14.2(23)[a]
2. Mooresville, N.C.: public, integrated	19.9(44)	11.6(14)
3. Greenville, N.C.: public, integrated	19.0(32)	14.6(20)
4. Beaufort, S.C.: public, integrated	20.5(18)	14.2(18)
5. Beaufort, S.C.: private, all Euro	21.0(36)	. . .
6. Albertson, N.Y.: public, all Euro	18.5(73)	. . .

NOTE.—*N*'s are given in parenthesis.
[a]The numbers of subjects reported here are the total numbers listed by Euro examiners prior to the random exclusion of subjects for the analysis of variance described in the text.

was significant at the .05 level. When this latter effect was further explored via *t* tests, significant differences ($p < .05$) were found between the following pairs of Euro group means: 3 versus 5, 4 versus 6, and 5 versus 6. It can be noted that all three of these comparisons involve the South Carolina groups and that, in each instance, the South Carolina means were higher than those with which they were compared. The mean score for the Winston-Salem Euro group was not significantly different from any of the other Euro group means.

DISCUSSION

The interpretation of the substantive findings of the present studies must be tempered by the usual cautionary statements concerning cross-sectional research designs. The assessment of developmental trends via such designs requires the assumption that there are no major factors influencing the research data other than those normally associated with increases in chronological age. In effect, we must assume that our first graders are subject to the same influences which our fourth graders were 3 years earlier, when they were first graders. This assumption may be more difficult to meet in the study of racial bias than in other areas of developmental research.

With the foregoing caveat in mind, we note that the pro-Euro/anti-Afro bias of preschool children (Williams et al. 1975) appears to persist into the early school grades. Among Euro-American children, pro-Euro bias appears to increase to the second-grade level and then to decline. Afro-American children, in general, appear to maintain a moderate degree of pro-Euro bias through the early school years, with no appreciable evidence of any age trends. Likewise, no evidence was found of any systematic increase in pro-Afro bias among the minority of Afro-American children displaying such bias. While the foregoing conclusions are based on data from children in a single elementary school in Winston-Salem, North Carolina, there appears to be no reason to believe that the findings are atypical, since it was found that the mean scores of the Winston-Salem second graders were generally comparable to those obtained with second graders in other geographical areas. On the other hand, the findings of the geographical area study did suggest that there may be modest differences in the degree of racial bias displayed by second graders in different geographic locations, for example, South Carolina versus New York state. There was no evidence, however, that the racial integration of the school influenced the general level of racial bias. Among the Euro-American groups in the second-grade study, the highest and the lowest mean PRAM II scores were obtained from children in all-Euro schools, with the means for Euro children in integrated schools falling at an intermediate level.

The moderately pro-Euro attitudes of Afro-American children in the early school grades must be distinguished from their racial preferences during these years. Morland (1972) has demonstrated that, while Afro preschoolers show a definite pro-Euro racial preference (e.g., in choice of playmates), this shifts to pro-Afro preference with the child's entry into the integrated public school situation. Thus, it appears that the typical early-school-age Afro-American child is pro-Afro in his racial preference while remaining somewhat pro-Euro in racial attitude. This analysis suggests that the problems of adequate self-concept development in Afro children, often thought to occur primarily in the preschool years, may instead be concentrated in the early school years, when the child has developed a preference for members of his own racial group but still evaluates Afro persons less positively than Euro persons.

With reference to methodology, the findings of the present study provide additional evidence that the PRAM II procedure is a useful method for the assessment of racial bias among children in the early school grades. The high degree of internal consistency of the measure provides assurance that true individual differences are being assessed and that PRAM II may be used to study the correlates of racial bias at this age level. For example, Mabe (1974) studied the PRAM II scores and sociometric scores of second graders in an integrated school and found a correlation of .52 between the degree of E+/A– bias and the frequency with which the children chose Euro-American associates. The fact that Series A and Series B of PRAM II constitute comparable short forms can be of value in studies (e.g., Best, Smith, Graves, & Williams 1975; Yancey 1972) in which pre-post designs are employed to assess the effects of procedures aimed at the modification of racial bias.

REFERENCES

Best, D. L. Race of examiner effects on the racial attitude responses of preschool children. Unpublished master's thesis, Wake Forest University, 1972.

Best, D. L., Smith, S. C., Graves, D. J., & Williams, J. E. The modification of racial bias in preschool children. *Journal of Experimental Child Psychology,* 1975, in press.

DiVesta, F. J. A developmental study of the semantic structures of children. *Journal of Verbal Learning and Verbal Behavior,* 1966, 5, 249–259.

Dunn, L. M. *Expanded manual for the Peabody Picture Vocabulary Test.* Circle Pines, Minn.: American Guidance Services, 1965.

Edwards, C. D., & Williams, J. E. Generalization between evaluative words associated with racial figures in preschool children. *Journal of Experimental Research in Personality,* 1970, 4, 144–155.

Gordon, L. H., & Williams, J. E. Secondary factors in the affective meaning system of the preschool child. *Developmental Psychology,* 1973, 8, 25–34.

Mabe, P. A., III. The correlation of racial attitudes as measured by the preschool racial attitude measure and sociometric choices for second-grade children. Unpublished master's thesis, East Carolina University, 1974

McAdoo, H. P. Racial attitudes and self-concepts of black preschool children. Unpublished doctoral dissertation, University of Michigan, 1970.

McAdoo, J. L. An exploratory study of racial attitude change in black preschool children using differential treatments. Unpublished doctoral dissertation, University of Michigan, 1970.

McMurtry, C. A., & Williams, J. E. The evaluation dimension of the affective meaning system of the preschool child. *Developmental Psychology,* 1972, 6, 238–246.

Morland, J. K. *Racial attitudes in school children: from kindergarten through high-school.* Final Report, Project 2-C-009, Office of Education, U.S. Department of Health, Education, and Welfare, November 1972.

Osgood, C. E., Suci, G. J., & Tannenbaum, P. H. *The measurement of meaning.* Urbana: University of Illinois Press, 1957.

Shanahan, J. K. The effects of modifying black-white concept attitudes of black and white first grade subjects upon two measures of racial attitudes. Unpublished doctoral dissertation, University of Washington, 1972.

Traynham, R. N. The effects of modifying color meaning concepts on racial attitudes in five- and eight-year-old children. Unpublished masters' thesis, University of Arkansas, 1974.

Vocke, J. M. Measuring racial attitudes in preschool Negro children. Unpublished master's thesis, University of South Carolina, 1971.

Walker, P. A. The effects of hearing selected children's stories that portray blacks in a favorable manner on the racial attitudes of groups of black and white kindergarten children. Unpublished doctoral dissertation, University of Kentucky, 1971.

Williams, J. E., Best, D. L., Boswell, D. A., Mattson, L. A., & Graves, D. J. Preschool Racial Attitude Measure II. *Educational and Psychological Measurements,* 1975, in press.

Williams, J. E., & Edwards, C. D. An exploratory study of the modification of color concepts and racial attitudes in preschool children. *Child Development,* 1969, 40, 737–750.

Williams, J. E., & Roberson, J. K. A method of assessing racial attitudes in preschool children. *Educational and Psychological Measurement,* 1967, 27, 671–689.

Yancey, A. V. A study of racial attitudes in white first grade children. Unpublished paper, Department of Education, Pennsylvania State University, 1972.

THINK IT THROUGH

Let us investigate the methods section of this article more closely by answering some specific questions. Answering these initial questions will help to make certain you are quite familiar with the topics covered and will allow you the opportunity to make a few predictions concerning the results of this research.

1. What was studied in this article and why do you think it was studied?
2. What is the PRAM II, how was it used, and why was it used?
3. Why did the authors use post-preschool children as participants?
4. If we wanted to investigate attitudes of 12- to 16-year olds toward light- and dark-skinned people, how would we have to modify the PRAM II to accomplish this?
5. Why did the authors use the terms Euro-American and Afro-American? Are these terms appropriate to use today or are there more contemporary terms?
6. What do you think the results of this study were? Think of several reasons to support your hypothesis.

When looking at this article, along with the others in this book, you should be struck by the simplicity by which the various researchers investigated their particular areas of interest. Once we have an idea, we only need to creatively develop appropriate methods to study that area of interest. The problem faced by most beginning, as well as many advanced, researchers is in developing those methods.

How can one determine the racial preferences of preschool children? One problem we have is that these children cannot read. Another problem is that we cannot just ask the child for their racial preference, since, even at their young age, they might give a socially desirable answer rather than a true answer. These are two problems we must address if we want to accurately study racial attitudes in children.

With these two problems in mind, we must use an instrument that does not rely on reading ability and that masks, to a certain extent, the true nature of our study. The PRAM II is just such an instrument. The PRAM II is a simple instrument the authors developed to help determine preferences in preliterate children for light- versus dark-skinned human figures. All one needs is a dark-skinned figure, a light-skinned figure, and 24 adjectives a child can use in describing these two figures. This is an ingenious, yet quite simple, procedure. You might be thinking right now, "Hey, I could have thought of that! That is easy." You are right on both counts; you could have thought of it, and it is easy!

Why did the authors use 24 adjectives and not 12 or 48? It is probably just a matter of preference. We could use almost any number of adjectives. We would just have to be careful not to use too many. If we had, say, over 100 adjectives, the child very likely would lose interest in the study; this is something we would want to avoid.

Now read the abstract, introduction, results, and discussion sections of the study, paying particular attention to the results section. Were you surprised with the results? Many people are. It would seem to be intuitive, for a variety of reasons, for us to believe that Caucasian children would have held more favorable attitudes toward members of their own ethnic group (E+/A–) and for African American children to have held more favorable attitudes toward their own ethnic group (E–/A+). This was not the case! Although the first belief was supported the second was not. It seems that, in general, both ethnic groups favored the Caucasian figure (at least as measured by the PRAM II).

The authors give several explanations for their findings. Do you agree with them? What other possible explanations could you give for the results? What would we find if we conducted this same study today? Have these attitudes changed in the past 20 years?

THINK IT THROUGH

Suppose we decided to explore children's attitudes on race today. What changes and modifications in the Williams, Best, & Boswell study would have to be undertaken in order to do so? What ethical concerns would we encounter if we were to conduct a modified replication of this study today?

This study would be simple to replicate today; no substantial changes would have to be made. Using the PRAM II, we could easily collect our data. The authors do not say so, but we would assume they received appropriate permission to conduct the study. Because we are studying children, we would have to secure the parents' permission to have their children take part in our study. Because this study is not overly intrusive, most parents would likely allow their children to participate. We would also have to obtain permission from the school system from which the children are drawn, and we would need IRB approval as well. Our study being simple and straightforward, our IRB would be very likely to give us its approval.

We would have to be sensitive concerning the language we use in describing a particular ethnic population. Terms such as Euro-American and Afro-American, appropriate in 1975, are no longer acceptable. Were the authors being prejudiced or biased in using these terms? No, they were not; these terms were acceptable when the study was conducted. If we were to replicate this study today, we would use the terms Caucasian and African American.

Instead of using human figures, what other methods could be employed to study racial attitudes in children? Could we use a story (which would be read to the children) in which the main character is a white or a black child? That is, could we make up a story of, say, a child playing in a field filled with flowers? The narrative portion of the story would be up to you. The critical manipulation of our study (the independent variable) would be the two versions of the story. In one version, our main character would be a black child and in the alternate version the child would be white. Would varying only the color of our main character make children of different ethnic backgrounds relate more or less positively to that character? Why not try it and find out?

Could we use Barbie and Ken dolls? Today, Barbie and Ken dolls come in a multitude of ethnic identities. Instead of using the type of human figures given in the PRAM II we could use different Barbies and Kens. (By doing so, we would control for such factors as height, facial features, girth, etc.) For an early study on preference with dolls we invite you to read Clark and Clark (1939). Were the Clarks able to control for the variables we would be able to control for by using both black and white Barbies and Kens?

Going back to an earlier question posed to you, what do you think would happen if we conducted this study today? Quite likely we would get very different results. The self-images of minorities have changed over the past 20 years (Spencer & Markstrom-Adams, 1990), and these changes should be reflected in the results of any such study done today. Today, particular ethnic groups would most likely identify and prefer their own respective ethnic groups.

Although the Williams et al study investigated African American and Caucasian racial attitudes, we could also study other ethnic groups. For example, it would be interesting to replicate this same study using Native American and Asian American children as participants. We could also investigate sex differences, or sex differences as well as racial differences. We could pose specific questions, such as "African American girls respond differently from African American boys when testing using the PRAM II?" or "Are African American girls different from Native American girls in their respective racial attitudes?" There are many possible parameters we could investigate by manipulating ethnicity and sex; some rather interesting findings would likely result from such manipulations.

Modifying the ethnicity dimension somewhat, we could also study the attitudes of children from predominately black schools versus those from predominately white schools (much of our knowledge regarding racial attitudes has been acquired from studies that used students in the latter category). We could investigate racial attitudes among children of various ethnic groups who attend private versus public schools. The differences between these populations would certainly yield interesting results.

We could also investigate different age groups to see if racial attitudes change dramatically as one gets older. For example, we could compare preschool children's attitudes with students in grade school, middle school, and high school. We could also use adults and the elderly as participants. What are the different ways we could go about studying these various age groups? One way would be to use a *cross-sectional* study. In a research project of this type, we would select, for example, 20 preschool children, 20 third graders, 20 seventh graders, and 20 high school seniors, and then compare the racial attitudes of these different groups at a single point in time. On the other hand, we could do a longitudinal study in which we would assess the changes in racial attitudes of a particular group over, say, a 20-year period. In a longitudinal study, we measure the attitudes of each person over a long period of time. We would not necessarily assess their attitudes every year. We might want to measure their attitudes every five years or so.

THINK IT THROUGH

Which type of research method do you think is used most frequently when studying developmental processes: the cross-sectional method or the longitudinal method? Why did you select the method you did?

If you chose the cross-sectional method, you are correct. If we took a cross-sectional approach in our study, we would have our results collected in a much shorter period of time when compared to the longitudinal approach. On the other hand, if we used the longitudinal approach, we would have to invest substantially more time and energy in collecting our data (perhaps as much as 20 years or more). When looking at changes in behavior over different age groups, most developmental researchers will employ the cross-sectional approach to save time and money.

When studying the racial attitudes of older participants, we would have to devise more appropriate devises (the PRAM II would not be suitable after the age of eight or so). One method we could employ to study people over the age of eight would be to have our participants come up with their own lists of adjectives for describing different ethnic groups. An approach similar to this was used by Niemann, Jennings, Rozelle, Baxter, and Sullivan (1994). They found that participants used very different adjectives in describing African Americans, Mexican Americans, Asian Americans, and Caucasians. They also found differences when they asked their participants to rate men and women from these different ethnic groups. What results would you obtain if you conducted a project like this in one of your psychology classes? What would your results be if you conducted this project in the city in which you reside? What other groups could you study using this method?

THINK IT THROUGH

Is there any way animals can be used in developmental studies related to racial attitudes? It may seem impossible, but it can be done. See if you can think of several ways we could introduce animals in studies of this type. What type of animals could you use?

You may have to stretch your imagination somewhat in this exercise. One such study idea would be to have children of different ethnic groups playing with dogs or cats and then ask the children taking part in our study which child was the "nicer" or "kinder" child. (Let us take an example of a Native American child versus an African American child playing with a puppy.) More specifically, we could have the children in our study watch a videotape of either a Native American or African American child playing with a puppy. The children playing with the animal would probably have to be videotaped, since, by doing so, we could control for some potentially strong confounding variables. For example, the animal would *have* to be played with in exactly the same manner by the two children to avoid an obvious confounding of the results. Likewise, the length of time the animal was played with, in what settings the animal is played with, and the temperament of the animal would have to be controlled. Such possible confounds could logically challenge the internal validity of our work. By using videotapes we would be able to standardize those variables needing control. We could then ask the children participating in our study (say, Native Americans and Asian Americans) to state which child on the two videotapes was kinder, gentler, nicer, and so on. We could also introduce sex as an independent variable and investigate attitudinal differences in boys and girls of different ethnic backgrounds.

THINK IT THROUGH

List five areas researched related to those mentioned above that can be researched and list three novel areas (not related to any of the above) that could also be researched. What types of materials and time would each of these eight areas require? Are there any ethical concerns in the studies you have proposed? If so, how can you go about eliminating these concerns?

Related areas:

1. _____

2. _____

3. _____

4. _____

5. _____

Novel ideas:

1. _____

2. _____

3. _____

After listing your various research ideas, have one of your professors read them and give you additional and alternate suggestions. If this is indeed an area of research in which you have an interest, you will find it exciting to develop and pursue your idea to fruition with the aid of your favorite professor and your ethics committee.

There are some additional readings you can do if you are interested in pursuing research in this area. We have listed several that should be of interest to you. And, do not hesitate to ask your professor for additional suggestions.

REFERENCES

Clark, K. B., & Clark, M. K. (1939). The development of consciousness of self and the emergence of facial identity in Negro pre-school schoolchildren. *Journal of Social Psychology, 10,* 591–599.

Niemann, Y. F., Jennings, L., Rozelle, R. M., Baxter, J., & Sullivan, E. (1994). Use of free responses and cluster analysis to determine stereotypes of eight groups. *Personality and Social Psychology Bulletin, 20,* 279–390.

Spencer, M. B., & Markstrom-Adams, C. (1990). Identity Processes among Racial and Ethnic Minority Children in America. *Child Development, 61,* 290–310.

Williams, J. E., Best, D. L., & Boswell, D. A. (1975). The Measurement of Children's Racial Attitudes in the Early School Years. *Child Development, 46,* 494–500.

ADDITIONAL READINGS

Harris, H. W., Blue, H. C., & Griffith, E. H. (Eds.). (1995). *Racial and ethnic identity: Psychological development and creative expression.* New York: Routledge.

Hirschfield, L. A. (1995). Do children have a theory of race? *Cognition, 54,* 209–252

South, S. (1993). Racial and ethnic differences in the desire to marry. *Journal of Marriage and the Family, 55,* 357–370.

CHAPTER 7

Memory Research Idea Development

When Wilhelm Wundt established psychology as a science in 1879, the study of mental processes was at the core of psychology's existence. Wundt and his disciple, E. B. Titchener, who taught at Cornell University, investigated the elements that comprised our thoughts and conscious awareness. Hermann von Ebbinghaus (1885) studied memory and forgetting. Gradually, however, the study of these cognitive processes gave way to a more behavioral approach. In 1913, John Watson pronounced that the study of consciousness was out and the study of behaviorism was in.

Although some researchers refused to accept the tenets of behaviorism, it has only been during the past two decades that the study of cognitive processes, such as thinking, has become generally accepted once again. The cognitive revolution in psychology has resulted in a dramatic increase in the amount of research being conducted in the general area of human learning and memory. No longer are researchers constricted to just observing behaviors; a whole new panorama of research topics has been opened to them.

Our featured article for this chapter deals with research on the topic of memory. In this paper, Bahrick, Hall, and Berger (1996) investigate the accuracy and distortion of memory for high school grades.

Accuracy and Distortion in Memory for High School Grades

Harry P. Bahrick, Lynda K. Hall, and Stephanie A. Berger
Ohio Wesleyan University

Abstract—The relation between accuracy and distortion of autobiographical memory content was examined by verifying 3,220 high school grades recalled by 99 college students. Accuracy of recall declined monotonically with letter grade, from 89% for grades of A to 29% for grades of D. The positive correlation between achievement and accuracy of recall is attributed to more frequent rehearsals of affectively positive content and to greater accuracy of reconstructive inferences based on homogeneous, generic memories. Most errors inflated the verified grade, and the degree of asymmetry of the error distribution is used as an index of the degree of distortion. Distortions are attributed to reconstructions in a positive, emotionally gratifying direction. Contrary to expectation, the percentage of accurate recall and the degree of asymmetry of the error distribution were uncorrelated. This finding indicates that the process of distortion does not cause forgetting of the veridical content. Rather, distortion reflects bias in reconstructive inferences that occur after the veridical content has been forgotten for other reasons.

During the past century, memory research focused primarily on the loss of memory content over time. Systematic modifications of memory content were also investigated, but methodological problems made this research more difficult and less popular. Gestalt theorists were the first to investigate distortions of content (Wulf, 1922/1938), and the classic research of Bartlett (1932) inspired current reconstructive views of memory (Bransford & Franks, 1972; Neisser, 1981), including accounts of reconstructive bias (Ross, 1989).

There is now abundant evidence that memory content can undergo systematic changes. Diverse paradigms have been developed to investigate changes that are either induced by experimental interventions, such as Loftus's (1975) modifications of eyewitness reports and Fischoff's (1975) hindsight effect, or induced by the subject, reflecting reconstructions of the autobiographical past in accord with current self-perceptions (Ross, 1989). However, integrative accounts of the circumstances that produce systematic distortion instead of unbiased forgetting and of the direction and degree of distortion associated with various situational and individual difference variables are still lacking.

Koriat and Goldsmith (1994) advocate research emphasizing the differences between quantity-oriented (number correct) and accuracy-oriented

Address correspondence to Harry P. Bahrick, Department of Psychology, Ohio Wesleyan University, Delaware, OH 43015.

(fidelity) approaches to memory assessment. The former approach characterizes traditional laboratory research on the amount of retention; the latter characterizes naturalistic investigations concerned with the degree of fidelity of the recalled content relative to the objective content. The present investigation describes a framework to promote research related to this distinction. We wanted to obtain measures of both aspects of retention in the same investigation so that the interrelations between the amount forgotten and the degree of distortion of forgotten content could be examined.

Grades received in school are a very suitable content for examining accuracy and distortion of autobiographical memory. The data are plentiful because most adults have received a large number of course grades in their secondary education. Encoding conditions for the data are fairly similar, and the data are usually comparably scaled so that direction and magnitude of errors of recall can be determined. The degree of retention is typically within a sensitive range that avoids floor or ceiling effects, and, finally, the accuracy of recall can usually be verified on the basis of archival records.

METHOD

Forty male and 59 female Ohio Wesleyan University freshmen and sophomores fulfilled a research requirement in an introductory psychology course by participating. Prior to completing a questionnaire about their high school grades (see the appendix), all participants gave written permission for the registrar to release their high school transcripts to the investigator in order to verify the recalled grades. We believe that this requirement controlled deliberate falsifications of recalled grades.

The questionnaire required participants to recall grades from all 4 years of high school in the following five content areas: mathematics, science, history, foreign language, and English. For each recalled grade, students rated their degree of confidence that the recall was accurate (on a 3-point scale) and their degree of present satisfaction with the grade (on a 5-point scale). If students did not recall having taken a particular course, they were instructed to mark an *X* instead of a grade.

We subsequently verified 3,220 grades from the registrar's records. Numerical grades were transformed into corresponding letter grades, and pluses and minuses were ignored in our verification.

RESULTS AND DISCUSSION

Accuracy of Recall

Table 7A–1 frequencies of recalled grades as a function of the verified letter grades. We discuss first the frequencies that indicate accurate recall, that is, correspondence between recalled grade and verified grade. The relevant fre-

Table 7A–1 Frequency of Recalled Grades by Actual Grades

Recalled grade	Actual grade					Total
	A	B	C	D	F	
A	1,110	357	35	1	—	1,503
B	127	843	230	20	—	1,220
C	3	108	296	28	1	436
D	1	8	24	21	3	57
F	—	—	—	3	1	4
Total	1,241	1,316	585	73	5	3,220

quencies are those in the diagonal cells (top left to bottom right) of Table 7A–1. All other cell frequencies represent various kinds of errors of recall that we examine later.

Overall, 71% of grades (i.e., 2,271 of the 3,220 grades) were recalled correctly. To determine the extent of forgetting during the 4 high school years, we calculated the mean percentage of course grades correctly recalled for courses taken in 9th, 10th, 11th, and 12th grades, respectively. These data are shown in the first two columns of Table 7A–2. Fewer grades were reported from the 12th grade than from the 3 earlier years because a number of students did not take mathematics or science courses during the last year in high school. Recall accuracy is slightly higher for grades from the last year of high school

Table 7A–2 Proportion of Accurately Recalled Grades as a Function of Year in High School, Letter Grade, Satisfaction, and Confidence

Year in high school		Letter grade		Satisfaction rating[a]		Confidence rating[b]	
Year	Proportion recalled	Grade	Proportion recalled	Rating	Proportion recalled	Rating	Proportion recalled
12	.73 (634)	A	.89 (1,241)	5	.75 (1,412)	3	.74 (2,052)
11	.70 (863)	B	.64 (1,316)	4	.67 (871)	2	.63 (893)
10	.70 (865)	C	.51 (585)	3	.68 (558)	1	.67 (213)
9	.70 (858)	D	.29 (73)	2/1	.65 (370)		

Note. The number of responses is in parentheses; discrepancies reflect missing data.
[a]Satisfaction was rated on a scale from 1 *(not very satisfied)* to 5 *(very satisfied)*.
[b]Confidence was rated on a scale from 1 *(not very confident)* to 3 *(very confident)*

than for the preceding 3 years. Assuming that virtually all grades would be correctly recalled immediately after being received, we can conclude that most forgetting occurs during the 1st year of retention interval.

Our data are in accord with classical retention functions and with our earlier findings (Bahrick, Hall, & Dunlosky, 1993). In another recent investigation of the accuracy of recalled grades, Schmela (1993) reported that German students in their 12th or 13th school year correctly recalled 57% of their grades from their 6th and 9th years of school. Recall from the 9th grade was 4% more accurate than recall from the 6th grade. Thus, the German students were somewhat less accurate than the students in our investigation, probably because of the larger variance of German grades. Almost none of our participants had poor high school records. Another reason for the difference may be that the transition to U.S. high schools is marked by context changes of buildings, curriculum, and peer group. These changes may render high school grades more discriminable from grades obtained in earlier years of school.

The percentage of accurately recalled grades as a function of the verified letter grade, the confidence rating, and the satisfaction rating is also shown in Table 7A–2. The relation between the degree of confidence and correct recall is in the expected direction, but modest. The same is true of the relation between expressed satisfaction with the grade and accuracy. Greater confidence and more satisfaction are associated with somewhat higher percentages of correct recall.

The most startling finding pertains to differences in the accuracy of retention of high versus low letter grades. Disregarding the data for grades of F ($N = 5$), recall accuracy monotonically declines from 89% for grades of A to 29% for grades of D. Past research (Koch, 1930; Thompson, 1985; Waters & Leeper, 1936) has generally shown that retention is best for experiences that are affectively pleasant, intermediate for experiences that are unpleasant, and worst for experiences that are neutral. The present findings are distinctive in that the order of recall accuracy monotonically reflects the degree of pleasantness associated with higher achievement. We believe that previous investigations may have confounded the degree or intensity of affect with the degree of importance, or the significance of the experience to the life of the individual. The confounding of emotionality and consequentiality of events has also been pointed out by Neisser (1982) in his critique of flashbulb memory research. Rubin and Kozin (1984) have shown that the most memorable autobiographical experiences are almost always rated high in personal importance or significance. Neutral autobiographical experiences not only lack affective attributes, but also generally lack significance. They have little impact on the quality of life and may therefore be less well encoded. In contrast, grades, regardless of their level, have equal significance. Each grade contributes equally to the overall record of achievement and, in turn, to future opportunities. The descending level of accuracy as a function of grade therefore reflects a descending degree of pleasantness, unconfounded by systematic covariance with significance.

We subjected the data in Table 7A–2 to a logistic regression analysis in which correct or incorrect recall of each grade was the dichotomized, dependent variable and year in high school, actual letter grade, and satisfaction and confidence levels were the independent variables. Product terms for the actual-grade-by-confidence and actual-grade-by-satisfaction interactions were added, as were 98 percent variables created to assess the contribution of individual differences to accuracy. Analyses were conducted hierarchically, entering the 98 contrast variables first, the four independent variables next, and the two interaction terms last.

The 98 contrast variables were significant as a set ($\chi^2[98, N = 3,155] = 636.82, p < .001$), indicating that the subjects differed in recall accuracy. After we controlled for individual differences, the four independent variables were significant as a set ($\chi^2[4, N = 3,155] = 176.58 \ p < .001$). Tests of each independent variable indicated significant effects for actual grade ($b = 1.00, \chi^2[1, N = 3,155] = 9.31, p < .01$), and satisfaction ($b = -.40, \chi^2[1, N = 3,155] = 56.61, p < .001$). Finally, the two interaction terms were significant as a set ($\chi^2[2, N = 3,155] = 192.50, p < .001$), although further analyses revealed that only the coefficient of the grade-by-satisfaction term was significant ($b = .78, \chi^2[1, N = 3,155] = 175.22, p < .001$). This interaction reflects the low accuracy of recall for grades other than A that received high satisfaction ratings. We discuss this interaction at a later point. Because the year in high school had no significant effect on accuracy, we pooled data in regard to this variable in subsequent analyses.

Individual Differences and Accuracy

The purpose of this part of the analysis was to find the extent to which individuals who were more satisfied with their grades, were more confident of their recall, or had a higher level of academic achievement were also more accurate in recalling their grades. Accordingly, we calculated for each participant the mean confidence rating for all correctly recalled grades. We then calculated the upper, middle, and lower terciles of the distribution of means so that participants were identified as high, middle, or low in their overall confidence of recall. We used the same procedure to identify those who were high, middle, or low in regard to their overall satisfaction with their correctly recalled grades. We also calculated the mean verified grade (grade point average, GPA) for each participant, based on the high school transcript, and identified those participants who were in each of four quartiles of the distribution for this index of academic achievement. Table 7A–3 gives the percentage of correctly recalled grades as a function of each of these individual difference variables. Separate values are given for verified grades of A, B, and C.

The data are consistent with Table 7A–2 in that higher letter grades were always recalled more accurately than lower grades. The row means also show that individuals with higher confidence, higher grade satisfaction, and higher academic achievement had more accurate recall. However, the effect of these

Table 7A–3 Proportion of Accurately Recalled Grades as a Function of Individual
Difference Variables and Actual Grade

Variable and level	Grade			
	A	B	C	M
Satisfaction tercile				
3 (4.7)	.89	.56	.53	.82
2 (4.0)	.73	.59	.50	.62
1 (3.2)	.72	.65	.56	.60
Confidence tercile				
3 (3.0)	.87	.50	.53	.75
2 (2.7)	.78	.69	.63	.68
1 (2.1)	.69	.61	.45	.61
Grade point average quartile				
4 (3.8)	.93	.57	.50	.89
3 (3.4)	.79	.60	.59	.68
2 (2.9)	.67	.62	.56	.61
1 (2.4)	.72	.62	.46	.55

Note. Values in parentheses are tercile or quartile means of individual difference variables.

individual difference variables is evident only in retention of grades of A. There is little or no effect on the retention of grades of B or C. It is noteworthy that students who are in the highest quartile of academic achievement were highly accurate in recalling grades of A (93%), but quite inaccurate in remembering grades of C (50%), even though they received very few Cs and one might therefore expect these grades toe recalled better as a result of their distinctiveness (Restorff, 1933).

To verify the statistical significance of our conclusions regarding the data in Table 7A–3, we correlated the percentage accuracy of each individual's recalled grades with the individual's mean satisfaction rating, mean confidence rating, and GPA. Separate correlations were computed for verified grades of A, B, and C. The accuracy of recalling grades of A correlated significantly with GPA ($r = .39$, $p < .01$), mean satisfaction ($r = .36$, $p < .01$), and mean confidence ($r = .22$, $p < .05$). The accuracy of recalling grades of B and C did not correlate significantly ($p > .05$) with any of these variables.

Two factors can account for the results pertaining to accuracy of recalled grades. One factor reflects the influence of affect. Higher grades are affectively pleasant; they are associated with the satisfaction of achievement motives. This condition reinforces rehearsals of the memory content and thus enhances retention of that content (Jersild, 1931). The rehearsal hypothesis is also supported by Rubin and Kozin (1984), whose subjects reported 6.7, 4.1, and 3.7

rehearsals, respectively, for the first, second, and third most memorable auto-biographical experiences.

The second factor involves reconstructive inferences. Students who have earned mostly As will infer that grades they cannot specifically recall are As, and their inferences are more likely to be correct than the inference of students who have earned an equal number of As, Bs, and Cs. Larger variance in past performance reduces the accuracy of inferences based on overall past performance.

The result of the interaction of these two factors is that higher grades are remembered more accurately than lower grades by all students, but the effect is enhanced for students who have earned mostly As. Our sample included no students whose academic records were uniformly poor, so our data cannot confirm the related prediction that poorer students have greater recall accuracy for low grades than do better students.

In addition, accuracy of recalling grades of A is enhanced by a ceiling effect, which precludes errors in an upward direction. However, this artifact does not apply to other grades and therefore accounts for only a small portion of the very large overall effect of grade level on recall accuracy.

Distortion of Recall

The preceding analyses have been limited to variations in accuracy of recall, as reflected in the diagonal cell frequencies of Table 7A–1. We now turn to analyses of distortion of recall based on the error frequencies reported in the remaining cells of Table 7A–1.

We define memory distortion as systematic changes of reported content with respect to verified content. Thus, memory of grades is distorted to the extent that reported grades are systematically higher or lower than verified grades. We calculated overall distortion scores and distortion scores for each participant based on the ratio of asymmetry of the error distribution. The numerator of the ratio was the number of recalled grades that were higher than verified grades. The denominator was the total number of errors in both directions. The ratio can vary from 0 to 1.0. An asymmetry ratio of .50 indicates no distortion; the number of incorrectly recalled grades that are higher than actual grades equals the number that are lower than actual grades. Ratios larger than .50 indicate systematic upward distortion, and a ratio of 1.0 indicates total distortion with all errors in the upward direction. Ratios smaller than .50 indicate downward distortion. Only errors in reporting grades of B, C, and D were included in calculating the ratio because grades of A and F can be distorted in only one direction and are therefore not suitable for calculating asymmetry of errors.

The cell frequencies in Table 7A–1 show that of 814 errors in recalling grades B, C, and D, 671 are in the upward direction and 143 are in the downward direction, for an overall asymmetry ratio of .82. Separate asymmetry ratios calculated for recall of individual letter grades are .75 for grades of B, .02 for grades of C, and .94 for grades of D. In the following analyses of the influence of individual difference variables on distortion, we first present asymmetry ratios based on errors in reporting verified grades of B only. The reasons for this limitation are that grades of C and D were nearly always distorted in the upward direction, so that asymmetry ratios based on these grades exhibit ceiling effects that render them insensitive to the effects of other variables.

Overall, 79 of the 99 subjects inflated their grades (ratios > .50), 13 subjects recalled all of their grades correctly, 1 subject had a symmetrical error distribution (ratio = .50), and 6 subjects deflated their grades (ratios < .50). Too few students deflated their grades to permit generalizations about characteristics associated with the direction of distortion, and all subsequent analyses focus on variations in the degree of distortion among the 80 subjects with the distortion ratios equal to or greater than .50.

Table 7A–4 relates the degree of asymmetry of errors in the recall of grades of B to individual difference variables. It is evident that the degree of asymmetry increases with confidence, with degree of grade satisfaction, and with academic achievement.

Table 7A–5 presents the same analyses based on asymmetry ratios that combine errors in reporting verified grades of B, C, and D. The effects of confidence, satisfaction, and GPA on distortion are in the same direction as those shown in Table 7A–4, but they are somewhat less pronounced because the added error data for grades of C and D yield asymmetry ratios close to 1.0 for all subgroups.

These findings are consistent with those of Schmela (1993), who also reported significantly greater distortion for students who show higher achievement and for those who indicate higher interest in the content. In our own prior investigation (Babrick et al., 1993), we reported the opposite trend. However, our earlier finding was based on a measure of asymmetry that included

Table 7A–4 Asymmetry Ratios for Actual Grades of B as a Function of Individual Difference Variables

Satisfaction		Confidence		Grade point average	
Tercile	Asymmetry ratio	Tercile	Asymmetry ratio	Quartile	Asymmetry ratio
3 (4.7)	.95	3 (3.0)	.87	4 (3.8)	.98
2 (4.0)	.80	2 (2.7)	.75	3 (3.4)	.91
1 (3.2)	.57	1 (2.1)	.65	2 (2.9)	.75
				1 (2.4)	.46

Note. Values in parentheses are tercile or quartile means of individual difference variables.

Table 7A–5 Asymmetry Ratios for Actual Grades of B, C, and D as a Function of Individual Difference Variables

Satisfaction		Confidence		Grade point average	
Tercile	Asymmetry ratio	Tercile	Asymmetry ratio	Quartile	Asymmetry ratio
3 (4.7)	.93	3 (3.0)	.92	4 (3.8)	.98
2 (4.0)	.88	2 (2.7)	.85	3 (3.4)	.91
1 (3.2)	.81	1 (2.1)	.84	2 (2.9)	.83
				1 (2.4)	.80

Note. Values in parentheses are tercile or quartile means of individual difference variables.

grades of A, and that measure severely constrained upward distortions of high achievers. When we recomputed asymmetry omitting errors for recall of grades of A, the results agreed with the present findings and those of Schmela.

We interpret individual differences in distortion on the basis of two factors, the first of which also applied to our interpretation of the results on accuracy of retention. Participants reconstruct or infer grades they cannot specifically recall in accord with relevant, generic memories, or what Flavell (1979) has called metacognitive knowledge. This assumption leads to the prediction that students with an outstanding academic record will infer a grade of A when a B has been forgotten. Students whose overall academic record is mediocre will be less likely to infer high grades on this basis. This differential effect on the asymmetry of errors of students with high versus low past achievement is in accord with the position of Ross (1989).

Although the data for recall of grades of A and F are not suitable for an asymmetry analysis, the frequency with which grades of A were recalled as Bs also exhibits this differential effect. For example, participants in the highest quartile of the GPA distribution recalled only 5% of their As as Bs, compared with 23% for participants in the lowest GPA quartile.

Beyond this differential effect, there is a second general effect that favors reconstructions in a positive, emotionally gratifying direction. Loftus (1982) has described this effect: "Memory naturally shifts in a positive or prestige-enhancing direction, perhaps for the purpose of allowing us to have a more comfortable recollection of the past" (p. 146). It has been methodologically difficult to quantify this positive reconstruction effect. In our data, the effect accounts for the overall asymmetry ratio of .82. It is important to note that 6 subjects distorted in the opposite direction and that conclusions regarding this subpopulation require a much larger sample.

Table 7A–6 shows the intercorrelations among the following individual difference variables: degree of asymmetry of the error distribution (based on grades of B, C, and D), percentage of correct recall, mean confidence, mean

Table 7A–6 Intercorrelations among Individual Difference Variables

Variable	Distortion	Accuracy	Satisfaction	Confidence
Distortion	—			
Accuracy	.156	—		
Satisfaction	.375*	.370*	—	
Confidence	.160	.157	.325*	—
Grade point average	.450*	.687*	.705*	.189

*$p < 01$.

grade satisfaction, and GPA. The table shows that degree of memory distortion is positively correlated with academic achievement and with grade satisfaction. This finding confirms the statistical significance of results in Table 7A–5 pertaining to satisfaction and GPA. The correlation between GPA and mean grade satisfaction is in the expected direction; that is, students who had higher grades were more satisfied with their grades, and our rationale relating higher GPA to greater accuracy and to more distortion therefore also applies to the effects of mean grade satisfaction shown in Tables 7A–2, 7A–4, and 7A–5. The correlation of GPA with grade satisfaction is attenuated because grade satisfaction does not accurately reflect the level of achievement. Grade satisfaction reflects the remembered grade, rather than the actual grade, and this fact explains the interaction between grade satisfaction and accuracy reported earlier. High satisfaction with grades that were actually B or C, but were recalled as A, attenuates the relationship between satisfaction and accuracy of recall.

The correlation between recall accuracy and degree of distortion is not statistically significant ($p > .05$), and this finding requires further discussion.

Relation Between Accuracy and Distortion

Our hypothesis was that distortion of memory content is an important cause of forgetting, that is, that systematic changes of the remembered content block access to the objective content. Our data do not support this conclusion. If distortions cause failures to recall the object content, then individuals who showed the greatest degree of distortion (highest asymmetry ratios) should also show the lowest recall accuracy. This is not the case. Even when GPA is held constant, the partial correlation between accuracy and degree of distortion of recall remains a low –.23.

The independence of degree of distortion from the amount of accurate retention is further illustrated by comparing the percentage of accurate recall and the asymmetry ratios for subjects in the highest and the lowest GPA quartiles. The data based on grades of B are most revealing. Table 7A–3 shows that the percentage of recall accuracy was .57 for the high achievers and .62 for the low achievers. Table 7A–4 shows that the distortion ratio was .98 for the high achievers and .46 for the low achievers. Thus, the two groups were very similar in accuracy, but extremely different in degree of distortion. If distortion of the objective content is a primary cause of failures to recall the objective content, then two groups extremely different in the degree of distortion should also differ in the percentage of accurate recall.

These data suggest that loss of objective memory content and distortion of that content are largely independent processes. Distortion does not cause forgetting in this situation, but generally occurs after the objective content has been lost for other reasons.

The investigation supports the conclusion that affective attributes associated with academic achievement have strong effects on the long-term retention of autobiographical content. High grades are recalled with much greater accuracy than low grades. Once the specific grade in a course has been forgotten, recall appears to be based on reconstructive inferences. Such inferences reflect relevant, metacognitive knowledge of past high or low academic achievements and a strong tendency to generate emotionally gratifying content (higher grades). As a result, correct recall of grades is based on specific memories and on successful inferences. Errors of recall are based on unsuccessful inferences, and these reflect the bias of positive reconstruction.

Our findings support the view that recall of autobiographical content reflects a combination of specific and generic memories. Generic memories provide the basis for inferences that can bring about distortions of content. Barring systematic interventions, such distortions do not appear to displace specific memories; rather, they supplement them and fill in the gaps when specific memories are lost.

ACKNOWLEDGMENTS

This research was supported by National Science Foundation Grant BNS-9119800 awarded to Harry P. Bahrick. We thank Andrew Tollafield and Kimberly Wagner for collecting and scoring data, the Ohio Wesleyan University Registrar's office for verifying the grades, Nadya Klinetob and Jeff Edwards for methodological advice, and Eugene Winograd, Thomas Nelson, and an anonymous reviewer for their valuable critiques of the manuscript.

REFERENCES

Bahrick, H. P., Hall, L. K., & Dunlowsky, J. (1993). Reconstructive processing of memory content for high versus low test scores and grades. *Applied Cognitive Psychology, 7,* 1–10.

Bartlett, F. C. (1932). *Remembering.* Cambridge, England: Cambridge University Press.

Bransford, J. D., & Franks, J. J. (1972). The abstraction of linguistic ideas: A review. *Cognition, 1,* 211–249.

Fischoff, B. (1975). Hindsight ≠ foresight: The effect of outcome knowledge on judgment under uncertainty. *Journal of Experimental Psychology: Human Perception and Performance, 1,* 288–299.

Flavell, J. H. (1979). Metacognition and cognitive monitoring: A new area of cognitive-developmental inquiry. *American Psychologists, 34,* 906–911.

Jersild, A. (1931). Memory for the pleasant as compared with the unpleasant. *Journal of Experimental Psychology, 14,* 284–288.

Koch, H. (1930). The influence of some affective factors upon recall. *Journal of Genetic Psychology, 4,* 171–190.

Koriat, A., & Goldsmith, M. (1994). Memory in naturalistic and laboratory contexts: Distinguishing the accuracy-oriented and quantity-oriented approaches to memory assessment. *Journal of Experimental Psychology: General, 123,* 297–315.

Loftus, E. F. (1975). Leading questions and the eyewitness report. *Cognitive Psychology, 7,* 560–572.

Loftus, E. F. (1982). Memory and its distortions. In A. G. Kraut (Ed.), *G. Stanley Hall Lectures* (pp. 119–154). Washington, DC: American Psychological Association.

Neisser, U. (1981). John Dean's memory: A case study. *Cognition, 9,* 1–22.

Neisser, U. (1982). Snapshots or benchmarks? In U. Neisser (Ed.), *Memory observed: Remembering in natural contexts* (pp. 43–48). San Francisco: Freeman

Restorff, H., von (1933). Analyse von Vorgaengen im Spurenfeld: I. Ueber die Wirkung von Bereichsbidungen im Spurenfeld [Analysis of processes in the trace system: I. The effect of concept formation in the trace system]. *Psychologische Forschung, 18,* 299–342.

Ross, M. (1989). Relation of implicit theories to the construction of personal histories. *Psychological Review, 96,* 341–357.

Rubin, D. C., & Kozin, M. (1984). Vivid memories. *Cognition, 16,* 81–95.

Schmela, M. (1993). Abiturienten erinnern sich an ihre alten Zeugnisnoten—Zur Qualitaet leitungsbezogener autobiographischer Erinnerungen [Pupils remember their former final grades: About the quality of achievement-related autobiographical memories]. *Zeitschrift für Paedogische Psychologie, 7*(1), 475–478.

Thompson, C. (1985). Memory for unique personal events: Effects of pleasantness. *Motivation and Emotion, 9,* 277–289.

Waters, R., & Leeper, R. (1936). The relation of affective tone to the retention of experiences of daily life. *Journal of Experimental Psychology, 19,* 203–215.

Wulf, F. (1938). Tendencies in figural variation. In W. D. Ellis (Ed. and Trans.). *A source book of gestalt psychology* (pp. 136–148). New York: Harcourt, Brace & World. (Reprinted from *Psychologische Forschung,* 1922, *1,* 133–373).

APPENDIX: QUESTIONNAIRE INSTRUCTIONS AND SAMPLE QUESTIONS[1]

Please fill in the letter grade received each semester in the following subjects. If you do not remember the exact grade, please use your best guess. In the "Confidence" column, please mark on a scale of 1 to 3 how confident you are that you are remembering the correct grade (1 = not very confident, 3 = very confident). In the "Satisfaction" column, please indicate on a scale of 1 to 5 how sat-

[1]The questionnaire we administered included identical question formats for reporting grades in the following courses: math, science, English, foreign language, and history.

isfied you are with your performance in that area each semester (1 = not very satisfied, 5 = very satisfied). If you did not take a class in a particular subject that
semester, please mark an "X" in the "Grade Received" column.

Math

Year	Semester	Grade Received	Confidence			Satisfaction				
			low		high	low				high
9th	first	_____	1	2	3	1	2	3	4	5
	second	_____	1	2	3	1	2	3	4	5
10th	first	_____	1	2	3	1	2	3	4	5
	second	_____	1	2	3	1	2	3	4	5
11th	first	_____	1	2	3	1	2	3	4	5
	second	_____	1	2	3	1	2	3	4	5
12th	first	_____	1	2	3	1	2	3	4	5
	second	_____	1	2	3	1	2	3	4	5

THINK IT THROUGH

Here some questions to help check your understanding of this article.
Write down your answers before reading further.

1. Why did the researchers specifically choose to study memory of grades?
2. What were the purposes of having the participants give written per-
    mission to release their high school grades?
3. When does most forgetting of grades occur?
4. What unusual finding do the authors report with regard to the mem-
    ory of high versus low grades? Why is this finding unusual? Why do the
    authors believe it occurred?
5. What is the relationship between accuracy of recall and satisfaction,
    confidence, and achievement? What qualification must be added to
    these conclusion?
6. What was the nature of the distortions in memory for grades? What is
    the relationship between distortion and satisfaction, confidence, and
    achievement?

What an interesting and relevant research project! We hope you enjoyed
reading it as much as we enjoyed selecting it. Let's see if your answers to the
Think It Through questions correspond to ours.

The researchers chose to study memory for high school grades so they could examine both *accuracy* (the number of grades remembered correctly) and *distortion* (the type of changes that were made in the memory of grades) in the same project. The participants signed a release in order to allow the researchers to gain access to their high school grades as well as to reduce the amount of deliberate falsification. As Bahrick, Hall, and Berger examined the participants' high school grades, they noted that the percent recalled was approximately 70% for Grades 9, 10, 11, and 12. Because the amount recalled did not decrease with time and because the participants had been out of high school for at least one year, it was determined that most forgetting for high school grades occurred during the first year following the receipt of the grades.

Because previous research (e.g., Thompson, 1985) has found that recall is best for pleasant events, next best for unpleasant events, and worst for neutral events, it was surprising to find the accuracy of recall declined from A to B to C to D. Assuming the receipt of a low grade, such as D, is unpleasant, past results would have predicted greater recall for the D grades than the Bs and Cs.

As satisfaction with grades, confidence in recall, and level of academic achievement increased, so did the accuracy of recall. In other words, students who were satisfied with their grades, had high confidence in their ability to recall their past grades, and were high academic achievers displayed better accuracy of recall. However, this relationship held true *only* for grades of A. This finding was especially intriguing. Because these high-achieving students made very few low grades, such as Cs, it is predictable they would remember these grades quite well because they are so distinctive.

So far, we have seen that this research produced some very interesting results with regard to the amount the students forgot about their high school grades: This is the accuracy component the investigators described at the beginning of the article. What about distortions or how the students remembered their grades? Again, this research produced some fascinating results. When distortion occurred, it tended to be in the direction of inflating the grade: "79 of the 99 subjects inflated their grades" (Bahrick et al., 1996, p. 268). It is interesting to note that the amount of distortion increased as the individual difference variables of satisfaction, confidence, and academic achievement became more pronounced. Of these three factors, level of academic achievement and grade satisfaction were most strongly related to grade distortion. Bahrick and his colleagues feel that the tendency for high-achieving students to inflate forgotten grades (e.g., B to A) and the general tendency to shift our memories in a positive direction may account for these distortions.

One important conclusion revealed by this research was that accuracy of recall and distortion of grades were independent processes. Contrary to the initial prediction, those students who had the greatest distortions were no less accurate than students who had low distortions.

THINK IT THROUGH

Where does this article leave us? Have we learned all there is to learn about students' memories for grades or are there still questions to be answered? Give some thought to this question and arrive at more than just a yes or no answer before reading further.

By now you should know the answer to the question we just posed. It is a *very* rare occasion when the results of a research project fail to prompt further research. The article you just finished reading prompts numerous possible follow up projects. Some of our ideas follow.

First, we thought it would be interesting to compare the recall of college freshmen with that of seniors. Will the memory of high school grades decline for seniors, compared to freshmen? Because a large number of grades are received during a student's college career, it is conceivable that the memory of college grades will interfere with the memory for high school grades (a retroactive interference effect). Because the participants tested by Bahrick and his colleagues were freshmen and sophomores, they were unable to make such comparisons.

Even though we are told that 40 male and 59 female students participated in the research on memory for high school grades, we are not given any information concerning similarities and differences between men and women. Hence, another idea for a follow-up study would be to see if sex differences exist in the memory for high school grades. If such differences are found, then it would be interesting to see if they are consistent over all courses or if they are limited to just a few, specific courses, as might be predicted by previous research. For example, a classic report by Maccoby and Jacklin (1974) contended that men and women differed in four areas: verbal ability, spatial ability, mathematical ability, and aggression (see also Halpern, 1992). It would be interesting to see if memory accuracy and distortion were in some way related to these proposed differences.

What about ethnicity? We might find interesting results when African Americans and Caucasians, or Native Americans and Latinos, are compared. Always remember that ethnicity can be an important variable for consideration.

Because the data reported by Bahrick and his colleagues came from students enrolled at a private university, it would seem relevant to determine if these results are generalizable to students at a variety of universities. Would similar results be obtained at large public universities or at institutions that do not have any formal admission requirements? If data such as these are being used to provide a view of how the general process of memory works, then similar results should be obtained from these other institutions. If differential results are obtained, then avenues for additional research will present themselves.

Extending this research to different types of colleges and universities prompts yet another follow-up study. What type of memory for high school grades do noncollegiate high school graduates have? In this instance, accuracy and distortion shown by men and women who opted not to attend college could be compared with the data generated by the collegiate participants. Of course, you have a wide range of potential participants to choose from; in fact, one can easily envision a series of studies evaluating the memory for grades of individuals having only a high school education from several areas and/or occupations in the general society. What were the cognitions involved for those students who distorted their grades on the high side versus those students who distorted their grades on the low side. These differences can provide the impetus for another set of interesting studies. Without question, the results of these studies will lead you to develop further research questions.

THINK IT THROUGH

List five ideas that are related to the ones we have described above that can be researched, and list three novel ideas (not related to any of the above) that could also be researched. What types of materials and time would each of these eight ideas require? Are there any special precautions or control procedures you will need to implement?

Related ideas:

1. _____

2. _____

3. _____

4. _____

5. _____

Novel ideas:

1. _____

2. _____

3. _____

After listing your various research ideas, have one of your professors read them and give you additional and alternate suggestions. If this is indeed an area of research in which you have an interest, you will find it exciting to develop and pursue your ideas to completion.

REFERENCES

Bahrick, H. P., Hall, L. K., & Berger, S. A. (1996). Accuracy and Distortion in Memory for High School Grades. *Psychological Science, 7,* 265–271.
Ebbinghaus, H. (1885). *On memory.* Leipzig: Duncker & Humblot.
Halpern, D. F. (1992). *Sex differences in cognitive abilities* (2nd ed.). Hillsdale, NJ: Erlbaum.
Maccoby, E. E., & Jacklin, C. N. (1974). *The psychology of sex differences.* Stanford, CA: Stanford University Press.

ADDITIONAL READINGS

Bartlett, F. C. (1932) *Remembering.* Cambridge, England: Cambridge University Press.
Jersild, A. (1931). Memory for the pleasant as compared with the unpleasant. *Journal of Experimental Psychology, 14,* 284–288.
Loftus, E. F. (1982). Memory and its distortions. In A. G. Kraut (Ed.), *G. Stanley Hall Lectures* (pp. 119–154). Washington, DC: American Psychological Association.
Watson, J. B. (1913). Psychology as the behaviorist views it. *Psychological Review, 20,* 158–177.

CHAPTER 8

Physiological Research Idea Development

In this chapter we examine research concerned with the relation between physiological effects and behavior. There are two basic ways to determine such relationships.

THINK IT THROUGH

What are these two approaches? Give this question some thought and write down possible answers before reading further.

First, the experimenter might directly manipulate a variable that changes the physiological nature of the test participants. For example, based on reports that humans exposed to lead in the environment displayed higher levels of emotionality (e. g., Baker, Feldman, White, & Harley, 1983; David, Clark, & Voeller, 1972), Nation and his colleagues (Nation, Baker, Fantasia, Ruscher, & Clark, 1987; Nation, Clark, Bourgeois, & Rogers, 1982) reasoned that laboratory rats administered lead in their food would also show increased levels of emotionality and even heightened aggression. Their results supported this prediction; the administration of lead altered the physiological makeup of the animals and made them more emotional and more aggressive toward aversive stimuli. Other researchers seek to change the physiological nature of their test participants by surgically removing or electrically stimulating a portion of the brain. For example, in a classic experiment, James Olds and Peter Milner (1954) examined the reinforcing effects of electrical stimulation of the brain. They found that rats would press the lever in a Skinner box hundreds of times an hour in order to receive brief but very pleasurable electrical stimulation of the brain following each lever press.

The second approach to investigating physiological effects and behavior is to identify a particular physiological state and then determine how those individuals displaying the specific physiological characteristics differ from individuals who do not display the designated characteristic. For example, two cardiologists, Meyer Friedman and Ray Rosenman (1974) published research indicating that a specific type of individual, the Type A personality, may be more prone to heart attacks than other individuals. The Type A individual is characterized as being aggressive, hostile, competitive, and having an exaggerated sense of time urgency. (The Type B individual is simply described as the opposite of the Type A.) All of these characteristics were originally thought to combine to make Type A individuals more susceptible to heart attacks.

Since the publication of that landmark research, hundreds of projects have investigated the specifics of the Type A behavior pattern. For example, it was shown that hostility is the main component of the Type A behavior constellation that leads to an increase in heart attacks (Barefoot, Dodge, Peterson, Dahlstrom, & Williams, 1989). Our feature article for this chapter is one of the studies that has further investigated this fascinating behavior pattern.

Our featured article is unique in several respects. First, it is a study done on a population outside the United States. Second, it recruits participants through a newspaper advertisement. Finally, the project did not test groups of participants; the results of testing only three participants are presented. As you may have learned, this approach constitutes a *single-subject research design.* In research of this nature, the experimenter first establishes a *baseline,* or naturally occurring frequency of the behavior that is to be modified; then, a treatment designed to change the frequency of this behavior is introduced. In order to be more certain the treatment is effective, the researcher may conduct a *multiple-baseline experiment.* In the multiple-baseline experiment, several dependent variables are recorded simultaneously and the experimenter is interested in the pattern of changes in these several responses. If they all change in a meaningful and predictable manner, then the researcher has increased confidence the experimental manipulation had the desired effect. If all the behavioral measures do not change as predicted, then some other factor(s) may be operating. Keep this feature in mind as you read the following article.

Application of Self-Control Procedures to Modifying Type A Behavior

Keiko Nakano
Keio University

The effects of the self-control procedure facilitating alternative behaviors on modifying speed and impatient behaviors of the Type A behavior pattern were evaluated with a multiple-baseline across meals arranged on a multiple-baseline across subjects design. The self-control procedure was a self-initiated approach designed with the intention of eliminating the antecedent stimuli evoking the time-urgent and chronically active behaviors at table and after meals. The multiple-baseline design could assess the capability of the self-control techniques to produce behaviorally significant changes of the target behaviors. The results indicated that the self-control treatment program of this study could help subjects to achieve significant increases in the number of minutes of eating and relaxing as well as clinically significant improvement in psychosomatic symptoms rated on daily logs following transfer to the self-control conditions. The effects of the self-control procedures were discussed in terms of acquisition of more adaptive behaviors.

The Type A behavior pattern, described as a hard-driving, hostile, competitive, and time-urgent response style (Friedman & Rosenman, 1974) has been identified as an important risk factor for coronary heart disease (Brand, Rosenman, Sholtz, & Friedman, 1976; Rosenman, Brand, Jenkins, Friedman, Straus, & Wurm, 1975). More recent studies have found some of these Type A characteristics are more strongly related to coronary heart disease. Booth-Kewley and Friedman (1987) suggested that hostility and anger were the only toxic components of the Type A behavior pattern. Wright (1988) has, however, indicated that time urgency (the everlasting struggle to achieve a great many goals in a short period of time) and persistent activation (the tendency to remain chronically active and tense) are also associated with coronary heart disease. Furthermore, Hecker, Chesney, Black, and Frautschi (1988) presented the evidence that hostility, immediateness, and competitiveness were related to coronary heart disease.

The Type A behavior pattern has also been hypothesized to be maladaptive self-control behavior (Glass, 1977) and was reported to relate to a wide variety of physical and psychosomatic symptoms. Howard, Cunningham, and Rechnitzer (1976) reported that Type A managers had more cardiovascular,

The Psychological Record, 1996, 46, 595–606. Used by permission of *The Psychological Record.*
I thank Dr. Masaya Sato for his helpful comments on this study. I am also grateful to the reviewers of a previous version of this article for their helpful comments. Requests for reprints should be addressed to Keiko Nakano, 3-10-21, Shakujiidai, Nerimaku, Tokyo 177, Japan.

gastrointestinal, and diabetic problems than Type B subjects who showed a relative absence of Type A attributes. Stout and Bloom (1982) administered a survey about upper respiratory symptoms in college students and found that Type A subjects reported more cold symptoms than Type B ones. Carmody, Hollis, Matarazzo, Fey, and Connor (1984) administered the Jenkins Activity Survey and the Cornell Medical Index to a large sample of a dietary intervention study. Significant positive correlations between Jenkins Activity Survey scores and physical symptoms were found. Woods and Burns (1984) found that Type A women reported significantly more symptoms of sleep disorders, respiratory symptoms, chest pains, and gastrointestinal problems. The Type A behavior pattern was reported to be an unfavorable characteristic for Japanese working environments (Hayano, Takeuchi, Yoshida, Jozuka, Mishima, & Fujinami, 1989) and was associated with physical symptoms such as headaches, acid stomach or indigestion, and insomnia (Nakano, 1990a).

Reduction of the risk of coronary heart disease in nonclinical populations by modifying their Type A behavior pattern (e.g., Kelly & Stone, 1987; Roskies, Kearney, Spevack, Surkis, Cohen, & Gilman, 1979; Suinn & Bloom, 1978) received great attention. Although a range of treatments from psychotherapy to cognitive restructuring has been applied to Type A individuals, behavioral treatments were demonstrated to be the most effective means of reducing the Type A behavior pattern (see, Suinn, 1982). Behaviorally oriented approaches are mostly based on various self-control procedures and are programmed to provide the opportunity for adapting more effective coping skills and relying less on Type A behavior.

A popular behavioral approach applied to Type A behavior is anxiety management training (Suinn, 1990). Suinn and Bloom (1978) first demonstrated that training healthy Type A subjects in anxiety management training led to significant reductions in Type A inventory scores and anxiety. Other studies (e.g., Hart, 1984; Kelly & Stone, 1987; Nakano, 1990b) which employed anxiety management training to modify the Type A behavior pattern also demonstrated significant reductions in Type A behaviors.

Levenkron, Cohen, Mueller, and Fisher (1983) compared the effectiveness of three treatments such as comprehensive behavior therapy, group psychotherapy, and brief information, for modifying the Type A behavior pattern among healthy subjects. The comprehensive behavior therapy program was a combination of active self-control, systematic desensitization, and altering internal dialogue. Among the self-control methods were removing one's wristwatch when unavoidably delayed, taking less work home in the evening, and adjusting personal schedules. Results showed that the comprehensive behavior therapy was most effective in reducing Type A behaviors. For Japanese subjects, several self-control techniques facilitating alternative behaviors were used to reduce Type A behaviors (Nakano, 1990b). The subjects showed significant reductions in the Type A inventory scores compared to controls.

Most studies on modifying the Type A behavior pattern tested the effects of treatments between groups with inventories such as the Jenkins Activity Survey (Jenkins, Zyzanski, & Rosenman, 1979). This type of experimental design fails to adequately assess the behaviorally significant changes through proposed modifying procedures (Barlow & Hersen, 1984). Barlow and Hersen suggested that single case experimental designs can more adequately demonstrate cause-effect relationship for treatment procedures.

Nakano (1990c) analyzed the effects of the operant self-control procedures which consisted of three phases, self-monitoring, self-evaluation, and self-reinforcement, through a single case experimental design. The study directly examined the changes in speed/impatient behaviors of the Type A behavior pattern in daily activities and demonstrated significant decreases in the behaviors following transfer to the self-reinforcement condition. Significant reductions in the Jenkins Activity Survey and physical symptoms scores from baseline to post-treatment were also indicated.

The results of the prior studies suggested that behavioral programs with a self-control component seemed to be most effective. Clinical researchers have, however, been unable to reach any consensus on the best method for the intervention in the Type A behavior pattern and on what specifically the target for the intervention should be. This variability in treatment approaches and target behaviors stems from the multifaceted components of the Type A behavior pattern. Each Type A subject might have a different adaptational problem and might need a different intervention approach. It can be implied that some of them need not carry out several self-control procedures, and others need not learn complicated self-management methods. A simple intervention program may be sufficient for their changing behaviors.

The purpose of the present study was to test the efficacy of a simple intervention program which was organized especially for the subjects' time-urgent and chronically active and tense behaviors. The intervention program was the self-control procedure through a self-initiated approach designed with the intention of eliminating the antecedent stimuli evoking the time-urgent and chronically active behaviors.

To assess the effects of this self-control procedure on target behaviors, a multiple-baseline design which behaviorally supports a cause-effect statement was used. Multiple-baseline strategies have been used by applied researchers with increased frequency when withdrawal and reversal designs have not been feasible. With the exception of Nakano's study (1990c), the investigations of the treatment effects of Type A behaviors have been between groups studies which used questionnaire scores as dependent variables. This study represents behavioral data which are complementary to those of the between groups studies which have demonstrated the statistical efficacy of self-control method for Type A behaviors.

METHOD

Subjects

Subjects responded to an advertisement in a community newspaper in Japan. They had some complaints of physical/psychosomatic symptoms and voluntarily attended a stress management training. The Jenkins Activity Survey of 1966 (Zyzanski & Jenkins, 1970) was used as a screening instrument. Among the participants of the stress management training, 12 persons had raw scores of more than 35 and 5 on the Jenkins Activity Survey and the speed/impatience subscale which were the mean scores of the subjects in Nakano's study (1990a). Three subjects who had problems in two out of six elements of speed/impatient behaviors: eating too fast and not relaxing after meals and getting busy were selected to participate in this self-control study, and they were willing to meet the requirements of this treatment program. Subject 1 was a 37-year-old married woman with no children. She was a translator. Subject 2 was a 47-year-old married woman with two children. She was a typist. Subject 3 was a 42-year-old woman, living with her father and son. Her father owned an apartment house next to their home. She was managing the business by herself. All three subjects had a college degree and were self-employed.

Dependent Measures

Target behaviors.   Eating too fast and not relaxing after meals and getting busy were target behaviors. Subjects began self-monitoring of these behaviors for a minimum of a week prior to the beginning of treatment and continued it throughout the treatment. They recorded the number of minutes of eating and relaxing per meal and additionally made brief notes about their behaviors, feelings, and thoughts. They recorded the time when they sat at the dining table and the time when they set to work on daily meal logs.

For the purpose of a reliability check, a family member was also instructed to record the subjects' number of minutes of eating and relaxing only for evening meals. They recorded the time when the subjects sat at the dining table and the time when they set to work per dinner on separate logs every day.

Psychosomatic symptoms.   The dependent variable to measure the severity of psychosomatic symptoms was a 1–5 rating scale (1 = no pains, 5 = severe pains). The symptoms of Subject 1 were sour stomach and stiff neck, and those of the Subjects 2 and 3 were headaches and stiff shoulders. They recorded the ratings on daily symptom logs.

Procedures

The program began with introductions and a review of confidentiality issues. The subjects were informed of the Type A behavior pattern, especially the speed/impatient factor, the relation between the Type A behavior pattern and psychosomatic symptoms, and a behavioral self-control rationale for the overall program. They were also taught appropriate self-monitoring skills of observing eating and relaxing behaviors. They were instructed to record the number of minutes of eating and relaxing per meal and the severity of psychosomatic symptoms along with feelings and thoughts on the daily logs throughout the treatment. Six weeks after the completion of the treatment, the subjects were asked to do the same recordings for a week as those of the treatment phases.

The treatment was the self-control procedures developed for this study, and the methods consisted of the following regimen: (a) fix the number of minutes of eating/relaxing per meal; (b) sit at the dining table during the time for eating; (c) do not read or work at meals; (d) plan how to spend the relaxing time after each meal, do not get busy, follow the plan, and have a relaxing time, for instance, listening to music, watching TV; (e) leave working places and spend the relaxing time somewhere else; (f) do not work, and do not even think about work during the relaxing time. The criteria of the eating/relaxing time per meal were constant across phases. These treatment methods were organized with the intention of eliminating the antecedent stimuli evoking the target behaviors. There was no contingency management of reinforcement or punishment in this treatment program.

The sequences of the self-control procedures administered to eating and relaxing behaviors per meal were changed for each subject. Subject 1 started them at breakfast, Subject 2 at lunch, and Subject 3 at dinner.

Experimental Design

To assess the effects of the self-control procedures on eating and relaxing behaviors, a multiple baseline across meals arranged on a multiple baseline across subjects design was used. Following baseline evaluation, self-control was carried out in sequence to the behaviors at three meals. For Subject 1, self-control was first applied to the behaviors at breakfast, subsequently to those at lunch, and to those at dinner. For Subject 2, it was first applied to the behaviors at lunch, secondly to those at dinner, and those at breakfast. For Subject 3, it was first applied to the behaviors at dinner, then to those at breakfast, and those at lunch.

The number of minutes of eating and relaxing per meal was used to evaluate the effects. The self-control procedures are assured to be effective when changes in minutes appear after their application.

The self-control procedures were also introduced separately in a multiple baseline across subjects design. The active treatment phases followed baselines which varied for each subject. This experimental design was applied to assess changes in psychosomatic symptoms which appeared as a result of the treatment. Subject 1 completed baseline data of a week and started the first self-control procedures. Subject 2 recorded baseline data for 2 weeks and started the first treatment. Subject 3 completed baseline data of three weeks and started the first treatment.

RESULTS

Figures 8A–1, 8A–2, and 8A–3 show the number of minutes of eating and relaxing per meal for Subjects 1, 2, and 3, respectively. During baselines, the number

Figure 8A–1 Minutes spent for eating and relaxing per meal during baseline and self-control conditions for Subject 1. To assess the effects of the self-control procedures on eating and relaxing behaviors, a multiple baseline across meals design was used. Following baseline evaluation, self-control was carried out in sequence to the behaviors at three meals. Self-control was first applied to the behaviors at breakfast, subsequently to those at lunch, and to those at dinner.

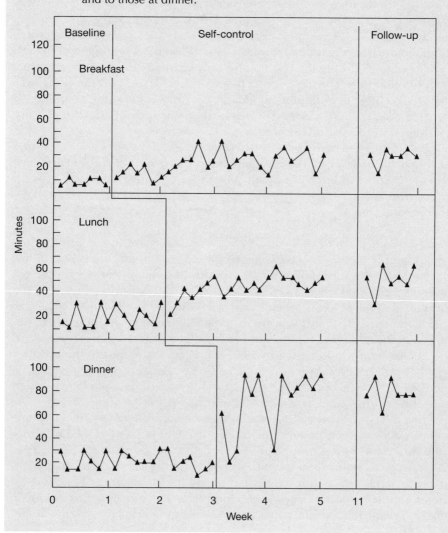

of minutes of eating and relaxing averaged 18.3, 23.6, and 25.2 for Subjects 1, 2, and 3, respectively. After carrying out the self-control procedures, the number of minutes of eating and relaxing increased. In the final week of the treatment phase the number of minutes of eating and relaxing increased to an average of 47.9, 56.0, and 61.0 in Subjects 1, 2, and 3, respectively. The increases were maintained at 12-week follow-up.

To assess accuracy of subjects' self-observation data, reliability analyses were conducted between subjects' data and their family members' observation

Figure 8A–2 Minutes spent for eating and relaxing per meal during baseline and self-control conditions for Subject 2. Self-control was first applied to the behaviors at lunch, secondly to those at dinner, and those at breakfast.

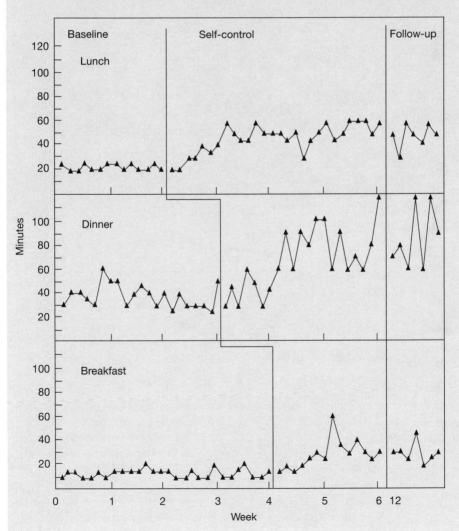

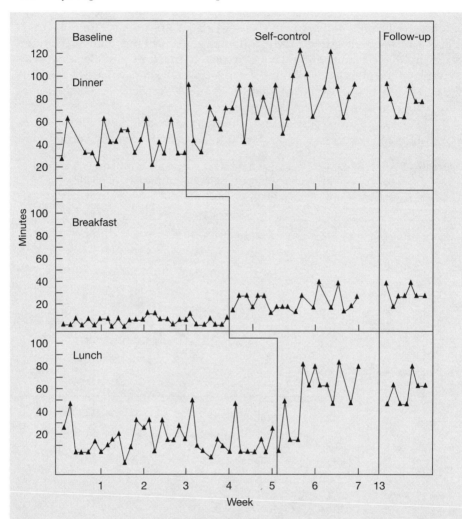

Figure 8A–3 Minutes spent for eating and relaxing per meal during baseline and self-control conditions for Subject 3. Self-control was first applied to the behaviors at dinner, then to those at breakfast, and those at lunch.

data. The family reliability check data showed marked agreements with the subjects' self-report data for minutes of eating and relaxing for evening meals. The Pearson correlations on each subject were $r = .96$, $r = .95$, and $r = .89$, (all $p < .001$). Reliability estimates on interobserver data accuracy of this study were highly significant. Therefore it seems reasonable to regard self-observation data in this study as accurate.

Figure 8A–4 depicts the results of the four phases of the analysis with regard to the severity of psychosomatic symptoms. The first phase was com-

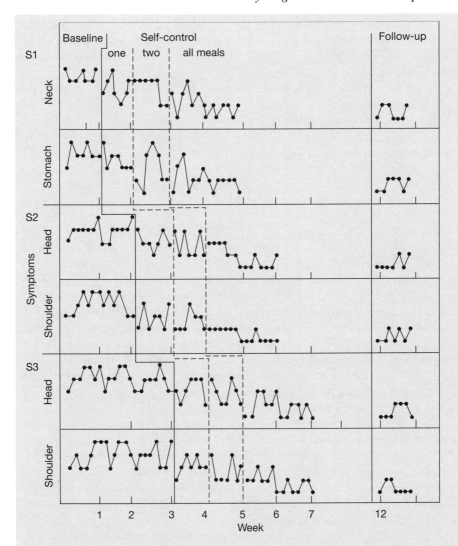

Figure 8A–4 Mean ratings of psychosomatic symptoms per day during baseline and self-control conditions across three subjects. To assess the effects of the self-control procedures on eating and relaxing behaviors, a multiple base-line across meals arranged on a multiple baseline across subjects design was used. Following baseline evaluation, self-control was carried out in sequence to the behaviors at three meals. The self-control procedures were introduced separately in a multiple baseline across subjects design. The active treatment phases followed baselines which varied for each sub-ject. The first phase was composed of all baseline conditions. The second phase consisted of the baseline conditions at two meals and the self-con-trol condition at a meal. The third phase consisted of a baseline condition and the self-control conditions at two meals. The final phase was com-posed of the self-control conditions. (1 = no pains; 5 = severe pains)

posed of all baseline conditions. The second phase consisted of the baseline conditions at two meals and the self-control condition at a meal. The third phase consisted of a baseline condition and the self-control conditions at two meals. The final phase was composed of the self-control conditions.

All three subjects gradually demonstrated reductions in the severity in psychosomatic symptoms following transfer to the self-control conditions and reported fewer symptoms at the end of the treatment and at 12-week follow-up. The results indicate that the self-control treatment, which significantly increased the minutes spent for eating and relaxing, seemed to be associated with the decreases in the severity of psychosomatic symptoms.

DISCUSSION

The effects of the self-control procedure facilitating alternative behaviors on modifying speed and impatient behaviors of the Type A behavior pattern were evaluated with a multiple-baseline across meals arranged on a multiple-baseline across subjects design. The self-control procedure was a self-initiated approach designed with the intention of eliminating the antecedent stimuli evoking the time-urgent and chronically active behaviors at table and after meals. The results indicated that the self-control treatment program of this study could help subjects to achieve behaviorally significant improvement in the behaviors of eating and relaxing as well as clinically significant improvement in psychosomatic symptoms. Multiple baseline designs demonstrated that the behavioral and clinical changes were not caused by passage of time, weekly sessions, nor self-observation.

The use of self-observation techniques in treatment evaluation has not been traditionally accepted because of the variable accuracy. In the present study, however, self-observation data were used for treatment evaluation because the subjects were not in naturally observable environments. To assess accuracy of subjects' self-observation data, reliability analyses were conducted between subjects' data and their family members' observation data. The family reliability check data showed marked agreements with the subjects' self-report data for minutes of eating and relaxing. Therefore it seems reasonable to regard self-observation data in this study, as accurate. Reliability analyses to assess accuracy of subjects' self-monitoring data of the severity in psychosomatic symptoms were not feasible. However self-monitoring has proven useful for assessing responses that are only accessible to the subjects and have gained in acceptance for the evaluation of behavioral intervention (Barlow & Hersen, 1984).

Suinn (1982) speculated that Anxiety Management Training provides a relaxation-based self-control technique which reduces the need for Type A behaviors. Self-reinforcement of operant self-control techniques was also demonstrated to decrease the need for Type A behaviors and to increase more adaptational self-control behaviors toward stressors (Nakano, 1990c). The present study indicated that a simple self-control procedure through a self-initiated approach designed with the intention of eliminating the antecedent stimuli evoking the time-urgent and chronically active behaviors could help Type A individuals to adapt relaxed behaviors at table and after meals and to reduce speed/impatient behaviors of the Type A behavior pattern.

The present study also pointed out the additional evidence that the reductions in speed/impatient behaviors of the Type A behavior pattern caused by the self-control procedures achieved clinically significant ameliorations in psychosomatic symptoms. Thus it could be concluded that the self-control procedures of this study provided Type A individuals with more efficient and adaptive behaviors.

The target behaviors of this study were, however, only eating and relaxing behaviors of the several elements of the multidimensional Type A behavior pattern. Researches have not yet demonstrated which factors of the Type A behavior pattern are pathogenic or symptom-related. Finding the most problematic element of the Type A behavior pattern for each Type A individual through self-observation, and then selecting suitable self-control procedures might be the most efficient and effective way of modifying the Type A behavior pattern.

The present study used the self-control strategy of antecedent stimuli regulation for modifying eating and relaxing behaviors of the Type A behavior pattern. The analyses conducted by a multiple-baseline across meals arranged on a multiple-baseline across subjects design behaviorally demonstrated that the self-control procedure had significant effects in reductions of Type A behaviors and facilitated clinically significant reductions in psychosomatic symptoms.

REFERENCES

Barlow, D. H., & Hersen, M. (1984). *Single case experimental designs: Strategies for studying human behavior.* New York: Pergamon Press.

Booth-Kewley, S., & Friedman, H. (1987). Psychological predictors of heart disease: A quantitative review. *Psychological Bulletin, 101,* 343–359.

Brand, R., Rosenman R., Sholtz R., & Friedman, M. (1976). Multivariate prediction of coronary heart disease in the Western Collaborative Group Study compared to the findings for the Framingham study. *Circulation, 53,* 344–355.

Carmody, T. P., Hollis, J. F, Matarazzo, J. D., Fey, S. G., & Connor, W. E. (1984). Type A behavior, attentional style, and symptom reporting among adult men and women. *Health Psychology, 3,* 45–61.

Friedman, M., & Rosenman, R. H. (1974). *Type A behavior and your heart.* New York: Knopf.

Glass, D. C. (1977). *Behavior patterns, stress and coronary heart disease.* Hillsdale, NJ: Lawrence Erlbaum.

Hart, K. E. (1984). Anxiety management training and anger control for Type A individuals. *Journal of Behavior Therapy and Experimental Psychiatry, 15,* 133–139.

Hayano, J., Takeuchi, S., Yoshida, S., Jozuka, H., Mishima, N., & Fujinami, T. (1989). Type A behavior pattern in Japanese employees: Cross-cultural comparison of major factors in Jenkins Activity Survey (JAS) responses. *Journal of Behavioral Medicine, 12,* 219–231.

Hecker, M., Chesney, M., Black, G., & Frautschi, N. (1988). Coronary-prone behaviors in the Western Collaborative Group Study. *Psychosomatic Medicine, 50,* 153–164.

Howard, J., Cunningham, D., & Rechnitzer, P. (1976). Health patterns associated with Type A behavior: A managerial population. *Journal of Human Stress, 2,* 24–33.

Jenkins, C. D., Zyzanski, S. J., & Rosenman, R. H. (1979). *Jenkins activity survey manual.* New York: Psychological Corporation.

Kelly, K. R., & Stone, G. L. (1987). Effects of three psychological treatments and self-monitoring on the reduction of Type A behavior. *Journal of Counseling Psychology, 34,* 46–54.

Levenkron, J. C., Cohen, J. D., Mueller, H. S., & Fisher, E. B. (1983). Modifying the Type A coronary-prone behavior pattern. *Journal of Consulting and Clinical Psychology, 15,* 192–204.

Nakano, K. (1990a). Hardiness, Type A behavior, and physical symptoms in a Japanese sample. *The Journal of Nervous and Mental Disease, 178,* 52–56.

Nakano, K. (1990b). Effects of two self-control procedures on modifying Type A behavior. *Journal of Clinical Psychology, 46,* 653–657.

Nakano, K. (1996c). Operant self-control procedure on modifying Type A behavior. *Journal of Behavior Therapy and Experimental Psychiatry, 21,* 249–255.

Rosenman, R. H., Brand, R. J., Jenkins, C. D., Friedman, M., Straus, R., & Wurm, M. (1975). Coronary heart disease in the Western Collaborative Group Study: Final follow-up of 8.5 years. *Journal of the American Medical Association, 233,* 872–877.

Roskies, E., Kearney, H., Spevack, M., Surkis, A., Cohen, C., & Gilman, S. (1979). Generalizability and durability of treatment effects in an intervention program for coronary-prone (Type A) managers. *Journal of Behavioral Medicine, 2,* 195–207.

Stout, C. W., & Bloom, L. J., (1982). Type A behavior and upper respiratory infections. *Journal of Human Stress, 8,* 4–7.

Suinn, R. M. (1982). Intervention with Type A behaviors. *Journal of Consulting and Clinical Psychology, 50,* 933–949.

Suinn, R. M. (1990). *Anxiety management training: A behavior therapy.* New York: Plenum.

Suinn, R. M., & Bloom, L. J. (1978). Anxiety management training for pattern A behavior. *Journal of Behavioral Medicine, 1,* 25–35.

Woods, P. J., & Burns, J. (1984). Type A behavior and illness in general. *Journal of Behavioral Medicine, 7,* 411–415.

Wright, L. (1988). The Type A behavior pattern and coronary artery disease. *American Psychologist, 43,* 2–14.

Zyzanski, S., & Jenkins, C. (1970). Basic dimensions of the coronary-prone behavior pattern. *Journal of Chronic Diseases, 22,* 781–795.

THINK IT THROUGH

Nakano's research is interesting and relevant to real-life problems for a number of reasons. Here are some questions that will help you check your understanding of this research. Give these questions some thought and write down your answers before reading further.

1. Other than being related to heart attacks, how else can the Type A behavior pattern be seen as a physiological state?
2. According to Nakano, how are Type A problems best treated?
3. In what major way does Nakano's study differ from many of the previous studies of change in Type A behavior?
4. What were the multiple baselines that Nakano observed?
5. What were the major findings of this research?
6. Although Nakano believes the single-case experimental approach is best suited to deal with Type A behaviors, it has not been universally accepted. What problems were encountered?

We hope you found you were able to answer most, if not all, of these questions after reading Nakano's article. Here are the answers we had in mind when we developed the questions.

In addition to being at greater risk for heart attacks, Type A individuals suffer from more colds, cardiovascular disorders, gastrointestinal problems, and diabetic problems than do their Type B counterparts. Moreover, Type A women have been shown to suffer from more sleep disorders and chest pains compared to Type B women. Finally, Nakano reports that Type A workers in Japan had more headaches, more acid stomach disturbances, more indigestion, and greater insomnia than Type B workers. The Type A behavior pattern truly involves a wide range of physiological processes. Because of its prevalence and potential impact on adaptive behavior, it is a physiological state worthy of sustained research attention.

Such a variety of potentially detrimental physical ailments indicates Type A behaviors are likely candidates for treatment and change. Nakano believes that behavioral treatments based on self-control procedures, such as learning how to cope with and rely less on Type A behaviors, are more effective in the treatment of Type A behaviors than other procedures, such as psychotherapy.

Unlike the authors of previous studies, Nakano did not use scores on questionnaires to evaluate changes in Type A behavior. Although a questionnaire was used initially to determine if an individual should be categorized as Type A, Nakano felt that *direct observation* of behavioral changes would yield more reliable and valid data. Therefore, the time (minutes) participants spent eating and relaxing during the three daily meals was recorded. A rating of the intensity of physical (psychosomatic) symptoms also was included as a dependent variable measure. Because four separate measures were recorded (time spent eating and relaxing during breakfast, lunch, and dinner; and the intensity of psychosomatic symptoms) this research clearly qualifies as a multiple-baseline approach. The fact that Nakano started the participants on their behavior-change regimens with different meals (i.e., Participant 1 began with breakfast, Participant 2 began with lunch, and Participant 3 began with dinner) is a control measure that ensures the effect is not linked to the specific meal at which the treatment is started. Using such a control strengthens Nakano's findings;

noticeable effects will be obtained, regardless of when the experimental procedure is initiated.

THINK IT THROUGH

Although Nakano's data supports the effectiveness of the single-case experimental approach in dealing with Type A behaviors, it has not been accepted by all researchers. Why? Give these issues some thought and write down your answers before reading further.

Researchers have not agreed on what is the best treatment or intervention strategy to deal with these behaviors. Even if a best strategy could be agreed on, researchers also have not agreed on the specific target behaviors that need to be changed. Moreover, it is arguable that such problems may never be resolved because it is arguable that each participant has a different adaptational problem that will require a different intervention strategy. Only continued research will provide answers to problems such as these.

Despite concerns, such as the ones we just mentioned, the results of Nakano's project indicate that self-control procedures are effective in modifying the speed and impatient components of the Type A behavior pattern. More specifically, all three participants displayed substantial increases in the time spent eating and relaxing during mealtimes. The number of somatic complaints also decreased during the experiment. The fact that time spent eating and relaxing during meals remained high and the number of psychosomatic complaints remained low during the follow-up period further attests to the effectiveness of the self-control procedure. The finding that the self-observation data provided by the participants was highly correlated with independent reports provided by family members indicates that the participants were quite accurate in the perceptions of their own behavior.

As we read this article, several research projects came to mind. Here are some of our ideas for future research in this area. First, there are characteristics of the participants that suggest several possible follow-up studies. For example, you should have noticed that all of the participant's in Nakano's project were all women. Would we obtain similar results if men served as our participants? What about educational level? All of Nakano's participants had college degrees. What results would be obtained with participants who have not gone to college? As Nakano's mailing address is Tokyo, Japan, we can assume the participants were Japanese. Will we obtain similar results when this study is conducted in different cultures?

A second source of several possible research projects is highlighted by considering Nakano's target behaviors. Modifying the time the participants took to eat and how much they relaxed during and after meals were selected for modification. Would the self-control technique be successful with other behaviors that are associated with the speed and impatience characteristics of the Type A individual? Some of the other behaviors you might choose to investigate are speaking too fast, demanding that others speak more rapidly, rushing when going shopping, and so on. Research projects of this nature are designed to establish the generality of the self-control procedure as a technique for dealing with the Type A characteristics of speed and impatience. If self-control also proves successful in modifying these aspects, then its generality is supported.

Considering the generality of the self-control technique suggests a third source of projects: the other characteristics of the Type A behavior pattern. Research could (and should) be conducted to determine if this treatment approach is successful with such characteristics as hostility and competitiveness. Once research has been started in these areas, you will find yourself involved in an increasingly wider range of projects as you seek to determine the generality of the self-control procedure *within* each of these areas. Yes, research definitely spawns additional research.

Should you choose to study Type A behavior in a research project of your own, we include the following scale and scoring instructions that have been employed to assess Type A behavior in college students (Krantz, Glass, & Snyder, 1974). We hope you find it helpful in your research. Should your research interests lean toward working with noncollege populations, you should consider using the Jenkins Activity Survey (Zyzanski & Jenkins, 1970) that was used by Nakano.

MODIFIED JENKINS ACTIVITY SURVEY*

1. How would your husband or wife (or closest friend) rate you?
    a. definitely hard-driving and competitive
    b. probably hard-driving and competitive
    c. probably relaxed and easy-going
    d. definitely relaxed and easy-going
2. How would you rate yourself?
    a. definitely hard-driving and competitive
    b. probably hard-driving and competitive
    c. probably relaxed and easy-going
    d. definitely relaxed and easy-going
3. How do you consider yourself compared to the average student?
    a. more responsible
    b. as responsible
    c. less responsible

---

*Source: From "Helplessness, Stress Level, and the Coronary-Prone Behavior Pattern" by D. S. Krantz, D. C. Glass, and M. L. Snyder, 1974, *Journal of Experimental Social Psychology, 10,* pp. 284–300.

4. Compared to the average student,
    a. I give much more effort
    b. I give the same amount of effort
    c. I give less effort
5. College has
    a. stirred me into action
    b. not stirred me into action
6. Compared to the average student,
    a. I am more precise
    b. I am as precise
    c. I am less precise
7. Compared to the average student,
    a. I approach life more seriously
    b. I approach life as seriously
    c. I approach life less seriously
8. How would most people rate you?
    a. definitely hard-driving and competitive
    b. probably hard-driving and competitive
    c. probably relaxed and easy-going
    d. definitely relaxed and easy-going
9. How would you rate yourself?
    a. definitely *not* having less energy than most people
    b. probably *not* having less energy than most people
    c. probably having less energy than most people
    d. definitely having less energy than most people
10. I frequently set deadlines for myself in courses or other things.
    a. yes   **b.** no   **c.** sometimes
11. Do you maintain a regular study schedule during vacations such as Thanksgiving, Christmas, and Easter?
    a. yes   **b.** no   **c.** sometimes
12. I hurry even when there is plenty of time
    a. yes   **b.** once in a while   **c.** sometimes
13. I have been told I eat too fast
    a. yes   **b.** once in a while   **c.** sometimes
14. How would you rate yourself?
    a. I eat more rapidly than most people
    b. I eat as rapidly as most people
    c. I eat less rapidly than most people
15. I hurry a speaker to the point.
    a. frequently
    b. once in a while
    c. never

16. How would most people rate you?
    a. definitely *not* doing most things in a hurry
    b. probably *not* doing most things in a hurry
    c. probably doing most things in a hurry
    d. definitely doing most things in a hurry
17. Compared to the average student,
    a. I hurry much less
    b. I hurry as much
    c. I hurry much more
18. How often are there deadlines in your courses?
    a. frequently   **b.** once in a while   **c.** never
19. Everyday life is filled with challenges to be met.
    a. yes   **b.** no   **c.** sometimes
20. I have held an office in an activity group or held a part-time job when in school.
    a. frequently   **b.** once in a while   **c.** never
21. I stay in the library at night while studying until closing.
    a. frequently   **b.** once in a while   **c.** never

SCORING AND NORMS FOR MODIFIED JENKINS ACTIVITY SURVEY

Give yourself one point for each answer that matches the following key:

1.	a or b	**2.**	a or b	**3.**	a	**4.**	a
5.	a	**6.**	a	**7.**	a	**8.**	a or b
9.	a or b	**10.**	a	**11.**	a	**12.**	a
13.	a	**14.**	a	**15.**	a	**16.**	c or d
17.	c	**18.**	a	**19.**	a	**20.**	a
21.	a						

Score	Classification
13+	A+
9–12	A–
8	borderline
4–7	B–
0–3	B+

THINK IT THROUGH

List five ideas that are related to the ones we have described above that can be researched and list three novel ideas (not related to any of the above) that could also be researched. What types of materials and time would each of these eight projects require? Are there any special precautions you will need to take or procedures you will need to implement?

Related ideas:

1. _____

2. _____

3. _____

4. _____

5. _____

Novel ideas:

1. _____

2. _____

3. _____

After writing down your various research ideas, have one of your professors read them and give you additional and alternate suggestions. If these are indeed areas of research in which you have an interest, you will find it exciting to develop and pursue your ideas to completion.

REFERENCES

Baker, E. L., Feldman, R. G., White, R. E., & Harley, J. P. (1983). The role of occupational lead exposure in the genesis of psychiatric and behavioral disturbances. *Acta Psychologica Scandinavia, 67* (Suppl. 303), 38–48.

Barefoot, J. C., Dodge, K. A., Peterson, B. L., Dahlstrom, W. G., & Williams, R. B., Jr. (1989). The Cook-Medley Hostility Scale: Item content and ability to predict survival. *Psychosomatic Medicine, 51,* 46–57.

David, O. J., Clark, J., & Voeller, K. (1972). Lead and hyperactivity. *Lancet, 2,* 900–903.

Friedman, M., & Rosenman, R. H. (1974). *Type A behavior and your heart.* New York: Knopf.

Krantz, D. S., Glass, D. C., & Snyder, M. L. (1974). Helplessness, stress level, and the coronary-prone behavior pattern. *Journal of Experimental Social Psychology, 10,* 284–300.

Nakano, K. (1996). Application of Self-Control Procedures to Modifying Type A Behavior. *The Psychological Record, 46,* 595–606.

Nation, J. R., Baker, D. M., Fantasia, M. A., Ruscher, A. E., & Clark, D. E. (1987). Ethanol consumption and free-operant avoidance performance following exposure to dietary lead. *Neurotoxicology, 8,* 561–569.

Nation, J. R., Clark, D. E., Bourgeois, A. E., & Rogers, J. K. (1982). Conditioned suppression in the adult rat following chronic exposure to lead. *Toxicology Letters, 14,* 63–67.

Olds, J., & Milner, P. (1954). Positive reinforcement produced by electrical stimulation of the septal area and other regions of the rat brain. *Journal of Comparative and Physiological Psychology, 47,* 419–427.

ADDITIONAL READING

Zyzanski, S., & Jenkins, C. (1970). Basic dimensions of the coronary-prone behavior pattern. *Journal of Chronic Diseases, 22,* 781–795.

CHAPTER 9

Abnormal Research Idea Development

The article selected for this chapter is a classic. Just because it is a classic does not preclude the emergence of new ideas. In fact, revisiting the old in light of new and recent knowledge can give us a veritable plethora of new research perspectives to pursue. "On Being Sane in Insane Places" by David Rosenhan is an investigation into the efficacy and accuracy of diagnoses in a psychiatric setting. The study points out that not only is a diagnosis many times ineffective, it can also lead to labeling and stereotyping the patient. This article provides an interesting and informative look into the multitude of problems associated with diagnosis and treatment.

On Being Sane in Insane Places

David L. Rosenhan

If sanity and insanity exist, how shall we know them?

The question is neither capricious nor itself insane. However much we may be personally convinced that we can tell the normal from the abnormal, the evidence is simply not compelling. It is commonplace, for example, to read about murder trials wherein eminent psychiatrists for the defense are contradicted by equally eminent psychiatrists for the prosecution on the matter of

SOURCE: D. L. Rosenhan, "On Being Sane in Insane Places," *Science,* Vol. 179, January 1973, pp. 250–258. Copyright 1973 by the American Association for the Advancement of Science. Reprinted by permission.

the defendant's sanity. More generally, there are a great deal of conflicting data on the reliability, utility, and meaning of such terms as "sanity," "insanity," "mental illness," and "schizophrenia."[1] Finally, as early as 1934, Benedict suggested that normality and abnormality are not universal.[2] What is viewed as normal in one culture may be seen as quite aberrant in another. Thus, notions of normality and abnormality may not be quite as accurate as people believe they are.

To raise questions regarding normality and abnormality is in no way to question the fact that some behaviors are deviant or odd. Murder is deviant. So, too, are hallucinations. Nor does raising such questions deny the existence of the personal anguish that is often associated with "mental illness." Anxiety and depression exist. Psychological suffering exists. But normality and abnormality, sanity and insanity, and the diagnoses that flow from them may be less substantive than many believe them to be.

At its heart, the question of whether the sane can be distinguished from the insane (and whether degrees of insanity can be distinguished from each other) is a simple matter: do the salient characteristics that lead to diagnoses reside in the patients themselves or in the environments and contexts in which observers find them? From Bleuler, through Kretchmer through the formulators of the recently revised *Diagnostic and Statistical Manual* of the American Psychiatric Association, the belief has been strong that patients present symptoms, that those symptoms can be categorized, and, implicitly, that the sane are distinguishable from the insane. More recently, however, this belief has been questioned. Based in part on theoretical and anthropological considerations, but also on philosophical, legal, and therapeutic ones, the view has grown that psychological categorization of mental illness is useless at best and downright harmful, misleading, and pejorative at worst. Psychiatric diagnoses, in this view, are in the minds of the observers and are not valid summaries of characteristics displayed by the observed.[3-5]

Gains can be made in deciding which of these is more nearly accurate by getting normal people (that is, people who do not have, and have never suffered, symptoms of serious psychiatric disorders) admitted to psychiatric hospitals and then determining whether they were discovered to be sane and, if so, how. If the sanity of such pseudopatients were always detected, there would be prima facie evidence that a sane individual can be distinguished from the insane context in which he is found. Normality (and presumably abnormality) is distinct enough that it can be recognized wherever it occurs, for it is carried within the person. If, on the other hand, the sanity of the pseudopatients were never discovered, serious difficulties would arise for those who support traditional modes of psychiatric diagnosis. Given that the hospital staff was not incompetent, that the pseudopatient had been behaving as sanely as he had been outside of the hospital, and that it had never been previously suggested that he belonged in a psychiatric hospital, such an unlikely outcome would support the view that psychiatric diagnosis betrays little about the patient but much about the environment in which an observer finds him.

This article describes such an experiment. Eight sane people gained secret ad mission to 12 different hospitals.[6] Their diagnostic experiences constitute the data of the first part of this article; the remainder is devoted to a description of their experiences in psychiatric institutions. Too few psychiatrists and psychologists, even those who have worked in such hospitals, know what the experience is like. They rarely talk about it with former patients, perhaps because they distrust information coming from the previously insane. Those who have worked in psychiatric hospitals are likely to have adapted so thoroughly to the settings that they are insensitive to the impact of that experience. And while there have been occasional reports of researchers who submitted themselves to psychiatric hospitalization,[7] these researchers have commonly remained in the hospitals for short periods of time, often with the knowledge of the hospital staff. It is difficult to know the extent to which they were treated like patients or like research colleagues. Nevertheless their reports about the inside of the psychiatric hospital have been valuable. This article extends those efforts.

PSEUDOPATIENTS AND THEIR SETTINGS

The eight pseudopatients were a varied group. One was a psychology graduate student in his 20s. The remaining seven were older and "established." Among them were three psychologists, a pediatrician, a psychiatrist, a painter, and a housewife. Three pseudopatients were women, five were men. All of them employed pseudonyms, lest their alleged diagnoses embarrass them later. Those who were in mental health professions alleged another occupation in order to avoid the special attentions that might be accorded by staff, as a matter of courtesy or caution, to ailing colleagues.[8] With the exception of myself (I was the first pseudopatient and my presence was known to the hospital administrator and chief psychologist and, so far as I can tell, to them alone), the presence of pseudopatients and the nature of the research program was not known to the hospital staffs.[9]

The settings were similarly varied. In order to generalize the findings, admission into a variety of hospitals was sought. The 12 hospitals in the sample were located in five different states on the East and West coasts. Some were old and shabby, some were quite new. Some were research-oriented, others not. Some had good staff-patient ratios, others were quite understaffed. Only one was a strictly private hospital. All of the others were supported by state or federal funds or, in one instance, by University funds.

After calling the hospital for an appointment, the pseudopatient arrived at the admissions office complaining that he had been hearing voices. Asked what the voices said, he replied that they were often unclear, but as far as he could tell they said "empty," "hollow," and "thud." The voices were unfamiliar and were of the same sex as the pseudopatient. The choice of these symptoms was occasioned by their apparent similarity to existential symptoms. Such symptoms are alleged to arise from painful concerns about the perceived meaninglessness of one's life. It is as if the hallucinating person were saying, "My life is empty and hollow." The choice of these symptoms was also determined by the *absence* of a single report of existential psychoses in the literature.

Beyond alleging the symptoms and falsifying name, vocation, and employment, no further alterations of person, history, or circumstances were made. The significant events of the pseudopatient's life history were presented as they had actually occurred. Relationships with parents and siblings, with spouse and children, with people at work and in school, consistent with the aforementioned exceptions, were described as they were or had been. Frustrations and upsets were described along with joys and satisfactions. These facts are important to remember. If anything, they strongly biased the subsequent results in favor of detecting sanity, since none of their histories or current behaviors were seriously pathological in any way.

Immediately upon admission to the psychiatric ward, the pseudopatient ceased simulating *any* symptoms of abnormality. In some cases, there was a brief period of mild nervousness and anxiety, since none of the pseudopatients really believed that they would be admitted so easily. Indeed, their shared fear was that they would be immediately exposed as frauds and greatly embarrassed. Moreover, many of them had never visited a psychiatric ward; even those who had, nevertheless had some genuine fears about what might happen to them. Their nervousness, then, was quite appropriate to the novelty of the hospital setting, and it abated rapidly.

Apart from that short-lived nervousness, the pseudopatient behaved on the ward as he "normally" behaved. The pseudopatient spoke to patients and staff as he might ordinarily. Because there is uncommonly little to do on a psychiatric ward, he attempted to engage others in conversation. When asked by staff how he was feeling, he indicated that he was fine, that he no longer experienced symptoms. He responded to instructions from attendants, to calls for medication (which was not swallowed), and to dining-hall instructions. Beyond such activities as were available to him on the admissions ward, he spent his time writing down his observations about the ward, its patients, and the staff. Initially these notes were written "secretly," but as it soon became clear that no one much cared, they were subsequently written on standard tablets of paper in such public places as the dayroom. No secret was made of these activities.

The pseudopatient, very much as a true psychiatric patient, entered a hospital with no foreknowledge of when he would be discharged. Each was told that he would have to get out by his own devices, essentially by convincing that staff that he was sane. The psychological stresses associated with hospitalization were considerable, and all but one of the pseudopatients desired to be discharged almost immediately after being admitted. They were, therefore, motivated not only to behave sanely, but to be paragons of cooperation. That their behavior was in no way disruptive is confirmed by nursing reports, which have been obtained on most of the patients. These reports uniformly indicate that the patients were "friendly," "cooperative," and "hibited no abnormal indications."

THE NORMAL ARE NOT DETECTABLY SANE

Despite their public "show" of sanity, the pseudopatients were never detected. Admitted, except in one case, with a diagnosis of schizophrenia,[10] each was discharged with a diagnosis of schizophrenia "in remission." The label "in remission" should in no way be dismissed as a formality, for at no time during any hospitalization had any question been raised about any pseudopatient's simulation. Nor are there any indications in the hospital records that the pseudopatient's status was suspect. Rather, the evidence is strong that, once labeled schizophrenic, the pseudopatient was stuck with that label. If the pseudopatient was to be discharged, he must naturally be "in remission"; but he was not sane, nor, in the institution's view, had he ever been sane.

The uniform failure to recognize sanity cannot be attributed to the quality of the hospitals, for, although there were considerable variations among them, several are considered excellent. Nor can it be alleged that there was simply not enough time to observe the pseudopatients. Length of hospitalization ranged from 7 to 52 days, with an average of 19 days. The pseudopatients were not, in fact, carefully observed, but this failure clearly speaks more to traditions within psychiatric hospitals than to lack of opportunity.

Finally, it cannot be said that the failure to recognize the pseudopatients' sanity was due to the fact that they were not behaving sanely. While there was clearly some tension present in all of them, their daily visitors could detect no serious behavioral consequences—nor, indeed, could other patients. It was quite common for the patients to "detect" the pseudopatients' sanity. During the first three hospitalizations, when accurate counts were kept, 35 of a total of 118 patients on the admissions ward voiced their suspicions, some vigorously. "You're not crazy. You're a journalist, or a professor [referring to the continual note-taking]. You're checking up on the hospital." While most of the patients were reassured by the pseudopatient's insistence that he had been sick before he came in but was fine now, some continued to believe that the pseudopatient was sane throughout his hospitalization.[11] The fact that the patients often recognized normality when staff did not raises important questions.

Failure to detect sanity during the course of hospitalization may be due to the fact that physicians operate with a strong bias toward what statisticians call the Type 2 error.[5] This is to say that physicians are more inclined to call a healthy person sick (a false positive, Type 2) than a sick person healthy (a false negative, Type 1). The reasons for this are not hard to find: it is clearly more dangerous to misdiagnose illness than health. Better to err on the side of caution, to suspect illness even among the healthy.

But what holds for medicine does not hold equally well for psychiatry. Medical illnesses, while unfortunate, are not commonly pejorative. Psychiatric diagnoses, on the contrary, carry with them personal, legal, and social stigmas.[12] It was therefore important to see whether the tendency toward diagnosing the sane insane could be reversed. The following experiment was arranged at a research and teaching hospital whose staff had heard these findings but doubted that such an error could occur in their hospital. The staff was informed that at some time during the following 3 months, one or more pseudopatients would attempt to be admitted into the psychiatric hospital. Each staff member was asked to rate each patient who presented himself at admissions or on the ward according to the likelihood that the patient was a pseudopatient. A 10-point scale was used, with a 1 and 2 reflecting high confidence that the patient was a pseudopatient.

Judgments were obtained on 193 patients who were admitted for psychiatric treatment. All staff who had had sustained contact with or primary responsibility for the patient—attendants, nurses, psychiatrists, physicians, and psychologists—were asked to make judgments. Forty-one patients were alleged, with high confidence, to be pseudopatients by at least one member of the staff. Twenty-three were considered suspect by at least one psychiatrist. Nineteen were suspected by one psychiatrist *and* one other staff member. Actually, no genuine pseudopatient (at least from my group) presented himself during this period.

The experiment is instructive. It indicates that the tendency to designate sane people as insane can be reversed when the stakes (in this case, prestige and diagnostic acumen) are high. But what can be said of the 19 people who were suspected of being "sane" by one psychiatrist and another staff member? Were these people truly "sane," or was it rather the case that in the course of avoiding the Type 2 error the staff tended to make more errors of the first sort—calling the crazy "sane"? There is no way of knowing. But one thing is certain: any diagnostic process that lends itself so readily to massive errors of this sort cannot be a very reliable one.

THE STICKINESS OF PSYCHODIAGNOSTIC LABELS

Beyond the tendency to call the healthy sick—a tendency that accounts better for diagnostic behavior on admission than it does for such behavior after a lengthy period of exposure—the data speak to the massive role of labeling in psychiatric assessment. Having once been labeled schizophrenic, there is nothing the pseudopatient can do to overcome the tag. The tag profoundly colors others' perceptions of him and his behavior.

From the one viewpoint, these data are hardly surprising, for it has long been known that elements are given meaning by the context in which they occur. Gestalt psychology made this point vigorously, and Asch[13] demonstrated that there are "central" personality traits (such as "warm" versus "cold") which are so powerful that they markedly color the meaning of other information in forming an impression of a given personality.[14] "Insane," "schizophrenic," "manic-depressive," and "crazy" are probably among the most powerful of such central traits. Once a person is designated abnormal, all of his other behaviors and characteristics are colored by that label. Indeed, that label is so powerful that many of the pseudopatients' normal behaviors were overlooked entirely or profoundly misinterpreted. Some examples may clarify this issue.

Earlier I indicated that there were no changes in the pseudopatient's personal history and current status beyond those of name, employment, and, where necessary, vocation. Otherwise, a veridical description of personal history and circumstances was offered. Those circumstances were not psychotic. How were they made consonant with the diagnosis of psychosis? Or were those diagnoses modified in such a way as to bring them into accord with the circumstances of the pseudopatient's life, as described by him?

As far as I can determine, diagnoses were in no way affected by the relative health of the circumstances of a pseudopatient's life. Rather, the reverse occurred: the perception of his circumstances was shaped entirely by the diagnosis. A clear example of such translation is found in the case of a pseudopatient who had had a close relationship with his mother but was rather remote from his father during his early childhood. During adolescence and beyond, however, his father became a close friend, while his relationship with this mother cooled. His present relationship with his wife was characteristically close and warm. Apart from occasional angry exchanges, friction was minimal. The children had rarely been spanked. Surely there is nothing especially pathological about such a history. Indeed, many readers may see a similar pattern in their own experiences, with no markedly deleterious consequences. Observe, however, how such a history was translated in the psychopathological context, this from the case summary prepared after the patient was discharged.

> This white 39-year-old male . . . manifests a long history of considerable ambivalence in close relationships, which begins in early childhood. A warm relationship with his other cools during his adolescence. A distant relationship to his father is described as becoming very intense. Affective stability is absent His attempts to control emotionality with his wife and children are punctuated by angry outbursts and, in the case of the children, spankings. And while he says that he has several good friends, one senses considerable ambivalence embedded in those relationships also.

The facts of the case were unintentionally distorted by the staff to achieve consistency with a popular theory of the dynamics of a schizophrenic reaction.[15] Nothing of an ambivalent nature had been described in relations with parents, spouse, or friends. To the extent that ambivalence could be inferred, it was probably not greater than is found in all human relationships. It is true the pseudopatient's relationships with his parents changed over time, but in the ordinary context that would hardly be remarkable—indeed, it might very well be expected. Clearly, the meaning ascribed to his verbalizations (that is, ambivalence, affective instability) was determined by the diagnosis: schizophrenia. An entirely different meaning would have been ascribed if it were known that the man was "normal."

All pseudopatients took extensive notes publicly. Under ordinary circumstances, such behavior would have raised questions in the minds of observers, as, in fact, it did among patients. Indeed, it seemed so certain that the notes would elicit suspicion that elaborate precautions were taken to remove them from the ward each day. But the precautions proved needless. The closest any staff member came to questioning these notes occurred when one pseudopatient asked his physician what kind of medication he was receiving and began to write down the response. "You needn't write it," he was told gently. "If you have trouble remembering, just ask me again."

If no questions were asked of the pseudopatients, how was their writing interpreted? Nursing records for three patients indicate that the writing was seen as an aspect of their pathological behavior. "Patient engages in writing behavior" was the daily nursing comment on one of the pseudopatients who was never questioned about his writing. Given that the patient is in the hospital, he must be psychologically disturbed. And given that he is disturbed, continuous writing must be a behavioral manifestation of that disturbance, perhaps a subset of the compulsive behaviors that are sometimes correlated with schizophrenia.

One tacit characteristic of psychiatric diagnosis is that it locates the sources of aberration within the individual and only rarely within the complex of stimuli that surrounds him. Consequently, behaviors that are stimulated by the environment are commonly misattributed to the patient's disorder. For example, one kindly nurse found a pseudopatient pacing the long hospital corridors. "Nervous, Mr. X?" she asked. "No, bored," he said.

The notes kept by pseudopatients are full of patient behaviors that were misinterpreted by well-intentioned staff. Often enough, a patient would go "berserk" because he had, wittingly or unwittingly, been mistreated by, say, an attendant. A nurse coming upon the scene would rarely inquire even cursorily into the environmental stimuli of the patient's behavior. Rather, she assumed that his upset derived from his pathology, not from his present interactions with other staff members. Occasionally, the staff might assume that the patient's family (especially when they had recently visited) or other patients had stimulated the outburst. But never were the staff found to assume that one of themselves or the structure of the hospital had anything to do with a patient's behavior. One psychiatrist pointed to a group of patients who were sitting outside the cafeteria entrance half an hour before lunch time. To a group of young residents he indicated that such behavior was characteristic of the oral-acquisitive nature of the syndrome. It seemed not to occur to him that there were very few things to anticipate in a psychiatric hospital besides eating.

A psychiatric label has a life and an influence of its own. Once the impression has been formed that the patient is schizophrenic, the expectation is that he will continue to be schizophrenic. When a sufficient amount of time has passed, during which the patient has done nothing bizarre, he is considered to be in remission and available for discharge. But the label endures beyond discharge, with the unconfirmed expectation that he will behave as a schizophrenic again. Such labels, conferred by mental health professionals, are as influential on the patient as they are on his relatives and friends, and it should not surprise anyone that the diagnosis acts on all of them as a self-fulfilling prophecy. Eventually, the patient himself accepts the diagnosis, with all of its surplus meanings and expectations, and behaves accordingly.[5]

The inferences to be made from these matters are quite simple. Much as Zigler and Phillips have demonstrated that there is enormous overlap in the symptoms presented by patients who have been variously diagnosed,[16] so there is enormous overlap in the behaviors of the sane and the insane. The sane are not "sane" all of the time. We lose our tempers "for no good reason." We are occasionally depressed or anxious, again for no good reason. And we may find it difficult to get along with one or another person—again for no reason that we can specify. Similarly, the insane are not always insane. Indeed, it was the impression of the pseudopatients while living with them that they were sane for long periods of time—that the bizarre behaviors upon which their diagnoses were allegedly predicated constituted only a small fraction of their total behavior. If it makes no sense to label ourselves permanently depressed on the basis of an occasional depression, then it takes better evidence than is presently available to label all patients insane or schizophrenic on the basis of bizarre behavior or cognitions. It seems more useful, as Mischel[17] has pointed out, to limit our discussion to *behaviors,* the stimuli that provoke them, and their correlates.

It is not known why powerful impressions of personality traits, such as "crazy" or "insane," arise. Conceivably, when the origins of and stimuli that give rise to a behavior are remote or unknown, or when the behavior strikes us as immutable, trait labels regarding the *behavior* arise. When, on the other hand the origins and stimuli are known and available, discourse is limited to the behavior itself. Thus, I may hallucinate because I am sleeping, or I may hallucinate because I have ingested a peculiar drug. These are termed sleep-induced hallucinations, respectively. But when the stimuli to my hallucinations are unknown, that is called craziness, or schizophrenia—as if that inference were somehow as illuminating as the others.

THE EXPERIENCE OF PSYCHIATRIC HOSPITALIZATION

The term "mental illness" is of recent origin. It was coined by people who were humane in their inclinations and who wanted very much to raise the station of (and the public's sympathies toward) the psychologically disturbed from that of witches and "crazies" to one that was akin to the physically ill. And they were at least partially successful, for the treatment of the mentally ill *has* improved considerably over the years. But while treatment has improved, it is doubtful that people really regard the mentally ill in the same way that they view the physically ill. A broken leg is something one recovers from, but mental illness allegedly endures forever.[18] A broken leg does not threaten the observer, but a crazy schizophrenic? There is by now a host of evidence that attitudes toward the mentally ill are characterized by fear, hostility, aloofness, suspicion, and dread.[19] The mentally ill are society's lepers.

That such attitudes infect the general population is perhaps not surprising, only upsetting. But that they affect the professionals—attendants, nurses, physicians, psychologists, and social workers—who treat and deal with the mentally ill is more disconcerting, both because such attitudes are self-evidently pernicious and because they are unwitting. Most mental health professionals would insist that they are sympathetic toward the mentally ill, that they are neither avoidant nor hostile. But it is more likely that an exquisite ambivalence characterizes their relations with psychiatric patients, such that their avowed impulses are only part of their entire attitude. Negative attitudes are there too and can easily be detected. Such attitudes should not surprise us. They are the natural offspring of the labels patients wear and the places in which they are found.

Consider the structure of the typical psychiatric hospital. Staff and patients are strictly segregated. Staff have their own living space, including their dining facilities, bathrooms, and assembly places. The glassed quarters that contain the professional staff, which the pseudopatients came to call "the cage," sit out on every dayroom. The staff emerge primarily for caretaking purposes—to give medication, to conduct a therapy or group meeting, to instruct or reprimand a patient. Otherwise, staff keep to themselves, almost as if the disorder that afflicts their charges is somehow catching.

So much is patient-staff segregation the rule that, for four public hospitals in which an attempt was made to measure the degree to which staff and patients mingle, it was necessary to use "time out of the staff cage" as the operational measure. While it was not the case that all time spent out of the cage was spent mingling with patients (attendants, for example, would occasionally emerge to watch television in the dayroom), it was the only way in which one could gather reliable data on time for measuring.

The average amount of time spent by attendants outside of the cage was 11.3 percent (range, 3 to 52 percent). This figure does not represent only time spent mingling with patients, but also includes time spent on such chores as folding laundry, supervising patients while they shave, directing ward cleanup, and sending patients to off-ward activities. It was the relatively rare attendant who spent time talking with patients or playing games with them. It proved impossible to obtain a "percent mingling time" for nurses, since the amount of time they spent out of the cage was too brief. Rather, we counted instances of emergence from the cage. On the average, daytime nurses emerged from the cage 11.5 times per shift, including instances when they left the ward entirely (range, 4 to 39 times). Late afternoon and night nurses were even less available, emerging on the average 9.4 times per shift (range, 4 to 41 times). Data on early morning nurses, who arrived usually after midnight and departed at 8 A.M., are not available because patients were asleep during most of this period.

Physicians, especially psychiatrists, were even less available. They were rarely seen on the wards. Quite commonly, they would be seen only when they arrived and departed, with the remaining time being spent in their offices or in the cage. On the average, physicians emerged on the ward 6.7 times per day (range, 1 to 17 times). It proved difficult to make an accurate estimate in this regard, since physicians often maintained hours that allowed them to come and go at different times.

The hierarchical organization of the psychiatric hospital has been commented on before,[20] but the latent meaning of that kind of organization is worth noting again. Those with the most power have least to do with patients, and those with the least power are most involved with them. Recall, however, that the acquisition of role-appropriate behaviors occurs mainly through the observation of others, with the most powerful having the most influence. Consequently, it is understandable that attendants not only spend more time with patients than do any other members of the staff—that is required by their station in the hierarchy—but also, insofar as they learn from their superiors' behavior, spend as little time with patients as they can. Attendants are seen mainly in the cage, which is where the models, the action, and the power are.

I turn now to a different set of studies, these dealing with staff response to patient-initiated contact. It has long been known that the amount of time a person spends with you can be an index of your significance to him. If he initiates and maintains eye contact, there is reason to believe that he is considering your requests and needs. If he pauses to chat or actually stops and talks, there is added reason to infer that he is individuating you. In four hospitals, the pseudopatient approached the staff member with a request which took the following form: "Pardon me, Mr. [or Dr. or Mrs.] X, could you tell me when I will be eligible for grounds privileges?" (or ". . . when I will be presented at the staff meeting?" or ". . . when I am likely to be discharged?"). While the content of the question varied according to the appropriateness of the target and the pseudopatient's (apparent) current needs the form was always a courteous and relevant request for information. Care was taken never to approach a particular member of the staff more than once a day, lest the staff member become suspicious or irritated. In examining these data, remember that the behavior of the pseudopatients was neither bizarre nor disruptive. One could indeed engage in good conversation with them.

The data for these experiments are shown in Table 9A–1, separately for physicians (column 1) and for nurses and attendants (column 2). Minor differences between these four institutions were overwhelmed by the degree to which staff avoided continuing contacts that patients had initiated. By far, their most common response consisted of either a brief response to the question, offered while they were "on the move" and with head averted, or no response at all.

The encounter frequently took the following bizarre form: (pseudopatient) "Pardon me, Dr. X. Could you tell me when I'm eligible for grounds priv-

Table 9A–1 Self-initiated contact by pseudopatients with psychiatrists and nurses and attendants, compared to contact with other groups

Contact	Psychiatric hospitals		University campus (nonmedical)	University medical center physicians		
	(1) Psychiatrists	(2) Nurses and attendants	(3) Faculty	(4) "Looking for a psychiatrist"	(5) "Looking for an internist"	(6) No additional comment
Responeses						
Moves on, head averted (%)	71	88	0	0	0	0
Makes eye contact (%)	23	10	0	11	0	0
Pauses and chats (%)	2	2	0	11	0	10
Stops and talks (%)	4	0.5	100	78	100	90
Mean number of questions answered (out of 6)	a	a	6	3.8	4.8	4.5
Respondents (No.)	13	47	14	18	15	10
Attempts (No.)	185	1283	14	18	15	10

[a]Not applicable.

ileges?" (physician) "Good morning, Dave. How are you today?" (Moves off without waiting for a response.)

It is instructive to compare these data with data recently obtained at Stanford University. It has been alleged that large and eminent universities are characterized by faculty who are so busy that they have no time for students. For this comparison, a young lady approached individual faculty members who seemed to be walking purposefully to some meeting or teaching engagement and asked them the following six questions.

1. "Pardon me, could you direct me to Encina Hall?" (at the medical school: ". . . to the Clinical Research Center?").
2. "Do you know where Fish Annex is?" (there is no Fish Annex at Stanford).
3. "Do you reach here?"
4. "How does one apply for admission to the college?" (at the medical school: ". . . to the medical school?)
5. "Is it difficult to get in?"
6. "Is there financial aid?"

Without exception, as can be seen in Table 9A–1 (column 3), all of the questions were answered. No matter how rushed they were, all respondents not only maintained eye contact, but stopped to talk. Indeed, many of the respondents went out of their way to direct or take the questioner to the office she was seeking, to try to locate "Fish Annex," or to discuss with her the possibilities of being admitted to the university.

Similar data, also shown in Table, 9A–1 (columns 4, 5, and 6), were obtained in the hospital. Here too, the young lady came prepared with six questions. After the first question, however, she remarked to 18 of her respondents (column 4), "I'm looking for a psychiatrist," and to 15 others (column 5), "I'm looking for an internist." Ten other respondents received no inserted comment (column 6). The general degree of cooperative responses is considerably higher for these university groups than it was for pseudopatients in psychiatric hospitals. Even so, differences are apparent within the medical school setting. Once having indicated that she was looking for a psychiatrist, the degree of cooperation elicited was less than when she sought an internist

POWERLESSNESS AND DEPERSONALIZATION

Eye contact and verbal contact reflect concern and individuation; their absence, avoidance and depersonalization. The data I have presented do not do justice to the rich daily encounters that grew up around matters of depersonalization and avoidance. I have records of patients who were beaten by staff for the sin of having initiated verbal contact. During my own experience, for example, one patient was beaten in the presence of other patients for having approached an attendant and told him, "I like you." Occasionally, punishment meted out to patients for misdemeanors seemed so excessive that it could not be justified by the most radical interpretations of psychiatric canon. Nevertheless, they appeared to go unquestioned. Tempers were often short. A patient who had not heard a call for medication would be roundly excoriated, and the morning attendants would often wake patients with, "Come on, you m——f——s, out of bed!"

Neither anecdotal nor "hard" data can convey the overwhelming sense of powerlessness which invades the individual as he is continually exposed to the depersonalization of the psychiatric hospital. It hardly matters *which* psychiatric hospital—the excellent public ones and the very plush private hospital were better than the rural and shabby ones in this regard, but, again, the features that psychiatric hospitals had in common overwhelmed by far their apparent differences.

Powerlessness was evident everywhere. The patient is deprived of many of his legal rights by dint of his psychiatric commitment.[21] He is shorn of credibility by virtue of his psychiatric label. His freedom of movement is restricted. He cannot initiate contact with the staff, but may only respond to such overtures as they make. Personal privacy is minimal. Patient quarters and possessions can be entered and examined by any staff member, for whatever reason.

His personal history and anguish is available to any staff member (often including the "gray lady" and "candy striper" volunteer) who chooses to read his
folder, regardless of their therapeutic relationship to him. His personal hygiene
and waste evacuation are often monitored. The water closets may have no doors.

At times, depersonalization reached such proportions that pseudopatients
had the sense that they were invisible, or at least unworthy of account. Upon
being admitted, I and other pseudopatients took the initial physical examinations in a semipublic room, where staff members went about their own business as if we were not there.

On the ward, attendants delivered verbal and occasionally serious physical abuse to patients in the presence of other observing patients, some of whom
(the pseudopatients) were writing it all down. Abusive behavior, on the other
hand, terminated quite abruptly when other staff members were known to be
coming. Staff are credible witnesses. Patients are not.

A nurse unbuttoned her uniform to adjust her brassiere in the presence
of an entire ward of viewing men. One did not have the sense that she was
being seductive. Rather, she didn't notice us. A group of staff persons might
point to a patient in the dayroom and discuss him animatedly, as if he were not
there.

One illuminating instance of depersonalization and invisibility occurred
with regard to medications. All told, the pseudopatients were administered
nearly 2,100 pills, including Elavil, Stelazine, Compazine, and Thorazine, to
name but a few. (That such a variety of medications should have been administered to patients presenting identical symptoms is itself worthy of note.) Only
two were swallowed. The rest were either pocketed or deposited in the toilet.
The pseudopatients were not alone in this. Although I have no precise record
on how many patients rejected their medications, the pseudopatients frequently found the medications of other patients in the toilet before they
deposited their own. As long as they were cooperative, their behavior and the
pseudopatients' own in this matter, as in other important matters, went unno-
ticed throughout.

Reactions to such depersonalization among pseudopatients were intense.
Although they had come to the hospital as participant observers and were fully
aware that they did not "belong," they nevertheless found themselves caught
up in and fighting the process of depersonalization. Some examples: a graduate student in psychology asked his wife to bring his textbooks to the hospital
so he could[16] catch up on his homework"—this despite the elaborate precautions
taken to conceal his professional association. The same student, who had trained
for quite some time to get into the hospital, and who had looked forward to
the experience, "remembered" some drag races that he had wanted to see on
the weekend and insisted that he be discharged by that time. Another pseudopatient attempted a romance with a nurse. Subsequently, he informed the staff
that he was applying for admission to graduate school in psychology and was
very likely to be admitted, since a graduate professor was one of his regular

hospital visitors. The same person began to engage in psychotherapy with other patients—all of this as a way of becoming a person in an impersonal environment.

THE SOURCES OF DEPERSONALIZATION

What are the origins of depersonalization? I have already mentioned two. First are attitudes held by all of us toward the mentally ill—including those who treat them—attitudes characterized by fear, distrust, and horrible expectations on the one hand, and benevolent intentions on the other. Our ambivalence leads, in this instance as in others, to avoidance.

Second, and not entirely separate, the hierarchical structure of the psychiatric hospital facilitates depersonalization. Those who are at the top have least to do with patients, and their behavior inspires the rest of the staff. Average daily contact with psychiatrists, psychologists, residents, and physicians combined ranged from 3.9 to 25.1 minutes, with an overall mean of 6.8 (six pseudopatients over a total of 129 days of hospitalization). Included in this average are time spent in the admissions interview, ward meetings in the presence of a senior staff member, group and individual psychotherapy contacts, case presentation conferences, and discharge meetings. Clearly, patients do not spend much time in interpersonal contact with doctoral staff. And doctoral staff serve as models for nurses and attendants.

There are probably other sources. Psychiatric installations arc presently in serious financial straits. Staff shortages are pervasive, staff time at a premium. Something has to give, and that something is patient contact. Yet, while financial stresses are realities, too much can be made of them. I have the impression that the psychological forces that result in depersonalization are much stronger than the fiscal ones and that the addition of more staff would not correspondingly improve patient care in this regard. The incidence of staff meetings and the enormous amount of record-keeping on patients, for example, have not been as substantially reduced as has patient contact. Priorities exist, even during hard times. Patient contact is not a significant priority in the traditional psychiatric hospital, and fiscal pressures do not account for this. Avoidance and depersonalization may.

Heavy reliance upon psychotropic medication tacitly contributes to depersonalization by convincing staff that treatment is indeed being conducted and that further patient contact may not be necessary. Even here, however, caution needs to be exercised in understanding the role of psychotropic drugs. If patients were powerful rather than powerless, if they were viewed as interesting individuals rather than diagnostic entities, if they were socially significant rather than social lepers, if their anguish truly and wholly compelled our sympathies and concerns, would we not *seek* contact with them, despite the availability of medications? Perhaps for the pleasure of it all?

THE CONSEQUENCES OF LABELING AND DEPERSONALIZATION

Whenever the ratio of what is known to what needs to be known approaches zero, we tend to invent "knowledge" and assume that we understand more than we actually do. We seem unable to acknowledge that we simply don't know. The needs for diagnosis and remediation of behavioral and emotional problems are enormous. But rather than acknowledge that we are just embarking on understanding, we continue to label patients "schizophrenic," "manic-depressive," and "insane," as if in those words we had captured the essence of understanding. The facts of the matter are that we have known for a long time that diagnoses are often not useful or reliable, but we have nevertheless continued to use them. We now know that we cannot distinguish insanity from sanity. It is depressing to consider how that information will be used.

Not merely depressing, but frightening. How many people, one wonders, are sane but not recognized as such in our psychiatric institutions? How many have been needlessly stripped of their privileges of citizenship, from the right to vote and drive to that of handling their own accounts? How many have feigned insanity in order to avoid the criminal consequences of their behavior, and, conversely, how many would rather stand trial than live interminably in a psychiatric hospital—but are wrongly thought to be mentally ill? How many have been stigmatized by well-intentioned, but nevertheless erroneous, diagnoses? On the last point, recall again that a "Type 2 error" in psychiatric diagnosis does not have the same consequences it does in medical diagnosis. A diagnosis of cancer that has been found to be in error is cause for celebration. But psychiatric diagnoses are rarely found to be in error. The label sticks, a mark of inadequacy forever.

Finally, how many patients might be "sane" outside the psychiatric hospital but seem insane in it—not because craziness resides in them, as it were, but because they are responding to a bizarre setting, one that may be unique to institutions which harbor nether people? Goffman[4] calls the process of socialization to such institutions "mortification"—an apt metaphor that includes the processes of depersonalization that have been described here. And while it is impossible to know whether the pseudopatients' responses to these processes are characteristic of all inmates—they were, after all, not real patients—it is difficult to believe that these processes of socialization to a psychiatric hospital provide useful attitudes or habits of response for living in the "real world."

SUMMARY AND CONCLUSIONS

It is clear that we cannot distinguish the sane from the insane in psychiatric hospitals. The hospital itself imposes a special environment in which the meanings of behavior can easily be misunderstood. The consequences to patients hospitalized in such an environment—the powerlessness, depersonalization, segregation, mortification, and self-labeling—seem undoubtedly countertherapeutic.

I do not, even now, understand this problem well enough to perceive solutions. But two matters seem to have some promise. The first concerns the proliferation of community mental health facilities, of crisis intervention centers, of the human potential movement, and of behavior therapies that, for all of their own problems, tend to avoid psychiatric labels, to focus on specific problems and behaviors and to retain the individual in a relatively nonpejorative environment. Clearly, to the extent that we refrain from sending the distressed to insane places, our impressions of them are less likely to be distorted. (The risk of distorted perceptions, it seems to me, is always present, since we are much more sensitive to an individual's behaviors and verbalizations than we are to the subtle contextual stimuli that often promote them. At issue here is a matter of magnitude. And, as I have shown, the magnitude of distortion is exceedingly high in the extreme context that is a psychiatric hospital.)

The second matter that might prove promising speaks to the need to increase the sensitivity of mental health workers and researchers to the *Catch 22* position of psychiatric patients. Simply reading materials in this area will be of help to some such workers and researchers. For others, directly experiencing the impact of psychiatric hospitalization will be of enormous use. Clearly, further research into the social psychology of such total institutions will both facilitate treatment and deepen understanding.

I and the other pseudopatients in the psychiatric setting had distinctly negative reactions. We do not pretend to describe the subjective experiences of true patients. Theirs may be different from ours, particularly with the passage of time and the necessary process of adaptation to one's environment. But we can and do speak to the relatively more objective indices of treatment within the hospital. It could be a mistake, and a very unfortunate one, to consider that what happened to us derived from malice or stupidity on the part of the staff. Quite the contrary, our overwhelming impression of them was of people who really cared, who were committed and who were uncommonly intelligent. Where they failed, as they sometimes did painfully, it would be more accurate to attribute those failures to the environment in which they, too, found themselves than to personal callousness. Their perceptions and behavior were controlled by the situation, rather than being motivated by a malicious disposition. In a more benign environment, one that was less attached to global diagnosis, their behaviors and judgments might have been more benign and effective.

REFERENCES AND NOTES

1. Ash, P., *Journal of Abnormal and Social Psychology*, 1949, *44*, 272; Beck, A. T., *American Journal of Psychiatry*, 1962, *119*, 210; Boisen, A. T., *Psychiatry*, 1938, *2*, 233; Kreitman, N., *Journal of Mental Science*, 1961, *107*, 876; Kreitman, N., Sainsbury, P., Morrisey, J., Towers, J., Scrivener, J., *ibid.*, p. 887; Schmitt, H. O., & Fonda, C. P., *Journal of Abnormal and Social Psychology*, 1956, *52*, 262; Seeman, W. *Journal of Nervous and Mental Disease*, 1953, *118*, 541. For an analysis of these artifacts and sum-

maries of the disputes, see Zubin, J., *Annual Review of Psychology*, 1967, *18*, 373; Phillips, L., & Dragnus, J. G., *ibid.*, 1971, *22*, 447.

2. Benedict, R., *Journal of General Psychology*, 1934, *10*, 59.

3. See in this regard Becker, H., *Outsiders: Studies in the sociology of deviance*. New York: Free Press, 1963; Braginsky, B. M., Braginsky, D. D., & Ring, K., *Methods of madness: The mental hospital as a last resort*. New York: Holt, Rinehart & Winston, 1969; Crocetti, G. M., & Lemkau, P. V., *American Sociological Review*, 1965, *30*, 577; Goffman, E., *Behavior in public places*. New York: Free Press, 1964; Laing, R. D., *The divided self: A study of sanity and madness*. Chicago: Quadrangle, 1960; Phillips, D. L., *American Sociological Review*, 1963, *28*, 963; Sarbin, T. R., *Psychology Today*, 1972, *6*, 18; Schur, E., *American Journal of Sociology*, 1969, *75*, 309; Szasz, T., *Law, liberty and psychiatry*. New York: Macmillan, 1963; *The myth of mental illness: Foundations of a theory of mental illness*. New York: Hoeber-Harper, 1963. For a critique of some of these views, see Gove, W. R., *American Sociological Review*, 1970, *35*, 873.

4. Goffman, E., *Asylums*. Garden City, N.Y.: Doubleday, 1961.

5. Scheff, T. J., *Being mentally ill: A sociological theory*. Chicago: Aldine, 1966.

6. Data from a ninth pseudopatient are not incorporated in this report because, although his sanity went undetected, he falsified aspects of his personal history, including his marital status and parental relationships. His experimental behaviors therefore were not identical to those of the other pseudopatients.

7. Barry, A. *Bellevue is a state of mind*. New York: Harcourt Brace Jovanovich, 1971; Belknap, I., *Human problems of a state mental hospital*. New York: McGraw-Hill, 1956; Caudill, W., Redlich, F. C., Gilmore, H. R., Brody, E. B., *American Journal of Orthopsychiatry*, 1952, *22*, 314; Goldman, A. R., Bohr, R. H., & Steinberg, T. A., *Professional Psychology*, 1970, *1*, 427; unauthored, *Roche Report 1* (No. 13), 1971, 8.

8. Beyond the personal difficulties that the pseudopatient is likely to experience in the hospital, there are legal and social ones that, combined, require considerable attention before entry. For example, once admitted to a psychiatric institution, it is difficult, if not impossible, to be discharged on short notice, state law to the contrary notwithstanding. I was not sensitive to these difficulties at the outset of the project, nor to the personal and situational emergencies that can arise, but later a writ of habeas corpus was prepared for each of the entering pseudopatients and an attorney was kept "on call" during every hospitalization. I am grateful to John Kaplan and Robert Bartels for legal advice and assistance in these matters.

9. However distasteful such concealment is, it was a necessary first step to examining these questions. Without concealment, there would have been no way to know how valid these experiences were; nor was there any way of knowing whether whatever detections occurred were a tribute to the diagnostic acumen of the staff or to the hospital's rumor network. Obviously, since my concerns are general ones that cut across individual hospitals and staffs, I have respected their anonymity and have eliminated clues that might lead to their identification.

10. Interestingly, of the 12 admissions, 11 were diagnosed as schizophrenic and one, with the identical symptomatology, as manic-depressive psychosis. This diagnosis has a more favorable prognosis, and it was given by the only private hospital in our sample. On the relations between social class and psychiatric diagnosis, see Hollingshead, A. deB., & Redlich, F. C., *Social class and mental illness: A community study*. New York: Wiley, 1958.

11. It is possible, of course, that patients have quite broad latitudes in diagnosis and therefore are inclined to call many people sane, even those whose behavior is patently aberrant. However, although we have no hard data on this matter, it was our distinct impression that this was not the case. In many instances, patients not only singled us out for attention, but came to imitate our behaviors and styles.

12. Cumming J., & Cumming, E., *Community Mental Health*, 1965, *1*, 135; Farina, A., & Ring, K., *Journal of Abnormal Psychology*, 1965, *70*, 47; Freeman, H. E., & Simmons, O. G., *The mental patient comes home*. New York: Wiley, 1963; Johannsen, W. J., *Mental Hygiene*, 1969, *53*, 218; Linsky, A. S., *Social Psychiatry*, 1970, *5*, 166.

13. Asch, S. E., *Journal of Abnormal and Social Psychology*, 1946, *41*, 258; *Social Psychology*. New York: Prentice Hall, 1952.

14. See also Mensh, I. N., & Wishner, J., *Journal of Personality*, 1947, *16*, 188; Wishner, J., *Psychological Review*, 1960, *67*, 96; Bruner, J. S., & Tagiuri, R., In G. Lindzey (Ed.), *Handbook of social psychology*. Cambridge, MA: Addison-Wesley, 1954, 2: 634–654; Brunner, J. S., Shapiro, D., & Tagiuri, R., In R. Tagiuri & L. Petrullo (Eds.), *Person perception and interpersonal behavior*. Stanford, CA: Stanford University Press, 1958, pp. 277–288.

15. For an example of a similar self-fulfilling prophecy, in this instance dealing with the "central" trait of intelligence, see Rosenthal, R., & Jacobson, L., *Pygmalion in the classroom*. New York: Holt, Rinehart & Winston, 1968.

16. Zigler, E., & Phillips, L., *Journal of Abnormal and Social Psychology*, 1961, *63*, 69. See also Freudenberg, R. K. & Robertson, J. P., *A.M.A. Archives of Neurology & Psychiatry*, 1956, *76*, 14.

17. Mischel, W., *Personality and assessment*. New York: Wiley, 1968.

18. The most recent and unfortunate instance of this tenet is that of Senator Thomas Eagleton.

19. Sarbin, T. R., & Mancuso, J. C., *Journal of Clinical and Consulting Psychology*, 1970, *35*, 159; Sarbin, T. R., *ibid.*, 1967, *31*, 447; Nunnally, J. C. Jr., *Popular conceptions of mental health*. New York: Holt, Rinehart & Winston, 1961.

20. Stanton, A. H., & Schwartz, M. S., *The mental hospital: A study of institutional participation in psychiatric illness and treatment*. New York: Basic Books, 1954.

21. Wexler, D. B., & Scoville, S. E., *Arizona Law Review*, 1971, *13*, 1.

22. I thank W. Miscel, E. Orme, and M. S. Rosenhan for comments on an earlier draft of manuscript.

What are your initial impressions about this article? Was it rather ingenious the way Dr. Rosenhan decided to study his concerns? Was he able to cover all of the concerns relating to diagnosis in this one study?

THINK IT THROUGH

Let us investigate this article more closely by answering some specific questions related to the article. Answering these initial questions will help to make certain we are quite familiar with the topics covered.

1. What was studied in this article and why was it studied?
2. How was it studied?
3. What diagnoses were psuedopatients given? Why was one psuedopatient diagnosed differently from the others?
4. What was the average length of stay for the psuedopatients? Why do you think there were differences in the length of stays for the individual psuedopatients?
5. Is this article suggesting that patients are better diagnostitions than professionals?
6. What ethical concerns would you encounter if you were to replicate this study today? Why were these same ethical concerns not as important in 1973?

Ethical considerations would be a primary concern in conducting this research today. Is it really ethical to feign an illness in an attempt to gain admittance into a mental institution? Is it ethical to use psuedopatients in the way this study used them? Is it ethical to tell administrators you will be sending psuedopatients to their facility in an attempt to determine the facility's accuracy in correctly diagnosing psychological disorders? The answer to these questions would generally be no. Does this mean Dr. Rosenhan was unethical in conducting this research? Absolutely not. Dr. Rosenhan used the ethical standards that were in existence at the time. Remember when we stated at the end of Chapter 1 that ethics are dynamic? Rosenhan's article is a prime example of this dynamic aspect of ethics. When this study was conducted, a significantly different set of ethical standards was in effect. Today, we, as experimenters, must be much more concerned with the participant's care and concerns. We are precluded from conducting research in which a person might come away harmed in some way (physically, psychologically, emotionally, etc.). With Rosenhan's study such harm could have happened. The administrators could have felt "duped" and as a result feel "stupid" for admitting a psuedopatient into their facility. A belief that one has made an egregious mistake in a diagnosis could ultimately cause an administrator to quit the psychological profession.

Might this study have had some effect on the administrator's future admission decisions? That is, might an administrator be less inclined to accept actual patients in the future (i.e., commit a Type 2 error)? Could such faulty decisions prove to be disastrous for actual patients who were not admitted to the hospital? Could one of these patients commit suicide or a murder because he or she was not admitted?

Obviously, the potential outcomes suggested are extreme and probably not likely to occur; they do point out serious ethical issues the researcher must be concerned. These issues must be investigated and considered thoroughly prior to conducting a study. If our participants (or people our participants might later come in contact with) could be potentially harmed by participating in our study, we must redesign our research to make certain our participants (and others) are protected.

Do such considerations suggest we could not do similar studies today? The answer to this question is a resounding no. However, we must first redesign our study. Let us look at a few ways we can take a new and different perspective on an existing piece of research. As you encounter the following questions, ask yourself if reframing the study using the suggested changes would render the study free of any ethical considerations. And, ask yourself what the cost would be (in terms of time and money) in making the suggested changes. Remember, the following questions are posed for suggestive purposes only; feel free to modify them and to develop additional ones. After all, that is what research idea generation is all about.

THINK IT THROUGH

Instead of studying psuedopatients hearing voices, what other types of symptoms could we investigate? Could we do the same study and have the psuedopatients state they have been experiencing visual hallucinations? Instead of having the participants state they are hearing sounds, we could have them feign seeing their dead mothers. What if we have the psuedopatients feign delusional symptoms rather than hallucinational symptoms? That is, we could have them state they believe themselves to be "Jesus Christ" or a werewolf. Would these changes in symptoms have any influence on admissions?

What other forms of feigned disorders could be studied (e.g., panic attack, phobic disorders, sexual dysfunctions)? How would these feigned disorders likely have changed the results of the original Rosenhan study? Would different disorders suggest different lengths of admission stays?

These are all interesting questions; however, as you have probably guessed, conducting the above studies in the same settings as the original study would present similar ethical considerations. We would be ethically prevented from conducting these studies. How, then, can one investigate psychological assessment in an experiment today?

When trying to overcome ethical problems in real-life settings one must generally turn to other, less intrusive means of investigation. For example, survey studies could be used when ethics are a concern. Surveys tend to be much less intrusive. The diagnosis issue could be studied by sending out a written scenario of a supposed hallucinational person (using the general format of the Rosenhan study) to selected professionals who are asked to make a diagnosis and suggest a course of treatment for that "person." We could also ask how long the person in our scenario could be expected to be confined in an institution. In other words, we could conduct the Rosenhan study but do it in written form. We could even compare the answers of professionals to our scenarios in private versus public institutions to investigate any differences that may exist. Alternatively, we could compare results between professionals, psychology students, and other types of "lay" participants. There is a veritable plethora of variations or independent variables we could study!

Are there any problems with this type of research? Absolutely. We have the problem of potentially low return rates (we would be lucky to have a return rate of 20 percent). Thus, our study may not be very representative of the actual population from which we would like to draw inferences. Also there is the problem of *demand characteristics* (Orne, 1962). We might be introducing artificial results on the part of our participants. That is, by the very nature of participating in a study the participant might say and do things they normally would not. They could be more cautious or careful knowing they were participating in a psychological study compared to what they would actually do if not in a study. Such artificial results would negate the validity and reliability of our study thus making it of little or no value.

We have, however, obviated the problem of ethics. As you can see, when you obviate one problem, you often are left with a different problem (or set of problems) to deal with.

What would be the correct approach to our problems? Should we cast aside ethical issues to make certain we achieve reliable and valid results, or do we concentrate on the ethical concerns and have problems generalizing our results? The answer here is an easy one. We must hold ethical concerns to be paramount. As a result we would have to deal with the reliability and validity concerns. No study is perfect; there are always "problems" with every study. We must decide which approach is best in light of all shortcomings. In other studies, we would have to deal with other problems, depending on the approach we decide to explore. Always consult your institution's ethics committee and your supervising professor for appropriate guidance in this area.

Using the scenario format, several other independent variables could be investigated. Geographical regions could serve as a variation on a theme. Are people more or less likely to be suggested for admission when we compare the results of professionals from the Midwest versus the West? If we sent our survey with scenario to different regions, perhaps we would obtain differential rates of suggested admission. Who knows? That is what research is all about: the process of answering.

What about sex and ethnicity? Do these two variables create differences in diagnosis for gaining admittance into a mental health facility? For example, are men more or less likely to be suggested for admission to a hospital when compared to women with the same symptoms? Are African Americans more or less likely to be admitted when compared to their Caucasian counterparts? These would be interesting variables worth investigating. They are also variables that have a high degree of editorial interest today. Likewise, we could vary the age of the person in our scenario. We might see differences when we state the person is 16 years of age versus 60 or 70.

As suggested above, another way to approach this study would be to ask "lay" people to judge the scenarios and suggest a diagnosis and length of stay. You could use the students in your advanced psychology class, or perhaps you could use the students in an introductory psychology course to serve as participants. This approach would have the benefit of saving time and money. You could do the study in a single class tomorrow at 10:00 A.M. thus saving time, and you would not have to send the survey out obviously saving on postage and related costs. You could get as many as 100 (or more) respondents in a single hour! However, you would be sacrificing professional insight in lieu of convenience by using lay participants. The decision on what type of participants to use is often a decision based on convenience rather than importance. Again, your professor can aid in the decisions as to the type of participants to use.

THINK IT THROUGH

How could we use animals in investigating diagnosis, labeling, and stereotyping? What type of animals should you use?

Using animals might, at first, seem to be an impossible method regarding the present study. However, it can be done! Remember, always think of different variations on a theme. How about asking human participants to train rats to run a maze or press a bar? We could randomly state to half of the participants their rat is "crazy"; it is suffering from a "rat form" of schizophrenia. The other half of the participants could be told their rats were "normal" or even bred for "superior rat intelligence." Comparing the groups could lead to some rather interesting and potentially provocative differences (see Rosenthal, 1966). So, we can even use nonhumans to investigate some of the issues Rosenhan raised.

Approaching this study from a different perspective, we could use our survey and scenario to investigate the following questions:

1. Do people know what schizophrenia is? Do they know the difference between schizophrenia and dissociative personality disorder? We could accomplish these goals by comparing psychology students with history students and/or the general population.
2. What is a typical hospital or institutional stay for different disorders? We could, with the aid of various institutions, investigate differential proposed lengths of stays for various disorders (e.g., phobic disorders, dissociative disorders, or psychotic disorders).
3. What do health related professionals feel about this type of study? That is, do they view it as being fraught with ethical concerns? Do they believe such studies can advance our field?
4. What effect does managed health care have on diagnosis and admissions?

THINK IT THROUGH

List five ideas that are related to those mentioned above that can be researched and list three novel ideas (not related to any of the above) that could also be researched. What types of materials and time would each of these eight areas require? Are there any ethical concerns in the studies you have proposed? If so, how can you go about eliminating these concerns?

Related ideas:

1. _____

2. _____

3. _____

4. _____

5. _____

Novel ideas:

1. _____

2. _____

3. _____

After writing down your various research ideas, have one of your professors read them and give you additional and alternate suggestions. If this is indeed an area of research in which you have an interest, you will find it exciting to develop and pursue your ideas to fruition with the aid of your favorite professor and your ethics committee.

There are some additional readings you can review if you are interested in pursuing research in this area. We have listed several that should be of interest to you. And, do not hesitate to ask your professor for additional suggestions.

REFERENCES

Rosenhan, D. L. (1973). On Being Sane in Insane Places. *Science, 179,* 250–258.

ADDITIONAL READINGS

Cooper, M. L. (1994). Motivations for alcohol use among adolescents: Development and validation of a four-factor model. *Psychological Assessment, 6,* 117–128.

Hare, R. D., Hart, S. D., & Harper, T. J. (1991). Psychopathy and DSM-IV criteria for antisocial personality disorder. *Journal of Abnormal Psychology, 100,* 391–398.

Patrick, C. J., Bradley, M. M. & Lang, P. J. (1993). Emotion in the criminal psychopath: Startle reflex modulation. *Journal of Abnormal Psychology, 103,* 523–534.

Spitzer, R. L. (1975). On pseudoscience in science, logic in remission, and psychiatric diagnosis: A critique of Rosenhan's "On being sane in insane places." *Journal of Abnormal Psychology, 84,* 442–452.

Szasz, T. (1974). *The myth of mental illness,* rev. ed. pp. 17–80. New York: Harper & Row.

CHAPTER 10

Researching Research

The following two chapters are included to cover additional areas within psychology and because the authors of this text are the authors of these final two articles. We have done this to give you suggestions as to how we have developed personal areas of research; to give you some personal insight into how some actual research was conceived and developed. We hope that by doing this, you will be able to understand the process of idea generation more deeply and be able to appreciate how "easy" it is to come up with an "original" idea for research.

The article selected for this chapter has two very important aspects. The first is that it is a study about researching research. Specifically, the article investigates the effects of postexperimental questionnaires in assessing suspiciousness on the part of experimental participants. The second is that this article takes two different and conflicting positions and blends them into one that shows that neither perspective is right or wrong; they are just approaching the same problem from two different viewpoints.

Detection of Suspiciousness as a Function of Pleas for Honesty

Joseph Horvat
Weber State College

An experimental study was conducted to assess the relative effect of two different sophistication levels of subjects (informed, naive) and three different pleas
for their honesty (personal, impersonal, control) on a postexperimental questionnaire designed to measure suspiciousness within the context of a deception
experiment. Results convincingly indicate that properly designed postexperimental techniques will accurately assess suspicions from truly suspicious subjects
while keeping naive subjects from falsely reporting suspicions.

There have been a conspicuous absence of postexperimental (PE) inquiry techniques in social psychology during recent years. This absence is particularly
striking in view of the strong concern with, and editorial demand for, manipulation checks of various sorts. It is surprising that this lack of concern with PE
inquiry techniques should follow the successful demonstration that some previous "truths" in social psychology were actually due to experimental artifacts
(Page & Scheidt, 1971).

When the problems of demand characteristics in deception research were
first dramatized by the work of Orne (1962), postexperimental questionnaires
(PEQs) were among the most apparent devices for assessing these problems.
Dramatic work in the PEQ field has been conducted with studies utilizing intentionally informed subjects to empirically test the validity of such inquiry techniques (e.g., Golding & Lichtenstein, 1970; Horvat, Dienstbier, La Velle, Flume,
& Creamer, 1985; Levy, 1967; Newberry, 1973; White & Schumsky, 1972). Col-
lectively these studies have suggested that although PEQs tend to be better
than using nothing when eliciting suspicions from subjects, they are actually
ineffective tools in discriminating truly suspicious from truly naive subjects. In
fact, the results of such studies have led Silverman (1977) to the conclusion
that "apparently, a sizeable proportion of subjects will be impervious to the best
efforts of experimenters to extract admissions of awareness after the fact" (p. 50).

The problem with such techniques does not end here, however, because
even when researchers are in agreement of the necessary utilization of PE techniques they are not in like agreement when it comes to the type of technique
to use. This can particularly be seen in the debate over the false positive versus the false negative problem. Page (1969, 1970, 1971, 1973; Page & Scheidt,
1971) has convincingly argued for the use of funnel type PEQs because he

believes that the only important potential problem when using PE inquiry techniques is the failure to identify truly suspicious or demand aware subjects (false negatives resulting in contaminated data). False positives (unsuspicious subjects misidentified as suspicious) merely result in the unnecessary elimination of subjects from the research. However, those researchers whose conclusions have been compellingly challenged by findings of high levels of subject suspicion or hypothesis awareness on extended PE techniques have generally protested that the misclassification of naive subjects is a problem of similar magnitude (e.g., Berkowitz, 1971; Staats, 1969). They suggest that extensive questioning in elaborate PEQs creates unambiguous demand characteristics for the false revelations of suspicion. They favor using only general questions in an attempt to elicit suspicions. Obviously, both lines of reasoning have merit. The ideal would be a procedure where the false positive as well as the false negative problems are addressed and minimized.

The present investigation attempts to solve past PE inquiry problems by developing a questionnaire that would successfully identify truly suspicious subjects while eliminating the problems of misidentifying truly naive subjects.

METHOD

Subjects

One hundred seventy-five male introductory psychology students participated in an experiment ostensibly to study the "effects of persuasive communication."

Design

A 2 × 3 between-groups factorial design was run with two levels of subject sophistication (naive, informed) and three levels of pleas (control, impersonal, personal). Subjects were run in small groups, with as many cells of the design being represented as there were subjects in each experimental session.

Procedure

The procedure was designed to resemble an experiment on racial prejudice under the guise of persuasive communication. Subjects were initially separated into different rooms and instructed to read some preliminary information. During this initial separation, half of the subjects were informed by a confederate (who had apparently just completed the same experiment) that the experiment was not about persuasive communication as the experimenter had stated, but rather "it is really about race prejudice."

When subjects completed this initial information they were seated, as a group, in a video presentation room. Partitions separated subjects so as not to allow conversation or viewing of each other. After watching a video presentation of four arguments by black and white speakers (to make the informing manipulation more salient), subjects rated the speakers on several dimensions. When subjects were finished with the ratings, the experiment proper took place.

Subjects received a booklet containing the PEQ that was prefaced with one of three different sets of instructions. The *personal plea* group received instructions that gave a request for their honesty on the questionnaire because "the research in which you have just participated was for the experimenter's dissertation." In addition the word "I" appeared where appropriate to give a more personal impression of the experiment to the subject. The *impersonal plea* group received the same instructions except that no mention of a dissertation was made and the word "they" was substituted for "I." The *control* group received only minimal instruction that essentially asked them to "answer the following questions."

Postexperimental Questionnaire

The questionnaire was 21 questions in length and was of the funnel variety (Page, 1969). The first question was very general: "Would you please write down anything you thought about the purpose of the experiment while you were participating in it." Successive questions were progressively more specific (e.g., "Did you form any suspicions or ideas that this study was really about racial prejudice?"). These latter questions came in three question sets of which the following is given as an example:

10. Did you form any suspicions or ideas that this study was really about racial prejudice?

No— Go To Next Page	Slight— Go To Question #11	Moderate— Go To Question #11	Very Much— Go To Question #11

11. What were those suspicions? _____.
    Go To Question #12.

12. When did you form those suspicions?

Before or During the Video	While Completing the Video Questionnaire	While Completing This Questionnaire

Go to Next Page

These question sets were on different pages, and the subjects were instructed not to go back to a previous page once it had been answered. The subjects were thus unable to view the entire questionnaire without turning pages;

the presence of the experimenter implicitly supported the verbal instruction to refrain from such behavior.

The final two pages of the questionnaire were included to assess suspicion of the actual purpose of the experiment (effectiveness of eliciting suspicions).

RESULTS

Of the 175 subjects who participated in the experiment 14 were dropped from the final analysis for the following reasons: 2 for volunteering (before the PEQ was administered) that they had received information from the confederate, 6 for being suspicious that the purpose of the experiment was to test the effectiveness of the questionnaire (3 in the informed/personal plea condition and 3 in the informed/impersonal plea condition), and 6 due to equipment failure. Thus, there was a total of 161 subjects in the analysis.

A conversion that can be utilized in PEQ studies is to give discrete suspicion scores ranging from 0 *(not suspicious)* to 4 *(highly suspicious)* to subjects depending on their level of suspicion. The subjects' suspicion scores were determined by two raters using this conversion with the raters remaining blind as to experimental conditions.[1] Furthermore, because it was felt that a rater's knowledge of a previous score on one section of the questionnaire might influence successive scoring, each section was scored without access to the remainder of the questionnaire. Between-rater reliabilities on the different sections of the questionnaire ranged from $r = .88$ to $r = .99$. The statistical analyses that follow are based on a third rater resolving differences that existed.

The suspicion scores over the different conditions (Table 10A–1) revealed a significant main effect for sophistication level, $F(1, 155) = 102.15$, $p < .001$, and a significant interaction between sophistical level and plea, $F(2, 155) = 4.50$, $p < .02$. As anticipated, the main effect of pleas was not significant, $F(2, 155) = 0.45$. It can be seen that all subjects in the informed/personal plea condition were classified as having some suspicions, with over half of those subjects being classified as very suspicious. In the remaining two informed conditions, there were a substantial number of subjects who were scored as having no suspicions.

Because experimenters generally eliminate moderate and very suspicious subjects (suspicion scores of 3 and 4, respectively) from data analysis, it is apparent in the present study that the personal plea condition was far more effective in detecting suspicions when compared to the other conditions, with that type of elimination process resulting in only 2 (6.7%) naive subjects being eliminated from analysis for their suspicions and only 4 (14.8%) informed subjects mistakenly retained as not suspicious. Comparable figures would be 4 (14.0%) and 10 (40.0%) in the impersonal plea conditions, and 6 (23.0%) and 7 (28.0%) in the control conditions.

[1]Complete scoring rules are available upon request.

Table 10A–1 Frequencies (F) and Percentages (P) of Suspicion Scores

Suspicion score[a]	Control		Impersonal plea		Personal plea	
	F	P	F	P	F	P
			Naive			
1	15	57.7	18	64.3	23	76.7
2	5	19.2	6	21.4	5	16.7
3	3	11.5	3	10.7	1	3.3
4	3	11.5	1	3.6	1	3.3
M		1.77		1.54		1.33
			Informed			
1	4	16.0	4	16.0	0	0.0
2	3	12.0	6	24.0	4	14.8
3	12	48.0	6	24.0	9	33.0
4	6	24.0	9	36.0	14	51.9
M		2.80		2.80		3.37

[a]Not suspicious (1), slightly suspicious (2), moderately suspicious (3), very suspicious (4).

As stated earlier, those who protest the use of funnel questionnaires due to the false negative problem tend to use questionnaires containing only one or two very general questions. If one were to compare the first page of the present study (which would replicate the type of questions these investigators ask) with the remaining funnel questions, a very impressive difference is found. When differentiating informed subjects as being *aware* (a suspicion score of 3 or 4) or *not aware* (a score of 0 or 1) of the informed purpose of the experiment (race prejudice), a significant difference was found between these two formats of questionnaires, $\chi^2(1, N = 161) = 26.60$, $p < .001$. That is, if only the first page had been used to elicit and assess suspicion scores, 24 informed subjects would have been detected as being suspicious, leaving 53 incorrectly identified. When using the funnel questions the majority of the informed subjects (56 of 77) were labeled correctly.

The first page on which a suspicion was admitted by subjects was analyzed over conditions. The mean page number on which a suspicion was first indicated from naive subjects in the control, impersonal plea, and personal plea conditions were 4.09, 2.50, and 2.71, respectively. Corresponding means across these same conditions for the informed subjects were 1.86, 1.92, and 1.74, respectively. These means represent a significant sophistication main effect,

$F(1, 90) = 17.92, p < .001$, with the interaction approaching significance, $F(2, 90)$ $= 2.94, p < .06$. The main effect of pleas was not significant, $F(2, 90) = 1.14$.

DISCUSSION

The present study approached the ideal in PE inquiry techniques by being able to avoid successfully both the false positive and false negative problems. Because suspicion scores for the informed subjects increased as one went from no plea to the personal plea and the reverse occurred with the naive subjects, the use of the personal plea seemed to have avoided both validity concerns. It is not, however, the plea alone that is responsible for this result. If it were, similar results should have been obtained when the suspicion scores on the first page (the general questions) of the questionnaire were analyzed, but this was clearly not the case. It is the combination of the personal plea with the funnel questions that avoids past PEQ problems.

It should be noted that even the naive subjects in the present study could have become suspicious that the study was about race prejudice. The results, however, indicate that when a naive subject does become suspicious those suspicions will be extracted with more accuracy using a personal plea for their honesty. Because the naive subjects in the control condition took an average of over four questions to reveal their suspicions and the naive subjects in the personal plea condition took an average of less than three questions, the former are probably revealing their suspicions after-the-fact. That is, they are probably displaying false positives due to the demand characteristics of the PEQ. Thus, Berkowitz's (1971) conclusion of the false positive problem is well justified looking at the naive subjects in the control condition. However, based upon the results obtained with the naive subjects in the personal plea condition, his conclusions lose justification. Comparing the number and percentage of naive subjects with suspicion scores of 3 or 4 in the control and personal plea conditions (6, 23% and 2, 7%, respectively) lends additional support to the notion that the present study was able to accurately identify naive subjects.

The studies of preinformation reviewed earlier found that the vast majority of subjects would not admit having illicit information. The use of a personal plea in the present investigation allowed identification of a sizeable percentage of informed subjects confessing their preinformation (81%). Results using the impersonal plea (32%) and no plea (16%) were consistent with previous findings. It is interesting to note two factors relating to this finding. First, all personal plea subjects who admitted moderate or strong suspicions did so before the direct question relating to preinformation was asked. This question, then, added nothing to the effectiveness of the PEQ in this condition. For the impersonal plea subjects that direct question changed the suspicion score to the moderate or strong level in 6 subjects and for 8 subjects in the control condition. Second, consistent with previous studies, subjects will not admit to being informed until a direct question pertaining to that information is asked. Of the 34 subjects who stated that they had been informed, 24 did not make this revelation until asked a direct question about that information. Although it can be argued that this result shows the general ineffectiveness of PE techniques, that argument is less than legitimate. It makes little difference why suspicious subjects are dropped from a study as long as they are dropped. Whether it be due to indicated suspicions or to the revelation of receiving important information is actually of little practical importance.

If the present study had been done for its supposed purpose (race prejudice), only the personal plea condition would have been effective in appropriately eliciting suspicions from subjects. It was not effective, unfortunately, in eliciting a strong indication of suspicions from 100% of the informed subjects. Nonetheless, it was far superior in eliciting suspicions when compared to previous studies. The present study would seem to justify a qualification change in Silverman's (1977) conclusion to now read "apparently, <few> subjects will be impervious to the *best* efforts of experimenters to extract admissions of awareness after the fact."

Making a study more personal for the subject can indeed help the conscientious experimenter extract valid results from reluctant subjects. Although this type of involvement is not exactly what Kelman (1967) and Jourard (1968) had in mind, a simple extrapolation from their conclusions indicates the correctness of such a statement. Researchers have neglected the postexperimental problem long enough. There is no valid reason for excluding systematic and detailed postexperimental inquiry techniques from research.

REFERENCES

Berkowitz, L. (1971). The "weapons effect," demanding characteristics, and the myth of the compliant subject. *Journal of Personality and Social Psychology, 20*, 332–338.

Golding, S. L., & Lichtenstein, E. (1970). Confession of awareness and prior knowledge of deception as a function of interview set and approval motivation. *Journal of Personality and Social Psychology, 14*, 213–223.

Horvat, J., Dienstbier, R., La Velle, D., Flume, M., & Creamer, K. (1985, August). *A comparison of postexperimental questionnaires.* Paper presented at the 93rd Annual Convention of the American Psychological Association, Los Angeles.

Jourard, S. M. (1968). *Disclosing man to himself.* Princeton, NJ: D. Van Nostrand.

Kelman, H. C. (1967). Human use of human subjects: The problem of deception in social psychological experiments. *Psychological Bulletin, 67*, 1–11.

Levy, L. H. (1967). Awareness, learning and the beneficent subject as expert witness. *Journal of Personality and Social Psychology, 6*, 365–370.

Newberry, B. J. (1973). Truth telling in subjects with information about experiments: Who is being deceived? *Journal of Personality and Social Psychology, 25*, 369–374.

Orne, M. T. (1962). On the social psychology of the psychological experiment: With particular reference to demand characteristics and their implications. *American Psychologist, 17*, 776–783.

Page, M. M. (1969). Social psychology of a classical conditioning of attitudes experiment. *Journal of Personality and Social Psychology, 11*, 177–186.

Page, M. M. (1970). Demand awareness, subject sophistication, and the effectiveness of a verbal "reinforcement." *Journal of Personality, 38,* 287–301.

Page, M. M. (1971). Effects of evaluation apprehension of cooperation in verbal conditioning. *Journal of Experimental Research in Personality, 5,* 85–91.

Page, M. M. (1973). On detecting demand awareness by postexperimental questionnaire. *The Journal of Social Psychology, 91,* 305–323.

Page, M. M., & Scheidt, R. H. (1971). The elusive weapons effect: Demand awareness, evaluation apprehension, and slightly sophisticated subjects. *Journal of Personality and Social Psychology, 20,* 304–318.

Silverman, I. (1977). *The human subject in the psychological laboratory,* New York: Pergamon Press.

Staats, A. (1969). Experimental demand characteristics and the classical conditioning of attitudes. *Journal of Personality and Social Psychology, 11,* 187–192.

White, H. A., & Schumsky, D. A. (1972). Prior information and "awareness" in verbal conditioning. *Journal of Personality and Social Psychology, 5,* 162–165.

What are your initial impressions about this article? How do you think the idea for this piece of research was conceived? Was it as a result of superior insight on the part of the author, or was it simply an attempt to answer a seemingly simple question? You might be surprised as to how easily the idea was conceived and developed.

As a graduate student, the author of this article was taking a course on research methods in social and personality psychology. While taking that course, he was required to read the Berkowitz (1971), Staats (1969), and the Page and Scheidt (1971) articles cited (as well as many others). After reading these three articles it was noted that there was considerable merit on both sides of the postexperimental questionnaire debate. Extensive postexperimental questionnaires could lead to the false reporting of suspicions from naive subjects under certain circumstances. Similarly, very general and nonprobing questionnaires could certainly fail to detect truly suspicious subjects.

The author remembered reading other social psychological research pertaining to the increase of participant's honesty when there is a specific request made by the experimenter for his or her honesty (Silverman, 1977). The author was actually surprised when he completed an exhaustive literature search that he was unable to find a single citation that had combined these ideas. By simply combining the two areas (funnel-type postexperimental questionnaires with a personal plea for the participant's honesty) the author was able to develop a specific research strategy to answer a specific research question. He developed a paradigm showing the relative merits of both postexperimental notions while, and at the same time, he uncovered a method that would be superior in reducing the reporting of false negative and false positive suspicions. The research idea ultimately conceived led to the author's dissertation and then to publication.

The author possesses no special insight into psychology and research. He, like his graduate counterparts, experienced considerable anxiety thinking about the inevitability of a dissertation topic. It was just a matter of finding an area in which he had an interest and following that area of interest to its logical conclusion. There is really nothing magical about idea generation at all. As we have been suggesting all along, you do not have to be a genius to develop a well-conceived research idea. You do not have to be overly sagacious either. By simply trying to answer a previously unanswered question, you can become a first-rate idea generator. You simply need to recognize a problem or void in contemporary research and then develop a simple strategy to answer that problem or fill that void. This is usually accomplished by reading published research. That is exactly what you have been doing while working through this text.

THINK IT THROUGH

Was the author able to cover all of the concerns relating to postexperimental questionnaires in this one study? Let us examine this article more closely and answer some specific questions related to the article. Investigating these initial questions will help make certain that we are quite familiar with the topics covered in the article.

1. What was studied in this article and why was it studied?
2. How was it studied?
3. What were the two differing viewpoints concerning postexperimental questionnaires posed by Berkowitz and Staats versus Page and Scheidt?
4. Do you believe postexperimental questionnaires are necessary in assessing suspicions on the part of participants within the framework of a deception experiment? Why or why not?
5. Do you think each of the two different views on postexperimental questionnaires have some validity? How could they both have validity?
6. What ethical concerns did the author confront in conducting the research? Were the ethical concerns adequately addressed?

One of the more interesting situations in psychological research is when there are two differing viewpoints to the same problem. This tends to be common in psychology, as it is in most behavioral and social sciences, since psychological results are often determined by the methods employed by the experimenter. Different methods often lead to different results. This is particularly true in the present study. In most instances of such conflicting viewpoints, both sides have some merit. This, then, would open the door for research ideas that try to bring the two conflicting views into harmony.

The Berkowitz and Staats argument is suggesting detailed postexperimental questionnaires in and of themselves are methods of developing false suspicions in otherwise naive participants. Page and Scheidt, on the other hand,

believes the only accurate means of assessing suspicions on the part of participants is to have very detailed, funnel-type questionnaires. Anything less is going
to open the experiment to logical criticism as to its validity.

Both sides are right! The general questionnaire is not sufficient to elicit
true suspicions in every instance (supporting Page and Scheidt), whereas the funnel questionnaire can elicit false suspicions on the part of some subjects (supporting Berkowitz and Staats). The ideal would be a procedure where we are able
to minimize the reporting of false suspicions while maximizing the reporting of
true suspicions. The problem, then, is simple: how do we develop a method
that will satisfy both camps? That is exactly what the current article attempted
to accomplish.

If you have an interest in this area (combining two opposing points of
view) we would suggest having you go to the library and read a social psychology text. Or, take a social psychology course. You will find enough conflicting
material to keep you in research ideas for the rest of your professional life. This
does not mean that social psychology has no idea what it is doing. On the contrary. Social psychology has considerably increased our general knowledge of
behavior. There are, however, many different approaches to the same problem
often resulting in conflicting results. Such conflicting results can give you a
cornucopia of ideas to research.

THINK IT THROUGH

Instead of studying the efficacy of postexperimental questionnaires within
the context of a supposed racial prejudice study what other types studies
could we use? Could we do the same study using weapons as the purported purpose of the study (as with Berkowitz's study)? If we did, would
this introduce any extraneous variables needing control? Or, could we
employ a similar paradigm under the auspices of some type of helping
behavior? That is, could we have a confederate relate to a prospective
participant the research in which they are about to take part is not really
about attraction as the experimenter would have him or her believe but
is instead about the likelihood of him or her helping a person suppos-
edly in some type of need. How could we study the postexperimental
questionnaire problem in a real-life situation?

What about gender and ethnicity? Do these two variables create differences in the results we would find on our postexperimental questionnaires?
The study presented used only males as participants. The reason for this was
to minimize the number of independent variables under investigation. Could
we redesign this study and use both genders? If we did, do you think we would
get different results from the two groups? Would males or females be more

likely to inform the experimenter of the illicit information received? What if we used male and female experimenters? Would participants be more likely to disclose the information received to one gender versus the other? Likewise, what if we varied the race of the experimenter and or the participants? What types of results would we obtain then?

The possibilities are endless. We could even vary the age of the participants. Are younger people (say under the age of 10) more or less likely to report remarks from a confederate when compared to older individuals (say people in their thirties)? We are only limited by the type of participants we have at our disposal and the time we want to invest. We could actually investigate all of these variables. Or could we?

THINK IT THROUGH

Let us assume you are a researcher wanting the definitive answer to all possible variations within the postexperimental questionnaire paradigm. You are interested in the gender of the participant and experimenter, the age of the participant, ethnicity on the part of the participant and experimenter, as well as the type of postexperimental questionnaire and different pleas for honesty. Would it be pragmatic to study all of these various variables? What would happen if you had two levels of gender of the experimenter (male, female), two levels of gender of participant (male, female), five levels of race of experimenter (African American, Native American, Asian American, Hispanic, Caucasian), the same five levels of race of participants, two levels of postexperimental questionnaire (general, funnel), two levels of age of participant (under the age of 10, over the age of 30) and two levels of pleas for honesty (control, personal). What would happen if you were to study all of these different variables at the same time?

Such a study would be a nightmare. Why? Could you actually manipulate all of the suggested variables? Probably not. It is unlikely you would be able to request specific races to participate without raising additional suspicions on the part of the participants as to what the study is investigating (i.e., increasing the demand characteristics of the study). And, assuming that you could, you would be working with a $2 \times 2 \times 5 \times 5 \times 2 \times 2 \times 2$ factorial design. How would one interpret any significant differences of the main effect in such a study? Even harder would be trying to interpret any interaction effect. Trying to research all possible combinations is just not practical. We must necessarily limit our concerns to those few variables that are of most concern to us.

THINK IT THROUGH

How could you use animals in investigating postexperimental question-naires? What type of animals could you use?

Using animals might, at first, seem to be an impossible method with the present study. However, it can be done! We could use a purported animal study (having students think the study is really about training pigeons to peck at a particular stimulus) and then have a confederate reveal the study is really about honesty and not pigeon pecking at all. By comparing the results of this study with studies using human participants we would be able to answer the question of when participants are more likely to reveal to experimenters the receiving of illicit information: when the study is using animals or when it is using humans. We might just come away with some interesting results!

Approaching this study from a different perspective, we could use our postexperimental questionnaires to investigate the following questions:

1. Are participants more or less likely to disclose receiving information from a confederate when the postexperimental questionnaire being used is in written form or when it is done face-to-face?
2. How detailed must a postexperimental questionnaire be in order to achieve its goal? Are three or four questions sufficient or do we need a questionnaire with eight or nine questions?
3. What do researchers feel about using postexperimental questionnaires? Do they believe it is worth the effort? Do they feel that such procedures are too intrusive?
4. What would the effect be where students are required to participate in several deception experiments each using personal pleas for honesty in disclosing suspicions? Would there be some type of habituation effect which would minimize the effect of the personal plea?

Finally, are there any ethical concerns when conducting deception experiments? As we discussed in Chapter 2, deception manipulations must be disclosed as soon as possible and the experiment must not induce any undue physical and/or psychological harm. Deception was used in the present experiment. It was felt it could not be avoided. The experimenter did obtain appropriate permission to proceed with the study by his university's institutional review board, he used appropriate methods, and he debriefed all participants as to the true nature of the experiment and why deception was employed. Thus, it appears all ethical concerns were anticipated and dealt with. We always must be highly concerned with ethics no matter what type of study we are conducting.

THINK IT THROUGH

List five ideas that are related to those mentioned above that can be researched and list three novel ideas (not related to any of the above) that could also be researched. What types of materials and time would each of these eight areas require? Are there any ethical concerns in the studies you have proposed? If so, how can you go about eliminating these concerns?

Related ideas:

1. _____

2. _____

3. _____

4. _____

5. _____

Novel ideas:

1. _____

2. _____

3. _____

After writing down your various research ideas, have one of your professors read them and give you additional and alternate suggestions. If this is indeed an area of research in which you have an interest, you will find it exciting to develop and pursue your idea to fruition with the aid of your favorite professor and your ethics committee.

There are some additional readings you can review if you are interested in pursuing research in this area. We have listed several that should be of interest to you. And, do not hesitate to ask your professor for additional suggestions.

REFERENCES

Berkowitz, L. (1971). The weapons effect, demand characteristics, and the myth of the compliant subject. *Journal of Social and Personality Psychology, 20,* 332–338.

Horvat, Joesph. (1986). Detection of suspiciousness as a function of pleas for honesty. *Journal of Personality and Social Psychology, 50,* 921–924.

Page M. M. and Scheidt. R. H. (1971). The elusive weapons effect: Demand awareness, evaluation apprehension, and slightly sophisticated subjects. *Journal of Personality and Social Psychology, 91,* 305–323.

Silverman, I. (1977). *The human subject in the psychological laboratory.* New York: Pergamon Press.

Staats, A. (1969) Experimental demand characteristics and the classical conditioning of attitudes. *Journal of Personality and Social Psychology, 11,* 187–192.

ADDITIONAL READINGS

Kelman, H. C. (1967). Human use of human subjects: The problem of deception in social psychological experiments. *Psychological Bulletin, 67,* 1–11.

Orne, M. T. (1962). On the social psychology of the psychological experiment: With particular reference to demand characteristics and their implications. *American Psychologist, 17,* 776–783.

CHAPTER 11

Some of the Best Research Ideas Come from Students

Do not think because you are "just a student" you cannot have important research ideas. The original idea on which the articles for this chapter are built was generated by a student. Yes, students *frequently* have excellent research ideas.

The ongoing research project described in the following articles had its inception toward the end of a fall day several years ago. Many of the students had left for the day; only a few individuals who were conducting research projects remained in the psychology department. A teaching assistant stopped in to chat after completing her daily research session. She was not in a pleasant mood because she had witnessed several students cheating on a test she gave that morning. The intensity of her indignation and her interest in the topic suggested academic dishonesty might be a worthwhile area to research. Following two subsequent conversations, the tentative outlines of a research project began to emerge.

THINK IT THROUGH

Imagine you are participating on one of these initial research meetings. What are some of the issues likely to be discussed. How will you resolve the questions that arise?

The topics of discussion at these formative sessions included consideration of such issues as how to define and measure academic dishonesty, who the participants would be, and the information that would be gathered. Following some pilot testing on our own campus to help refine our survey, we expanded our efforts and began to survey students at other schools. The following article describes how we answered the questions that came up at those initial research meetings. We hope you find the project and our results interesting.

Academic Dishonesty: Prevalence, Determinants, Techniques, and Punishments

Stephen F. Davis
Emporia State University

Cathy A. Grover
Texas A&M University

Angela H. Becker
Texas A&M University

Loretta N. McGregor
Southern Arkansas University

Data from more than 6,000 students regarding the prevalence, causes, techniques, faculty and institutional responsibility, deterrent measures, and punishment dimensions of academic dishonesty are presented.

Academic dishonesty is a perennial problem in higher education. Although scholarly reports of academic dishonesty have appeared for more than 60 years, a concerted research effort was mounted only during the past 20 years. This increased interest may reflect the fact that "cheating has become one of the major problems in education today" (Singhal, 1982, p. 775). For example, Haines, Diekhoff, LaBeff, and Clark (1986) stated that "student dishonesty on college campuses throughout the nation has been widely recognized as epidemic" (p. 342).

Published accounts suggest that these statements may be accurate and that cheating has escalated recently. Drake (1941) reported a cheating rate of 23%, whereas Goldsen, Rosenberg, William, and Suchman (1960) reported rates of 38% and 49% for 1952 and 1960, respectively. Hetherington and Feldman (1964) and Baird (1980) reported cheating rates of 64% and 76%, respectively. Jendreck (1989) placed the typical rate between 40% and 60% but noted other rates as high as 82% (Stern & Havlicek, 1986) and 88% (Sierles, Hen-

Used by permission of Lawrence Erlbaum Associates, Publishers.

drickx, & Circle, 1980). Clearly, we need more research designed to understand academic dishonesty and how to deal with it.

METHOD

Four years ago, we developed a 21-item survey. Students take 10 to 15 min to complete the questionnaire anonymously. The first three questions deal with general attitudes toward cheating. For example, Question 1 asks "Is it 'wrong' to cheat?," and Question 2 is "Should students go ahead and cheat if they know they can get away with it?" Question 3 asks "Should students try to cheat even when they know that their chances of getting away with it are very slim?"

Question 4 deals with whether the student has cheated in high school and/or college. If the answer is yes, students answer Question 5 about how they cheated. Question 6 through 9 ask whether the student has been caught cheating, who detected the incident, the penalty involved, and if the student had knowledge of the penalty before cheating.

Questions 10 through 13 concern students' intent when allowing someone else to cheat from their exam. Questions 14 through 18 ask students to react to two hypothetical situations that entail either little or much effort and preparation for a test.

Question 19 taps students' opinions about the instructor's concern with cheating. Questions 20 and 21 concern appropriate measures for preventing cheating and dealing with offenders. This questionnaire has been administered to more than 6,000 students at large state schools ($n = 8$), medium state schools ($n = 8$), large private schools ($n = 5$), small private schools ($n = 8$), and 2-year schools ($n = 6$).

PREVALENCE

Most students say that it is wrong to cheat. For example, the percentage of students answering yes to the question "Is it wrong to cheat?" has never been below 90%. This opinion contrasts sharply with the mean percentage of students who report having cheated in either high school or college or both (76%). Rates of cheating in high school range from 51% reported by women at a small state university to 83% reported by men at a large state university. These high school cheating rates are to be contrasted with those reported at the collegiate level. A low of 9% was reported by one sample of women at a small private liberal arts college; a high of 64% was reported by men at a small regional university. There is a significant decrease in the incidence of cheating from high school to college, smallest $\chi^2(1, N = 183) = 3.96$, $p < .05$. Except for extending the range of collegiate cheating downward, our data are similar to those reported by Jendrick (1989).

Gender and institutional affiliation influence cheating. Women consistently report lower cheating rates that men in high school and college. This difference was statistically reliable, smallest $\chi^2(1, N = 167) = 4.61$, $p < .05$, in all but one instance. The percentages of men and women at small, private liberal arts colleges who reported having cheated in college are significantly lower, smallest $\chi^2(1, N = 218) = 4.23$, $p < .05$, than those reported by their counterparts at larger state and private institutions.

DETERMINANTS

What factors influence academic dishonesty? Are certain students more likely to cheat than others?

Situational Determinants of Cheating

Drake (1941) suggested that stress and the pressure for good grades are important determinants of academic dishonesty. Keller (1976) reported that 69% of the students in his study cited pressure for good grades as a major reason for cheating. Baird (1980) and Barnett and Dalton (1981) indicated that these pressures are important and that faculty members may not fully comprehend the stress experienced by their students.

Large, crowded classes that use only multiple-choice exams foster cheating (Houston, 1976). Computerized test banks that enable instructors to scramble the order of test questions may help alleviate this problem.

Answers to Question 5 suggest why students allow other students access to their answers during an exam. The most popular reason, "because he/she was a friend," was cited by a low of 76% in one sample and a high of 88% in another. On a positive note, the percentage of students allowing others to cheat for monetary considerations ranged from a low of .30% to a high of only 8.00%. A sampling of some other reasons is interesting and instructive because such statement reflects similar comments by several students.

1. He was bigger than me.
2. I knew they needed to do good in order to pass the class. I felt sorry for them.
3. I wouldn't want them to be mad at me.
4. She was damn good-looking.
5. Because they might let me cheat off of them sometime.
6. No particular reason. It doesn't bother me because I probably have it wrong and so will they.
7. I knew they studied and knew the material, but test taking was really difficult.
8. Just to do it. I didn't like the teacher, and I knew if I got caught nothing would happen.

Keith-Spiegel (1990) corroborated several of these sentiments. For example, she indicated that.

1. We put a lot of pressures on our students.
2. Young people see huge reinforcing properties in cheating. It's everywhere.
3. A new view of academic ownership appears to be emerging among our students. One student thought that buying a term paper justified his claiming somebody else's work as his own.
4. Our students have a new view about cheating. One respondent saw nothing wrong with a student cheating from another student's exam when the two had arranged a collusion.

Dispositional Determinants of Cheating

Students' beliefs that "everyone cheats" (Houston, 1976, p. 301) or that cheating is a normal part of life (Baird, 1980) encourage cheating. The adage "cheaters never win" may not apply in the case of academic dishonesty. With cheating rates as high as 75% to 87% (e.g., Baird, 1980; Jendreck, 1989) and detection rates as low as 1.30% (Haines et al., 1986), academic dishonesty is reinforced, not punished. Even when cheating is detected, swift and appropriate punishment may not follow. Singhal (1982) suggested ". . . that most educational units in a college do not pay adequate attention to cheating and moreover do not have techniques to deal with cheating if it is detected" (p. 775).

Personality research has identified some characteristics of those who cheat. For example, students with lower intelligence cheat more than students with higher intelligence (Hetherington & Feldman, 1964; Johnson & Gormly, 1971; Kelly & Worrell, 1978). Crowne and Marlowe (1964) reported a positive relation between the need for social approval and frequency of cheating. Eve and Bromley (1981) reported a negative relation between internalized social control and frequency of cheating. Eisenberger and Shank (1985) demonstrated that students with a high personal work ethic were more resistant to cheating that students with a low personal work ethic.

Results from studies of the relation between gender and academic dishonesty are inconsistent. Several authors (e.g., Hetherington & Feldmen, 1964; Johnson & Gormly, 1971; Kelly & Worrell, 1978; Roskens & Dizney, 1966) reported higher levels of cheating by men, but Jacobson, Berger, and Millham (1970) reported the opposite outcome. Several others (e.g., Fischer, 1970; Houston, 1977; Karabenick & Srull, 1978; Vitro & Schoer, 1972) observed no reliable gender differences. Our data support the proposition that men cheat more than women.

Responses to the two hypothetical situations that involved cheating from another person's examination (Questions 14 to 18) indicated that women reacted more intensely than men. On a scale ranging from *that's great* (1) to *very angry* (7), women had significantly higher scores, smallest $F(1, 468) = 5.72$,

$p < .05$, than did men. The lowest mean for women was 5.06 for Question 13: "What would your reaction be if you were to find out that a classmate has been, is presently, or plans to cheat on an exam?"

The hypothetical situations also showed that different situations engendered different degrees of emotionality. When students perceived the situation as innocuous, they reported lower anger scores. Thus, Question 15—"Given that 'You have not studied well for your exam and at best you only know the material well enough to earn a D,' how would you feel about someone else cheating off of your paper?"—yielded means from a low of 4.73 for one sample of men to a high of 5.57 for one sample of women. When cheating was perceived as having a direct bearing on or relation to the respondent, anger increased. Thus, Question 18—"Given that 'You have put many hours into studying for your test and you are certain you are going to get a very high grade,' how would you feel about a student cheating and doing better than you?"—yielded means from a low of 5.85 for one sample of men to a high of 6.63 for one sample of women.

CHEATING TECHNIQUES

To catch the academic thieves, we must know their modus operandi. Our surveys indicated that approximately 80% of the cheaters copied from a nearby paper or used crib notes. The remaining 20% provided some food for thought. Items 1 to 5 represent composite statements; Items 6 to 9 are unique approaches to cheating:

1. We worked out a system of hand and feet positions.
2. Each corner of the desk top matched an answer—A, B, C, or D. We simply touched the corner we thought was the right answer.
3. I had a copy of the test and looked up the answers ahead of time and memorized them.
4. We traded papers during the test and compared answers.
5. Opened my book and looked up the answers.
6. I hid a calculator down my pants.
7. The answers were taped recorded before the test and I just took my Walkman to class and listened to the answers during the test.
8. I've done everything from writing all the way up my arm to having notes in a plastic bag inside my mouth.
9. I would make a paper flower, write notes on it, and then pin it on my blouse.

This sample of methods indicates that faculty members may not be able to afford the luxury of reading a book, writing, or grading papers during an examination. If we could only harness these students' creative energies in a more productive manner!

FACULTY AND INSTITUTIONAL RESPONSIBILITY

Question 19 deals with whether faculty should be concerned with academic dishonesty. The concept of scholastic integrity provides a compelling affirmative. Paradoxically, students who cheat agree. No sample produced fewer than 90% "yes" answers to the question "Should an instructor care whether or not students cheat on an exam?"

Unfortunately, such concerns may not always be translated into appropriate actions. For example, Keith-Spiegel (1990) reported that 21% of her faculty respondents had ignored evidence of cheating and that 30% of this number believed that this was an appropriate reaction. What prompts such reactions from faculty? Confronting students in these situations creates possibly undesirable consequences. A student's career may be ruined. The faculty member may become entangled in lengthy litigation. Like students' views about ownership of term papers and the appropriateness of cheating, faculty views about detection and intervention may have changed.

DISCOURAGING CHEATING IN THE CLASSROOM

Question 20 is "What measures will deter or discourage cheating in the classroom?" Regardless of the size and type of institution, our respondents had definite ideas about what should be done. The most desirable deterrent was the use of separate forms of the test. This measure was followed closely by these preferred deterrents (in order of preference):

1. Simply informing the students why they should not cheat.
2. Arranging seating so that students are separated by empty desks.
3. Walking up and down the rows during the test.
4. Constantly watching the students.

The less preferred deterrents (in order of preference) included:

1. Announcing "do not cheat."
2. Having assigned seats.
3. Having all essay exams.
4. Requiring students to leave their belongings outside the classroom during an examination.

Preferred deterrents, such as having separate forms of the exam and separating students by an empty desk, have merit. In contrast, unless faculty do not routinely discuss cheating with each class, one must question the impact of simply informing students why they should not cheat. Common sense suggests that some of the less preferred methods might be effective, but implementing them can be difficult. For example, students dislike taking all essay tests, and faculty dislike grading them. Personal items might be left in the front of the lecture hall, but retrieving them as the students finish their examinations may cause undue commotion. Legitimate reasons for not having assigned seats are less obvious.

PUNISHMENT

Question 21 is "What should be done if someone is caught cheating?" Substantial percentages of our samples believed that nothing should be done until after the test. This way one's class is not disrupted and the culprit is not publicly humiliated. Delayed action is a less effective deterrent and may even signal tacit condonation.

The most popular "punishment" suggested by our respondents was for the instructor to tell students to keep their eyes on their own paper. The efficacy of this approach is questionable. Likewise, one might question the advisability of simply taking the test away and allowing the student to start over. Nevertheless, more than 20% of the students endorsed these two options. Perhaps the students favoring these alternatives are those who have cheated.

Another 20% endorsed giving a failing grade to someone caught cheating. This viewpoint may represent the opinion of those who have not cheated.

CONCLUSIONS

Our results indicate that several factors are important determinants of cheating. For example, in addition to pressures for good grades, students stress, ineffective deterrents, and condoning teachers, our respondents demonstrate a diminishing sense of academic integrity.

Consider also data that appeared in the October 30, 1989 issue of *Newsweek.* The Pinnacle Group, Inc., an international public relations firms, surveyed 1,093 high school seniors about how far they would stretch ethical standards to get ahead in the business world. Some results of this survey were:

1. When asked if they would be willing to face 6 months probation on an illegal deal in which they made $10 million, 59% of the students responded either "definitely yes" or "maybe."
2. Thirty-six percent indicated they would plagiarize in order to pass a certification test.
3. Sixty-seven percent said they would inflate their business-expense reports.
4. Fifty percent said they would exaggerate on an insurance damage report.
5. Sixty-six percent said they would lie to achieve a business objective.
6. Forty percent indicated they would accept a gift from a supplier worth more than $100; 23% would accept $500 in cash from a supplier; 32% would accept a free vacation.

These alarming results are consistent with statements from several of our respondents. One student said: "Generally when someone cheats, it's like adultery. What they don't know, ain't going to hurt 'em." Another student said: "I will never be caught." Still another student indicated that "cheating in high school is for grades, cheating in college is for a career." Clearly, many students in the Pinnacle Group survey and in our samples lack integrity, academic or otherwise. Hence, their behavior is influenced by external pressures.

Forsyth, Pope, and McMillan (1985) reported an attributional analysis of academic dishonesty. When they compared the causal inferences of cheaters and noncheaters, the external attributions of cheaters were significantly greater than those of noncheaters. Equally relevant is their finding that external attributions made by the cheaters for the dishonest act were significantly greater in number than those made by a group of uninvolved observers. In short, cheaters excuse their cheating.

Although preventive measures deter cheating in specific situations, they will not succeed in the long run. Only when students develop a stronger commitment to the educational process and when they possess or activate an internalized code of ethics that opposes cheating will the problem have been dealt with effectively. Achieving this goal is unlikely as long as the educational system remains unchanged.

Before our students will internalize standards and apply them, the institutions and their faculties must openly and uniformly support such ethical behaviors. According to Fass (1986),

> Academic and professional ethics must be widely understood and supported throughout the institution if a college or university is to be regarded as a community in which it is legitimate to hold students to the highest standards of behavior in their academic works. (p. 35)

Is your college such an institution? Recent data suggest that many colleges and universities do not belong in this category. Academic dishonesty policies at various institutions were studied by collecting a sample of 200 college catalogs (Weaver, Davis, Look, Buzzanga, & Neal, in press). The catalogs containing information about responsibility indicated that faculty were obligated to inform students of academic dishonesty policies. Hence, written policies confirm the students' sentiments that faculty members should be concerned with academic dishonesty. However, the strength of this obligation may not be pervasive. Of the 200 catalogs surveyed, only 55% (63 public institutions and 47 private institutions) contained relevant policy statements. Although catalogs are not the only printed source for such policies, a disturbing message is that many institutions may not wish to become involved in such matters. Hence, responsibility is deferred to individual departments and faculty members. In addition to the mixed messages that independent policies send to students, Keith-Spiegel's (1990) report suggests how individual faculty may choose to view this situation.

According to Fass (1986),

> If a policy academic dishonesty does not exist already, a college or university should undertake to develop one. This process will focus attention and discussion on the ethical issues involved, and will provide a basis for regular, ongoing education about academic ethics. If the institutions are reluctant to address this issue and assume responsibility, who can fault the faculty for following suit? (p. 35)

The challenge is clear. Are institutions and their faculties willing to accept it?

REFERENCES

Baird, J. S., Jr. (1980). Current trends in college cheating. *Psychology in the Schools, 17,* 515–522.

Barnett, D. C., & Dalton, J. C. (1981). Why college students cheat. *Journal of College Student Personnel, 22,* 545–551.

Crowne, D. P., & Marlowe, D. (1964). *The approval motive.* New York: Wiley.

Drake, C. A. (1941). Why students cheat. *Journal of Higher Education, 12,* 418–420.

Eisenberger, R., & Shank, D. M. (1985). Personal work ethic and effort training affect cheating. *Journal of Personality and Social Psychology, 49,* 520–528.

Eve, R., & Bromley, D. G. (1981). Scholastic dishonesty among college undergraduates: Parallel test of two sociological explanations. *Youth and Society, 13,* 3–22.

Fass, R. A. (1986). By honor bound: Encouraging academic honesty. *Educational Record, 67,* 32–35.

Fischer, C. T. (1970). Levels of cheating under conditions of informative appeal to honesty, public affirmation of value and threats of punishment. *Journal of Educational Research, 64,* 12–16.

Forsyth, D. R., Pope, W. R., & McMillan, J. H. (1985). Students' reactions after cheating: An attributional analysis. *Contemporary Educational Psychology, 10,* 72–82.

Goldsen, R. K., Rosenberg, M., William, R., Jr., & Suchman, E. (1960). *What college students think.* Princeton, NJ: Van Nostrand.

Haines, V. J., Diekhoff, G. M., LaBeff, E. E., & Clark, R. E. (1986). College cheating: Immaturity, lack of commitment, and the neutralizing attitude. *Research in Higher Education, 25,* 342–354.

Hetherington, E. M., & Feldman, S. E. (1964). College cheating as a function of subject and situational variables. *Journal of Educational Psychology, 55,* 212–218.

Houston, J. P. (1976). The assessment and prevention of answer copying on undergraduate multiple-choice examinations. *Research in Higher Education, 5,* 301–311.

Houston, J. P. (1977). Four components of Rotter's internal–external scale and cheating behavior. *Contemporary Educational Psychology, 2,* 275–283.

Jacobson, L. I., Berger, S. E., & Millham, J. (1970). Individual differences in cheating during a temptation period when confronting failure. *Journal of Personality and Social Psychology, 15,* 48–56.

Jendreck, M. P. (1989). Faculty reactions to academic dishonesty. *Journal of College Student Development, 30,* 401–406.

Johnson, C. D., & Gormly, J. (1971). Achievement, sociability and task importance in relation to academic cheating. *Psychological Reports, 28,* 302.

Karabenick, S. A., & Srull, T. K. (1978). Effects of personality and situational variation in locus of control on cheating: Determinants of the "congruence effect." *Journal of Personality, 46,* 72–95.

Keith-Spiegel, P. (1990, April). *Ethical conflicts between students and professors.* Paper presented at the annual meeting of the Western Psychological Association, Los Angeles.

Keller, M. (1976, August). Academic dishonesty at Miami. *Student Life Research, Miami University,* pp. 1–16.

Kelly, J. A., & Worrell, L. (1978). Personality characteristics, parent behaviors, and sex of the subject in relation to cheating. *Journal of Research in Personality, 12,* 179–188.

Roskens, R. W., & Dizney, H. F. (1966). A study of unethical behavior in high school and college. *The Journal of Educational Research, 59,* 321–324.

Sierles, F., Hendrickx, I., & Circle, S. (1980) Cheating in medical school. *Journal of Medical Education, 55,* 124–125.

Singhal, A. C. (1982). Factors in students' dishonesty. *Psychological Reports, 51,* 775–780.

Stern, E. B., & Havlicek, L. (1986). Academic misconduct: Results of faculty and undergraduate student surveys. *Journal of Allied Health, 5,* 129–142.

Vitro, F. T., & Schoer, L. A. (1972). The effects of probability of test success, test importance, and risk of detection on the incidence of cheating. *Journal of School Psychology, 10,* 269–277.

Weaver, K. A., Davis, S. F., Look, C. T., Buzzanga, V. L., & Neal, L. (in press). Academic dishonesty in college catalogs. *College Student Journal.*

NOTES

1. We thank Charles L. Brewer and three anonymous reviewers for their excellent suggestions and their patience in the preparation of this article.

2. Requests for reprints, copies of the cheating survey, and more extensive data sets should be sent to Stephen F. Davis, Department of Psychology, Emporia State University, Emporia, KS 66801.

THINK IT THROUGH

To ensure you have a good grasp of this article, here are some questions to answer.

1. How was academic dishonesty defined? Why was it defined in this manner?

2. How was academic dishonesty measured? Why was this method selected? What potential problem is associated with this method of measurement?

3. How did the respondents feel about cheating? Was there anything paradoxical about their feelings and their behavior?

4. What is the relationship between size of school and prevalence of cheating in college?

5. What two most methods are used most frequently to cheat on exams? What are some of the more unusual methods that have been used?

6. Why was the survey administered to such a large number of students at such a variety of schools?

Academic dishonesty was defined as cheating on an examination. This definition was adopted in order to make the research manageable. Can you imagine how immense the project would have been if we attempted to conduct research on *all* aspects of academic dishonesty? What other forms of academic dishonesty could we have investigated? In addition to cheating on an exam, we also would have to consider plagiarism, copying homework, changing (or completely fabricating) data on laboratory reports, and turning in term papers that were purchased. Studying cheating on examinations has proved sufficient to support active research in this area for 10 years. These other topics await research.

Self-report was used to measure cheating. Although other techniques that involved the actual detection of cheating could have been employed, we selected self-report because of its ease and convenience. The researcher can obtain responses from a much larger sample of participants if all that is required is the distribution, completion, and retrieval of surveys. The major problem associated with this procedure (as we have discussed in previous chapters) concerns the validity of the responses. The researcher has no way of knowing if the respondents are being truthful; they may well be cheating on a cheating survey!

What about the feelings and behaviors of the respondents? Even though no sample fell below 90 percent in answering *yes* to the question "Is it wrong to cheat?" the respondents' behaviors were not in agreement. Over 50 percent of the students sampled reported cheating in high school. Substantial numbers reported cheating in college.

Is the same rate of cheating found at all colleges and universities? No. Analysis of the responses revealed a negative relation between size of school and amount of self-reported cheating. Students at small, private liberal arts colleges reported the lowest rates of cheating on examinations.

Although a variety of cheating techniques were reported by the respondents, the two most popular ones were copying from another student's paper and using cheat sheets. Among the other, more unusual techniques were writing notes on a paper flower that was pinned on the blouse, using a system of hand and feet positions to indicate questions and answers, hiding a calculator down one's pants, and tape recording the answers prior to the examination and then listening to the answers during the examination.

Why was the survey administered to such a large number of students (over 6,000) at so many different schools? We were intimately concerned with *external validity*—the ability to generalize results beyond the specific participants in a study and the setting in which the research was conducted. By testing a large number of participants at a variety of schools across the country, we hoped to increase the external validity of our project.

THINK IT THROUGH

Now it's your turn to generate some additional research ideas. Carefully consider the article you have just finished reading. There are at least two questions we failed to ask with this piece of research. What are these questions? Are there any other issues that should be investigated?

Although the findings that as many as 83 percent of the respondents had cheated in high school and as many as 64 percent had cheated in college were disturbing, we finally realized that figures such as these did not, by themselves, provide a complete picture of cheating on examinations. We had forgotten to include a question about *frequency* of cheating on our original survey! In short, we had no way of telling how many respondents were repeat offenders or the number of repeat offenses these respondents committed.

A closer inspection of our data indicated that even though we had acquired considerable knowledge concerning the more general pressures or determinants that resulted in cheating, we really had little information concerning the specific reasons *why* students cheated. Obviously, further research was needed! When you conduct a piece of research, you often, if not always, will find the results of one study suggest additional studies that need to be done. Research is ongoing. None of the research presented in this text is definitive; rather, it is a self-perpetuating process.

Because the focus of the follow-up study necessitated the addition of questions to ascertain the number of repeat offenders and the number of offenses they committed, we decided to critically examine the entire survey that was used in the first study. As a result of this scrutiny, the survey was reduced from 21 to 7 items. We feel the revised survey, which takes 10 minutes to complete, adequately addresses the main issues concerning cheating on examinations we are interested in studying. Several years later, we are still using the revised survey.

In the following article, you will see how we answered the questions of the number of repeat offenders and the number of offenses they commit. Read carefully; we will have some questions for you once you have finished.

Additional Data on Academic Dishonesty and a Proposal for Remediation

Stephen F. Davis
Emporia State University

H. Wayne Ludvigson
Texas Christian University

In this article, we present data from 2,153 upper division undergraduate students regarding the frequency of cheating, reasons for cheating, and influence of penalties on cheating. We also discuss how a model that develops an internalized code of ethics will counteract academic dishonesty.

Cheating has become a major concern on many college campuses (Fishbein, 1993; Haines, Diekhoff, LaBeff, & Clark, 1986; Singhal, 1982). Jendreck (1989) and Davis, Grover, Becker, and McGregor (1992) indicated that between 40% and 60% of their student respondents reported cheating on at least one examination. McCabe and Bowers (1994) corroborated these data at non-honor-code institutions, but they found that students at institutions having honor codes had lower self-reported cheating rates. In addition, Davis et al. reported that students at small, private liberal arts colleges reported lower cheating rates.

Davis et al. (1992) and McCabe and Bowers (1994) also discussed techniques used to cheat. Although the most popular techniques were copying from a nearby paper and using crib notes, more unusual techniques included trading papers during the test or using intricate patterns of hand and foot position.

Most of the students in Davis et al.'s (1992) study thought that instructors should care whether students cheat. To discourage cheating during a test, students favored the instructor's use of separate forms of the test, informing students about the penalties for cheating, separating students by an empty desk, walking up and down the rows, and constantly watching the students.

Although Davis et al.'s (1992) study provided information about the percentage of cheaters, cheating techniques, and in-class deterrents, it provided no information about the number of repeat offenders or the number of repeated offenses. In this study, we corrected this deficit. The fear of being caught and the influence that this fear has on one's decision to cheat also received attention in this study, as did the effect of announcing strict penalties at the beginning of the semester. Finally, we sought to ascertain why students cheat.

METHOD

Participants

A total of 2,153 undergraduates (675 men and 1,478 women) enrolled in upper division courses voluntarily participated in this study. All students were classified as either juniors or seniors and were surveyed during regular class sessions.

Materials

We devised a seven-item questionnaire that takes 10 min or less to complete. The first two questions dealt with whether the respondent had cheated at least once, the frequency of cheating, and whether the person had been caught cheating in high school (Question 1) and college (Question 2). Question 3 required a yes or no answer to the question, "Do you fear being caught cheating?" If the respondents answered yes to Question 3, they rated this fear on a 7-point scale ranging from *minimally fearful* (1) to *very fearful* (7). Using a 7-point scale ranging from *minimal influence* (1) to *great influence* (7), they further indicated (Question 4) the extent to which this fear influences whether they will cheat.

Students also responded yes or no to Question 5, "If a professor has strict penalties for cheating and informs the class about them at the beginning of the semester, would this prevent you from cheating?" Question 6 requested a listing of penalties most likely to prevent the individual from cheating. The final question dealt with reasons for cheating. The respondents also provided information about their sex; age; academic major; year in school; and if they hold a job (if so, they were asked to list the number of hours they work each week). All questionnaires were completed anonymously.

Procedure

The 71 samples were obtained from private and public institutions located in 11 different states. The class size of the 71 classes surveyed ranged from 19 to 53 students. Enrollment at the institutions surveyed ranged from approximately 3,000 to more than 30,000. A faculty contact at each institution assumed responsibility for distributing, collecting, and returning the informed consent documents and completed questionnaires. All data were gathered in accord with institutional review board principles at all participating institutions.

RESULTS

Frequency of Cheating

More than 70% in each sample (lowest = 71% and highest = 79) reported cheating in high school, and the percentage of men and women who cheated did not differ. Self-reports of cheating in college fell within the 40% to 60% range (lowest = 42% and highest = 64%). Corroborating Davis et al.'s (1992) results, there was a consistent and reliable trend for a higher percentage of the men in each sample to report cheating in college, $t(140) = 2.07$, $p < .05$.

More than 80% of the students who reported cheating at least once in high school reported cheating on several occasions during high school (lowest = 83% and highest = 88%). Nearly 50% of those in each sample who reported cheating in college also reported doing so on more than one occasion (lowest = 45% and highest = 53%). The average number of transgressions was 7.88 in high school and 4.25 in college. In both instances, more men than women were repeat offenders, smallest $t(140) = 2.13$, $p < .05$.

Virtually all (98.64%) students who reported cheating on several occasions in college had also cheated on several occasions in high school. This result contrasts with the findings that (a) of the students who reported cheating once in high school, only 24.36% reported cheating in college on no more than one occasion; and (b) of the students who did not cheat in high school, only 1.51% reported cheating in college on no more than one occasion.

The Influence of Announced Penalties

In response to the question concerning whether the instructor's announcement of strict penalties at the beginning of the semester would deter cheating, more than 40% of each sample of men responded no (lowest = 42% and highest = 47%). Contrarily, less than 10% of each sample of women answered no to this question (lowest = 4% and highest = 7%). A closer inspection of these no respondents indicated that the majority in each sample reported cheating in college (for men, lowest = 82% and highest = 96% for women, lowest = 93% and highest = 100%).

Reasons for Cheating

The most frequently cited reason for cheating (29.25%) was "I do study, but cheat to enhance my score." "My job cuts down on study time" (14.28%) and "usually don't study" (13.60%) also were frequently cited reasons for cheating.

Other reasons included "I cheat so my GPA looks better to prospective employers" (8.16%), and "I feel pressure from parents to get good grades so I cheat" (6.80%). Various other reasons, such as "pass the class," "class is too hard," "nervous," "only if I'm not sure of my answers," and "if I blank out and someone else's paper is in clear sight," accounted for 18.36% of the reasons for cheating. The number of references to external factors/pressures is noteworthy.

DISCUSSION AND REMEDIATION

One message from these data is clear: Although cheating in college is a major problem that needs attention, there is an equally pressing need to discourage cheaters, especially repeat offenders, in high school. The extrapolation from cheating in college to cheating in real life also has been documented (Sims, 1993). Our data contradict McCabe's contention (see Pavela, 1993) that academic dishonesty is learned during one's collegiate career and is largely determined by its social acceptability at a given institution.

Our data also indicate that, in general, professor-announced penalties have more influence on female students than male students. Moreover, the threat of strict penalties appears to have a greater impact on women who have cheated in college than men who have cheated in college.

Although measures to render cheating difficult, such as those discussed by Davis et al. (1992), should reduce cheating, they do not solve the problem. Indeed, our data suggest that external deterrents will fail in the long run. Alternatively, the existence of ethical–moral–religious systems of social control, from apparently early in our species's history, tell us that only when students have developed a stronger commitment to the educational process and an internalized code of ethics that opposes cheating will the problem be eradicated.

How do we facilitate appropriate internal controls? A Skinnerian analysis (cf. Nye, 1992, p. 65, for a useful discussion) suggests two possible strategies: (a) Manipulate the relevant contingencies of reinforcement, and (b) encourage the learning of relevant rules. In both cases, we aim to produce or strengthen dispositions that naturally resist tendencies to cheat.

Although manipulation of the contingencies of reinforcement surrounding cheating would seem, at first glance, to be difficult, the work of Eisenberger (1992) and Eisenberger and Shank (1985) is encouraging. For example, students trained on high-effort tasks, for which they received only modest reinforcement, displayed substantial resistance to cheating compared with students trained on low-effort tasks (Eisenberger & Shank, 1985). In short, Eisenberger (1992) concluded, from a rich source of data, that long-term training in effortful tasks contributes to durable industriousness, a work ethic that naturally resists cheating. In this context, the spectacle over the last 20 to 30 years of substantial grade inflation and associated pressures to reduce the necessity for effortful student behavior (e.g., through student-controlled contingencies influencing what teachers expect from students, the most obvious being universal student evaluation of teaching) is depressing. If we have an epidemic in cheating, we can apparently lay part of the blame on a deterioration of our own standards for student conduct.

Fishbein (1993) provided another view of manipulating relevant reinforcement contingencies. here he argued that one way to "fundamentally alter [improve] the climate of academic integrity [is] by increasing the volume of cases handled by legitimate university disciplinary procedures and by making enforcement more widespread and equitable" (p. A52). Having codified penalties that take seriousness of offense and number of offenses into account, Fishbeing delineated a streamlined procedure. This proposed system may have merit, but it awaits verification in the academy.

The second strategy, encouraging relevant rule learning or, even better, encouraging a world view, life theory, or philosophy that naturally resists cheating has probably seen diminished use as standards have deteriorated. Resistance to such teaching may arise from an understandable reluctance of instructors to impose their values on others. However, the values implied by a world view that naturally opposes cheating may be nearly universally accepted in all education.

Such a world view relevant to education and opposed to academic dishonesty (Ludvigson, 1992) establishes the goal of understanding as central (necessary but not sufficient) for success and general well-being. Perhaps a casual picture of the following sort would be helpful:

Understanding . . .
    (is required for . . .) $\rightarrow$ Competence
                        and
Competence . . .
    (is required for . . .) $\rightarrow$ Success
                        and
Success . . .
    (is required for . . .) $\rightarrow$ Self-reliance
                        and
Self-reliance . . .
    (is required for . . .) $\rightarrow$ Happiness

Given its central role, students must learn that understanding does not entail rote memorization, although some things must be memorized, or the learning of isolated facts, although facts must be learned. In contrast, understanding requires the construction of a personal theory of what is to be understood. That is, if students are to understand something, they must build their own theories in their own heads and not just parrot others'. Such a theory will yield a new perspective that permits generalization of inferences to new situations. It will permit the student to know what is important about the subject and what is not.

Pertinent for resistance to cheating, students must be convinced that building a good personal theory, just as in science, is a continuing process of testing and revising the theory. Testing the theory is critical for a good theory. Recitation, listening to lectures, and exams are all ways of testing one's personal theory. Cheating in the process of theory construction leaves one bereft of understanding. Cheating during exams deprives students of an opportunity to test their theory. Students who aim for understanding must take every opportunity to be tested. We believe that such a philosophy of education, if taught with conviction, just may lessen cheating.

REFERENCES

Davis, S. F., Grover, C. A., Becker, A. H., & McGregor, L. N. (1992). Academic dishonesty: Prevalence, determinants, techniques, and punishments. *Teaching of Psychology, 19*, 16–20.

Eisenberger, R. (1992). Learned industriousness. *Psychological Review, 99*, 248–267.

Eisenberger, R., & Shank, D. M. (1985). Personal worth ethic and effort training affect cheating. *Journal of Personality and Social Psychology, 49*, 520–528.

Fishbein, L. (1993, December 1). Curbing cheating and restoring academic integrity. *The Chronicle of Higher Education*, p. A52.

Haines, V. J., Diekhoff, G. M., LaBeff, E. E., & Clark, R. E. (1986). College cheating: Immaturity, lack of commitment, and the neutralizing attitude. *Research in Higher Education, 25*, 342–354.

Jendreck, M. P. (1989). Faculty reactions to academic dishonesty. *Journal of College Student Development, 30*, 401–406.

Ludvigson, H. W. (1992, November). *Cheating: What to do?* Paper presented at the Southwest Regional Conference for Teachers of Psychology, Fort Worth, TX.

McCabe, D. L., & Bowers, W. J. (1994). Academic dishonesty among males in college: A thirty year perspective. *Journal of College Student Development, 35*, 5–10.

Nye, R. D. (1992). *The legacy of B. F. Skinner.* Pacific Grove, CA: Brooks/Cole.

Pavela, G. (1993). Donald L. McCable on academic integrity: What the latest research shows. *SYNTHESIS: Law and Policy in Higher Education, 5*, 340–343.

Sims, R. L. (1993). The relationship between academic dishonesty and unethical business practices. *Journal of Education for Business, 68*, 207–211.

Singhal, A. C. (1982). Factors in students' dishonesty. *Psychological Reports, 51*, 775–780.

NOTES

1. We appreciate the assistance of Charles L. Brewer and three anonymous reviewers on the final draft of this article.

2. Requests for reprints should be sent to Stephen F. Davis, Department of Psychology, Emporia State University, Emporia, KS 66801–5807.

THINK IT THROUGH

Here are some questions about the second article that will help you put this research in perspective.

1. How are the results of the second project similar to those of the first study?
2. How do the results of the two projects differ? What are some possible reasons for these differences?
3. With regard to repeat offenders, describe one trend that appears to be developing.
4. What reasons do students give for cheating?

The results of the second study agree with those of the first project by showing that (a) the majority of the respondents reported cheating in high school, and (b) between 40 and 60 percent of the respondents reported cheating in college.

The results of the second study differed from those of the first study in several ways. First, there were no samples in which the self-reported rate of cheating in college fell below 40 percent. This result is to be contrasted with the results of the first study in which rates as low as 9 percent were observed. The reason for this difference is because all of the schools tested in the second study had enrollments of 3,000 or more students. Thus, it would appear cheating rates are higher at schools that have larger enrollments.

A second difference between the two studies concerned the determination of the percentage of repeat offenders and the number of times they have cheated. Clearly, many students cheat on a regular basis in high school. Of the 40 to 60 percent who report cheating in college, it is discouraging to find half of this group also report cheating on a regular basis. The finding that students who cheated on multiple occasions in high school also cheated on multiple occasions in college suggests this behavior is likely to continue after the students complete their undergraduate degrees.

A third difference between the two studies concerns examining the effect of the professor announcing strict penalties at the beginning of the semester. It was somewhat surprising to find a high percentage of the respondents, especially men who cheated on multiple occasions, felt they would not be influenced by such penalties.

The second study also provides insight into the specific reasons students have for cheating. Is it surprising to you to read that students who also hold jobs are tempted to cheat? Likewise, the perceived need to have a high GPA to obtain admission to graduate school, obtain a job, or please parents is not surprising. The number of external pressures experienced by contemporary students is substantial and probably growing. The power of such external pressures suggests cheating on examinations will likely be part of higher education for years to come.

THINK IT THROUGH

List five ideas related to those given above that can be researched and three novel ideas that could also be researched. What types of materials and time would each of these eight ideas require? Are there any ethical concerns in the studies you have proposed? If so, how can you go about eliminating these concerns?

Related ideas:

1. _____

2. _____

3. _____

4. _____

5. _____

Novel ideas:

1. _____

2. _____

3. _____

After writing down your various research ideas, have one of your professors read them and give you additional or alternate suggestions. If this is indeed an area of research interest, you will find it exciting to develop and pursue your ideas to fruition.

In recent years, our own research in this area has involved the following: exploring the relation of personality traits (such as Type A behavior, see Chapter 8) and cheating on examinations, investigating cheating on examinations by collegiate athletes, grade-school children, and graduate students, and evaluating the prevalence of cheating on examinations in other cultures. If you are interested in this area, you may review some of the additional readings that follow.

REFERENCES

Davis, S. F., Grover, C. A., Becker, A. H., & McGregor, L. N. (1992). Academic Dishonesty: Prevalence, Determinants, Techniques, and Punishments. *Teaching of Psychology, 19,* 16–20.

Davis, S. F., & Ludvigson, H. W. (1995). Additional Data on Academic Dishonesty and a Proposal for Remediation. *Teaching of Psychology, 22,* 119–121.

ADDITIONAL READINGS

Davis, S. F., Noble, L. M., Zak, E. N., & Dreyer, K. K. (1994). A comparison of cheating and learning/grade orientation in American and Australian college students. *College Student Journal, 28,* 354–356.

Davis, S. F., Pierce, M. C., Yandell, L. R., Arnow, P. S., & Loree, A. (1995). Cheating in college and the Type A personality: A reevaluation. *College Student Journal, 29,* 493–497.

Drake, C. A. (1941). Why students cheat. *Journal of Higher Education, 12,* 418–420.

Forsyth, D. R., Pope, W. R., & McMillan, J. H. (1985). Students' reactions after cheating: An attributional analysis. *Contemporary Educational Psychology, 10,* 72–82.

Huss, M. T., Curnyn, J. P., Roberts, S. L., Davis, S. F., Yandell, L., & Giordano, P. (1993). Hard driven but not dishonest: Cheating and the Type A personality. *Bulletin of the Psychonomic Society, 31,* 429–430.

Jendreck, M. P. (1989). Faculty reactions to academic dishonesty. *Journal of College Student Development, 30,* 401–406.

CHAPTER 12

In Closing

You have come a long way since Chapter 1! You investigated eight different psychological studies that will help you develop your own research ideas. Congratulations! With the knowledge you have gained from the readings and exercises in this text, it should almost be second nature to now develop a research idea on your own. You can be proud of your accomplishments.

THINK IT THROUGH

We want you to spend just a few minutes and reflect on the last 10 chapters and answer a few questions pertaining to them. Think about each question and write down the first answers that come to your mind.

1. How can you go about developing research ideas now that you have completed this text? What approaches to research have you learned that will now carry over to the development of other research ideas not discussed in the text?
2. What are some potential sources of participants you can utilize in studies you develop? What are the ethical considerations involved in using each type of participant?
3. What sorts of materials does research involve? Is conducting research something that is expensive and beyond the means of most students?
4. What are some of the important aspects of research you have learned about while reading this text?

Let us answer these questions sequentially and in a bit of detail. First, as we discussed in Chapter 1, as you go through the texts for your various courses in psychology (or for any class for that matter) you will be reading about a vast array of different research topics. You only need to look at the reference section of one of your texts to see how true this statement is. As you read your different texts you are certain to encounter topics which perk your interest. When you come across one of these areas, jot down the reference or references to which your author refers. Go to the back of the book for the entire citation and take that citation to your library. Look up the article and read it at your leisure. You will be surprised how many other excellent articles will be referred in the original one you read; these are articles you should obtain copies of. After reading these additional articles, ask yourself what questions have not been answered by them. Doing so will help you develop new ideas you can research yourself! That is exactly what we have tried to help you with in our text; to help you develop ideas from previously published research. We have tried to show you how easy this process actually is.

In answering the second question, just think back to the research cited in the last 10 chapters. We have had you read articles using bees *(Apis mellifera)*, children, mice, psuedopatients, and college students as participants. We have presented research using African American participants and Caucasian participants. Furthermore, the research presented has used participants from the United States and Japan. Your only limitation to the type of participant you decide to use in one of your studies is your own imagination. You can certainly use students at your institution as participants. You can also use students in your local grade school, middle school, and high school. Do you live in a part of the country where bees are scarce or inappropriate for your study? If you do, how about using flies, fruit flies, grasshoppers, mice, dogs, cats, or cows? Always remember, however, when conducting any type of research, you must conduct your research having the highest regard for the participants in your study (refer to Chapter 1). Whether using animals, humans, insects, or other types of participants, you must make certain they are protected at every step in the research process. Adults are treated differently when compared to children (Chapter 6) and animals are treated differently when compared to humans (Chapter 4). When in doubt about the ethics and methods of your particular study, always consult your faculty advisor and make certain you receive approval for your research from your institutional review board.

How did you answer the third question? Remembering the studies in Chapters 3 through 10, the materials required by the various researchers were as diverse as matchboxes to questionnaires to human figures. The studies we have selected to include are those which can be done with no budget at all or with a very modest budget. In fact, with the exception of the Rosenhan article (Chapter 10), the studies presented can be carried out with a minimal amount of money and material; most of the equipment used in the studies presented can easily and happily be provided by your department. Thus, "good" research does not require a great deal of money and/or other resources. What successful research does require is ingenuity and familiarity. Money *does not* have to be a limiting force in competent and interesting research. You only need to review the materials needed for the research in Chapter 3 to realize research can be done on a shoestring budget.

In answering the final question, we hope you have learned anyone can conduct research! If you are at a community college or a prestigious research institution, the main requirement to carry out a competent research project is just an idea and appropriate motivation. With the help of this book, you have developed the skills to be able to carry out research in many different areas. As we stated earlier, we will never be able to answer all of the questions posed by researchers in psychology. Thus, our ideas for research in psychology (as in other areas as well) are limitless.

THINK IT THROUGH

Let us assume you have carried out your research project to its logical conclusion. That is, you have completed your research and have it in written form. Now what do you do? Think of some possible sources available to you for the dissemination of your research findings.

The one thing all researchers hope is to have their research published. You might think your research is not worthy of publication; you may well be wrong. There are many sources available for students to have their research published. One is to submit your research to an American Psychological Association journal. There are several APA journals that are published; several of these journals published the research we selected to include in this text. You should know, however, the rejection rate of such journals is quite high (as high as 93% for the *American Psychologist,* which is the premier journal in psychology). This does not mean you should not attempt to have your research published by one of these journals. It does mean you should be reasonable about your chances for publication in one of these fine journals. Always consult your faculty advisor for help as to the appropriateness of where to submit your research for publication consideration.

There are even divisional journals of the APA that accept manuscripts for publication consideration. There are currently 49 different divisions within APA, and several have their own journal. When you arrive at the point of submitting your manuscript for possible publication, look at the different divisional journals for appropriate venues for your research.

The American Psychological Society also offers opportunities to publish research. The competition is great for journal space here as well. However, if you and your advisor feel your research is good enough for consideration, send it in for review. You might be surprised!

Psi Chi (The National Honor Society in Psychology) has recently begun publishing research by students. The first managing editor for that journal is Dr.

Stephen Davis who, coincidentally, happens to be one of the authors of this text! This is a quarterly journal that publishes a variety of empirical research on a variety of topics. It is the premier journal dedicated to publishing student research. Other journals dedicated to publishing student research include *Modern Psychological Studies* and *Der Zeitgeist, Student Journal for Psychology.*

Perhaps your research is not of the quality for publication (do not worry, most research is not published!). You have other viable options for professional development. For example, you can submit your research for presentation at one of the national psychological conventions. Both the American Psychological Association and the American Psychological Society hold annual meetings that provide a forum for presenting your research in a paper, poster, or symposium format. Being selected to present one's research at one of these conventions is an accomplishment of which even the seasoned researcher can be proud. Psi Chi also accepts articles for presentation at these conventions. If you are a member of Psi Chi and your paper is accepted for presentation, you are not only rewarded by having your research accepted for presentation after a rigorous review process, but you are also rewarded by an official "Certificate of Appreciation" presented at a ceremony during the convention.

Going to one of these national conventions is an exceptional opportunity, not only to present your research, but to have the experience of hearing others presenting their research. However, such national conventions can be expensive; you have your travel, hotel, and meals to pay for. As a result, many of these conventions may be beyond the means of many students. Do not despair! There are other options available.

Every region has a convention where students are allowed (and encouraged) to submit research for presentation consideration. Each regional convention also has a Psi Chi paper competition where Psi Chi students can submit a paper (or papers) for presentation. Psi Chi also sponsors several awards to help defray costs associated with traveling to these conventions. You do not have to belong to a particular region to submit a paper to that region. For example, if you live in Kansas you are able to submit a paper to any one of the regional conventions. The Midwestern Psychological Association always has its convention in Chicago. However, if SWPA (Southwestern Psychological Association) happens to have its convention in Dallas, Texas, one year, it might be more economical for you to travel to Dallas (versus Chicago) that year for a presentation. You might want to travel to the Western Psychological Association (in 1993, its convention was in Hawaii). Scheduled meeting dates, times, places, and contact persons are published in the *American Psychologist* and in the *Eye on Psi Chi.*

If regional conventions are not your fancy, you could consider presenting your research at one of the many conferences devoted entirely to student research. There are several of these annual conferences around the nation. Again, you can ascertain the dates, times, places, and contact persons by reading the *Eye on Psi Chi* or *Teaching of Psychology.* Among these conferences are the Southeastern Undergraduate Psychology Research Conference, Arkansas Symposium for Psychology Students, ILLOWA Undergraduate Psychology Conference, Mid-America Undergraduate Psychology Research Conference, Great Plains Students' Psychology Conference, Delaware Valley Undergraduate Research Conference, and University of Winnipeg Undergraduate Psychology Research Conference.

You have a plethora of opportunities for the publication and/or presentation of your research. You should be proud of the research you have completed, and that pride should extend to sharing your findings with the larger psychological community. You do not have to be intimidated by presenting your research. Remember, all of us had to make our *first* presentation at some point. Although that initial presentation may be challenging, it is an experience that lasts a lifetime!

Index

Italic page references indicate biblio-graphic references.